WAR AND THE MEDIA

Reporting Conflict 24/7

Edited by
Daya Kishan Thussu and Des Freedman

SAGE Publications

London ● Thousand Oaks ● New Delhi

ISBN 0-7619-4312-9 (hbk)
ISBN 0-7619-4313-7 (pbk)
© Daya Kishan Thussu and Des Freedman 2003 Compilation and Introduction
© Aijaz Ahmad 2003 Chapter 1   © Ted Magder 2003 Chapter 2
© Jean Seaton 2003 Chapter 3   © Frank Webster 2003 Chapter 4
© John Downey and Graham Murdock 2003 Chapter 5
© Robin Brown 2003 Chapter 6   © Philip M. Taylor 2003 Chapter 7
© Daya Kishan Thussu 2003 Chapter 8
© Greg Philo, Alison Gilmour, Susanna Rust, Etta Gaskell,
Maureen Gilmour and Lucy West 2003 Chapter 9
© Noureddine Miladi 2003 Chapter 10   © Jonathan Burston 2003 Chapter 11
© Bruce A. Williams 2003 Chapter 12   © Cynthia Weber 2003 Chapter 13
© Jayne Rodgers 2003 Chapter 14
© Howard Tumber and Marina Prentoulis 2003 Chapter 15
© Nik Gowing 2003 Chapter 16   © Kieran Baker 2003 Chapter 17
© Yvonne Ridley 2003 Chapter 18   © Gordon Corera 2003 Chapter 19
First published 2003
Reprinted 2003, 2005

WAR AND THE MEDIA

CONTENTS

ABOUT THE EDITORS

Daya Kishan Thussu teaches in the Media and Communications Department of Goldsmiths College, University of London. He has a PhD in International Relations from Jawaharlal Nehru University, New Delhi and is a former Associate Editor of Gemini News Service, a London-based international news agency. He is the author of *International Communication – Continuity and Change* (2000); editor of *Electronic Empires – Global Media and Local Resistance* (1998) and co-author (with Oliver Boyd-Barrett) of *Contra-Flow in Global News* (1992), published in conjunction with UNESCO. He is currently writing a book entitled *Infotainment* (Sage).

Des Freedman teaches in the Media and Communications Department of Goldsmiths College, University of London. He is currently researching media and communications policy and is especially interested in the political and economic contexts of policy making. His most recent publication is *The Television Policies of the Labour Party, 1951–2001* (2003) and he is currently writing a book on the new media, *Patterns of Media Change* (Arnold).

NOTES ON CONTRIBUTORS

Aijaz Ahmad is a Visiting Professor at the Centre for Political Studies, Jawaharlal Nehru University (JNU) New Delhi and a Visiting Professor of Political Science at York University in Toronto. He has held the Rajiv Gandhi Chair at the School of Social Sciences (JNU) and was for five years a Professorial Fellow at the Nehru Memorial Museum and Library in New Delhi. Ahmad has lectured widely around the world, and apart from numerous essays in international journals, his major publications include *In Theory: Classes, Nations, Literatures* (1992) and *Lineages of the Present: Ideological and Political Genealogies of Contemporary South Asia* (2000), both published by Verso. Ahmad has also edited *Ghazals of Ghalib* (Columbia University Press, 1971) and *Selected Writings on the National and Colonial Questions, Marx & Engels* (Delhi, LeftWord Books, 2001).

Kieran Baker is a former Senior International Editor with CNN. He was a Field Producer with CNN for over a decade, and most recently served in Israel, Pakistan and Afghanistan. Since 2002 Baker has been working for Fox News as a Coordinating Producer for International Projects and is currently serving as a visiting lecturer on the Cardiff University Broadcast Journalism course.

Robin Brown is Senior Lecturer in International Communications in the Institute of Communications Studies, University of Leeds. He is currently Director of the Institute. His research interests revolve around the role of communications in international politics. Among recent publications are 'Public Diplomacy, Information Operations and Spin: The US and the Politics of Perception Management' in *Journal of Information Warfare* and 'The Contagiousness of Conflict: E.E. Schattschneider as a Theorist of the Information Age' in *Information, Communication and Society*.

Jonathan Burston is Assistant Professor in the Faculty of Information and Media Studies at the University of Western Ontario in Canada. He writes on labour and globalization in the entertainment industries and on the performing body in digital space and time. Recent work on these topics includes 'Whose Hollywood? Changing Forms and Relations Inside the North American Entertainment Economy', with Ted Magder, in *Continental Order? Integrating North America for Cybercapitalism* (2001), and 'Spectacle, Synergy and Megamusicals: The Global-Industrialization of the Live Entertainment Economy' in *Media Organisations in Society* (2000). A full-length book treatment of this second article is forthcoming from Duke University Press. Burston's current research is on Siliwood, Las Vegas, multi-media convergence and the coming era of digitally produced 'synthespianism'.

Gordon Corera is a foreign affairs reporter and producer on BBC Radio 4's *Today* programme.

John Downey teaches communications and media studies in the Department of Social Sciences at Loughborough University. He has a long-standing interest in the impact of new information and communications technologies on patterns of power. His books include *Technocities* (edited with Jim McGuigan).

Etta Gaskell is a graduate of Economic and Social History at Glasgow University and subsequently worked as a researcher in the Glasgow University Media Group.

Alison Gilmour is an undergraduate student in Sociology at the University of Glasgow and also works as a researcher in the Glasgow University Media Group.

Maureen Gilmour is a teacher and also works as a researcher in the Glasgow University Media Group.

Nik Gowing is a main presenter for *BBC World* TV at BBC News. He is also a regular speaker and published analyst on the challenges of handling real-time information in times of crisis.

Ted Magder is Associate Professor in the Department of Culture and Communication at New York University where, between 1996–2001, he was also the Director of Communication Studies. He is the author of *Canada's Hollywood: Feature Films and the Canadian State* and *Franchising the Candy Store: Split-Run Magazines and a New International Regime for Trade in Culture* as well as numerous articles on the political economy of the cultural industries and the international trade in media products. He has served as a special advisor to the Centre for Communication in New

York City. In 2001 he was the Malim Harding Distinguished Visitor at the University of Toronto.

Noureddine Miladi is a researcher and visiting lecturer at the Centre of Communication and Information Studies, University of Westminster. His research interests revolve around Arab broadcasting, its problems, development and prospects. He is currently finishing his PhD on the Al-Jazeera satellite channel.

Graham Murdock, Reader in the Sociology of Culture at Loughborough University, is well known internationally for his general research in media and cultural analysis and his work on the relations between communications systems, coercion and political conflict. His books include the path-breaking study, *Televising 'Terrorism': Political Violence in Popular Culture* (written jointly with Philip Schlesinger and Philip Elliott).

Greg Philo is Research Director of the Glasgow University Media Group (www.gla.ac.uk/departments/sociology/media.html) and Professor of Communication at Glasgow University. His most recent book (with David Miller) is *Market Killing* (Pearson/Longman, 2001).

Marina Prentoulis is a PhD candidate in the Department of Government, University of Essex. She works as a Visiting Lecturer at City University, London. Her research interests include the history and sociology of journalism, political communications and discourse analysis.

Yvonne Ridley is a freelance journalist, broadcaster and peace campaigner. She was chief reporter of the *Sunday Express* when she was captured by the Taliban on September 28, 2001. Before this, she worked as an investigative journalist, often doing undercover assignments, for the *News of the World*, the *Sunday Times*, the *Observer* and the *Independent on Sunday*.

Jayne Rodgers is Lecturer in International Communications at the University of Leeds, where she teaches courses on global broadcasting and international affairs. She is the author of *Spatializing International Politics – Analysing Activism on the Internet* (Routledge, 2003).

Susanna Rust is a graduate of Geography and Politics at the University of Edinburgh and is currently working as a researcher in the Glasgow University Media Group.

Jean Seaton is Professor of Media History at the University of Westminster. She has written extensively about media history and politics including *The Media of Conflict: War Reporting and Representations of Ethnic Violence* (1999, as co-editor), *Power without Responsibility* (with James Curran, 1997) and the forthcoming *Carnage and the Media*.

Philip M. Taylor is Professor of International Communications at the University of Leeds. He lectures regularly at military educational establishments on both sides of the Atlantic, including the Defence Intelligence and Security School at Chicksands and the Joint Services Command Staff College (UK), SHAPE and the United States Air Force Special Operations University. His publications include *Munitions of the Mind* (1995) and *Global Communications, International Affairs and the Media since 1945* (1997).

Howard Tumber is Professor of Sociology and Dean of the School of Social Sciences, City University, London. He is the author of several books and articles on the sociology of journalism and news media. His most recent works are *Media Power, Policies and Professionals* (Routledge, 2000) and *News: A Reader* (OUP, 1999). He is a founder and co-editor of the journal *Journalism: Theory, Practice, Criticism*.

Cynthia Weber is Professor of International Studies and Director of the Centre for International Studies at the University of Leeds. Her work, located at the intersections of International Studies, Gender and Sexuality Studies, Cultural Studies, and American Studies, addresses such topics as sovereignty, intervention, hegemony, and US foreign policy.

Frank Webster is Professor of Sociology, City University, London, and Docent in the Department of Journalism and Mass Communication, University of Tampere. He was Professor of Sociology at Oxford Brookes University (1990–98) and the University of Birmingham (1999–2002). Recent publications include: *Culture and Politics in the Information Age* (2001), *Theories of the Information Society* 2nd edition (2002), *The Virtual University?* (2002, with Kevin Robins), *Environmentalism: Critical Concepts* (5 volumes) (2002, with David Pepper and George Revill), *The Information Society Reader* (2003), and *Manuel Castells: Sage Masters of Modern Thought* (3 volumes) (2003). He is currently working on a book, *Information, Capitalism and Uncertainty*.

Lucy West is an undergraduate student in Sociology at the University of Glasgow and also works as a researcher in the Glasgow University Media Group.

Bruce A. Williams is Research Professor in the Institute of Communications Research at the University of Illinois at Urbana – Champaign. Currently, he is a Visiting Scholar in the Department of Social Psychology at the London School of Economics and Politics as well as a

Fellow at the Stanhope Center. His research interests focus on the role of the mass media in shaping public discourse as well as on citizen participation in environmental policymaking. His most recent book, *Democracy, Dialogue, and Environmental Disputes: The Contested Languages of Social Regulation* (with Albert Matheny), published by Yale University Press, was named best book published on environmental politics in 1996 by the American Political Science Association. He is finishing a book entitled *And the Walls Came Tumbling Down: The Eroding Boundaries Between News and Entertainment and What They Mean for Mediated Politics in the 21st Century* (with Michael Delli Carpini).

LIST OF TABLES AND FIGURES

INTRODUCTION

Daya Kishan Thussu and Des Freedman

The French novelist Albert Camus once remarked that 'naming things badly adds to the misfortunes of the world.' By calling for a 'war on terrorism', the United States has initiated an open-ended and global conflict – one that can be directed against any adversary, anywhere in the world. How this war is framed and represented in the media thus becomes a crucial area of inquiry for both academics and professionals.

The post-Cold War period was hailed as an era of global peace and economic prosperity; a triumph of market capitalism and of 'globalization' of Western democracy (Hoge and Rose (eds) (2002)). This promised peace dividend has not materialized. The 'majority world' – full of zones of conflict and host to many a 'failed' and 'rogue' state – has largely failed to benefit from globalization. Apart from the wars in the former Yugoslavia, most of the post-Cold War conflicts – intra-rather than inter-state – have taken place in the global South (see Table I.1), with Africa witnessing 19 major armed conflicts. According to the Stockholm International Peace Research Institute, of the 57 major armed conflicts in 45 countries during 1990–2001, only three were inter-state – Iraq/Kuwait, India/Pakistan and Eritrea/Ethiopia – the rest were internal conflicts over territory or resources (SIPRI, 2002).

Post-Cold War conflicts can be divided into three categories: where genuine geo-strategic and economic interests are involved (a key example being the war over Iraq which many see as being fought for control of oil); conflicts emanating out of ethnic and nationalistic politics, as witnessed in the wars in former Yugoslavia and in parts of central Asia; and the 'invisible' conflicts, which may have claimed millions of lives – wars in Sudan and the Democratic Republic of Congo (DRC) are prime examples – but rarely register on international media radars, which tend to cover only the conflicts where the West, led by the United States, is seen to be a peace-maker.

Table I.1 Continuing conflicts – top ten by number of deaths

Country	Since	Main parties to conflict	Deaths
Democratic Republic of Congo	1998–	Govt. vs. RCD; RCD-ML (1)	2.5 million
Sudan	1983–	Govt. vs. NDA (2)	2 million
Angola	1975–	Govt. vs. UNITA (3)	0.5 million
Algeria	1992–	Govt. vs. FIS and GIA (4)	up to 150,000
Russia	1991–	Govt. vs. Chechen rebels	up to 70,000
Sri Lanka	1983–	Govt. vs. LTTE (5)	62,000
Sierra Leone	1990–	Govt. vs. RUF (6)	43,000
Columbia	1960–	Govt. vs. FARC (7)	35,000
India	1989–	Govt. vs. Kashmiri rebels (8)	35,000
Israel/Palestine	1948–	Govt. vs. Palestinian groups	13,000

1. Rassemblement Congolais pour la démocratie and Rassemblement Congolais pour la démocratie-Mouvement de libération.
2. National Democratic Alliance
3. Uniao Nacional Para a Independencia Total de Angola
4. Front Islamique du Salut; Groupe Islamique Armé
5. Liberation Tigers of Tamil Eelam
6. Revolutionary United Front
7. Fuerzas Armadas Revolucionarias de Colombia
8. Hizbul Mujahideen, Lashkar-e-Toyeba

Source: SIPRI Yearbook 2002 and press reports

Radical Islam as the new global 'enemy'?

One major political development of the post-Cold War era has been the replacement of communism as the pre-eminent threat to Western interests with a radicalized Islam. In this version of international politics, influenced by the discourse of the 'clash of civilizations' and strengthened by the events of 11 September 2001, militant Islam represents characteristics that are inimical to a modern, secular and rational market-democracy (Karim, 2002). Militant Islam is projected as a transnational threat, exemplified by shadowy networks such as Al-Qaeda, with its alleged links with 'rogue' states like Iraq. An undifferentiated view of Islamic militancy seems to dominate the discourse, in which Lebanon's Hizbullah, Palestinian Hamas, Indonesia's Jemaah Islamiyah, Abu Sayyaf group in the Philippines and Chechen rebels, are all linked as part of a seamless transnational terror network. The fear that the weapons of mass destruction may fall in the hands of such networks is at the heart of the US security agenda (*International Security*, 2001).

Resentment against the West, and particularly the US, is profound in the Arab world, largely because it is seen as controlling the region's energy resources, being unjust to the Palestinians and propping up corrupt regimes (Ali, 2001). The globalization of a market economy and,

Table I.2 Major US post-Cold War military interventions

Year	Country	Name of operation	Type of operation
1989	Panama	*Just Cause*	Aerial bombing, ground troops
1991	Iraq	*Desert Storm*	Aerial bombing, ground troops
1992	Somalia	*Restore Hope*	Aerial bombing, ground troops
1994	Haiti	*Uphold Democracy*	Naval, ground troops
1995	Bosnia	*Joint Endeavour*	Aerial bombing
1998	Iraq	*Desert Fox*	Aerial bombing, missiles
1999	Yugoslavia	*Allied Force*	Aerial bombing
2001	Afghanistan	*Enduring Freedom*	Aerial bombing, special forces

with it, Western consumer culture is further weakening the traditional Arab way of life – 9/11 was arguably the most extreme reaction against the excesses of globalization.

In the global era, the US has laid claim to be the world's 'policeman', intervening to uphold its version of human rights and liberal democracy (Haass, 1999; Von Hippel, 2000; *Orbis*, 2001; Price and Thompson (eds) 2002). The pattern of US involvement has varied vastly – from no military intervention at all (Rwanda) to transfer of power to a pro-US regime (Afghanistan), to the creation of a protectorate (Kosovo) (see Table I.2).

However, non-intervention in situations where human rights have been grossly violated, such as Angola, Rwanda, Sudan, DRC or Chechnya, indicates that interventions are not solely or even largely dictated by such lofty ideals and have been influenced by geo-strategic and political interests (Mermin, 1999).

The contours of a global empire

In the twenty-first century version of imperialism, one can detect echoes of the 'informal empires' of the nineteenth century, when economic control and military coercion masked overt foreign rule. An example of this is China during the nineteenth century when extraterritorial legal privileges for European colonial powers and a free trade regime imposed by them severely stunted China's growth. Does the overwhelming US power – both coercive and of the 'soft' variety – justify the label of an informal empire?

One plank of this informal empire is the notion of 'global governance,' particularly through the United Nations Security Council, which, nearly 60 years after its inception, still does not have any veto-wielding representation from Latin America, Africa or the Arab world. The undermining of state sovereignty coupled with increasing powers to new Western-sponsored international legal and human rights regimes and the globalization of the discourse of market democracy, are the main features of this trend (Chesterman, 2001; *International Organization*, 2000). One manifestation of such indirect governance is that the 'international community' (the US) has the right to 'regime-change' and the burden of 'nation-building' in failed states (Ikenberry, 2002; Ajami, 2003).

Economically, the triumvirate of the World Bank, the International Monetary Fund and the World Trade Organization has created a global system that tends to serve the interests of transnational corporations, most of which are based in the West. Their fundamentalist neo-liberal economic prescriptions, handed down by the 'ayatollahs of the IMF and World Bank' have restructured the economies of the developing world in a fashion that suits primarily the interests of transnational capital (Ali, 2001: 195).

The third plank of this informal empire is the US military domination of the globe. US supremacy in the skies has become increasingly important in the post-Cold War world. As Table I.2 shows, aerial bombing is the most common form of US military intervention and the bombing of Kosovo was the first conflict in history where victory was achieved solely on the basis of airpower. The Kosovo conflict also transformed NATO, whose rapid reaction units can be airlifted anywhere on the globe to defend imperial interests.

With the deployment of increasingly sophisticated and militarized space systems, the US is all set to have 'full-spectrum dominance,' for the collection of intelligence, communication and transmission of information, navigation and weapons delivery. In 2001, the US had nearly 110 operational military-related satellites, accounting for more than 60 per cent of all military satellites orbiting the earth. In addition, the US's decision to withdraw from the Anti-Ballistic Missile Treaty and its plans for a ballistic missile defence system makes the 'weaponization' of outer space a major concern (Pike, 2002). A new 'space cadre' is being created with the purpose of establishing global vigilance and the ability to strike anywhere in the world (US Government, 2002).

A fourth plank of the informal empire is US superiority in the field of global entertainment and information networks (Herman and McChesney, 1997; Thussu (ed.) 1998; Thussu, 2000). The US-dominated mass media play a central role in the legitimization of the imperial discourse, especially significant during the time of a conflict (Metzl, 1997; Price and Thompson (eds) 2002; Kaufman, 2002).

Reporting conflict – the role of the media

Three key narratives concerning the role of mainstream media in communicating conflict can be identified: as critical observer, publicist and, most recently, as battleground, the surface upon which war is imagined and executed. The idea that journalists are impartial and independent monitors of military conduct is cherished by many media professionals and liberal commentators. It assumes that correspondents are able and willing to shrug off ideological and organizational restrictions to keep a watchful eye on the activities of military combatants. It also implies that journalists are prepared to confront the arguments of powerful voices in government and the military who are responsible for both strategic and tactical decisions in a time of war.

The most celebrated example of this 'adversarial' conception of the journalist's role is US coverage of the Vietnam War where the uncensored and brutal portrayal of American casualties undermined public support and effectively 'lost the war'. One of the key turning points of the war was the transmission of a special report by the country's most celebrated news anchor, Walter Cronkite of CBS. Having just returned from a visit to Vietnam, he argued that the war was a 'bloody stalemate' and that outright military victory was virtually impossible. Upon watching this, President Johnson is alleged to have remarked to his aides that 'it is all over' (Ranney, 1983: 5). Broadcast coverage of (US) corpses and critical comments about US involvement were argued to have transformed public opinion. Television pictures of Vietnam, according to President Nixon, 'showed the terrible human suffering and sacrifice of war. . .the result was a serious demoralization of the home front, raising the question whether America would ever again be able to fight an enemy abroad with unity and strength of purpose at home' (quoted in Hallin, 1986: 3).

The 'adversarial' model suggests that the prying eyes and investigative reports of committed journalists force governments to be more open in their justifications for war and more transparent in their conduct of military operations. According to this logic, the recent expansion in the number of media outlets and volume of news has simply fuelled the 'watchdog' role of the media. Increased competition forces reporters to go beyond the handouts and briefings to discover an original story that their rivals may not have discovered. 'Truth' therefore becomes an important commodity in the era of rolling news.

This account of the media's 'fourth estate' role has been subjected to extensive critique, most urgently in coverage of conflict. Celebrated studies of war reporters, notably Philip Knightley's *The First Casualty* (1989), emphasize the public relations value of most reportage that legitimates government perspectives and narratives. Knightley describes how British correspondents covering World War One blurred the distinction between military and civilian personnel by wearing army uniforms and consenting to being accompanied by official army 'guides'. Far from adopting a critical or oppositional viewpoint, this model suggests that correspondents are more likely to publicize and reinforce official sources on which reporters choose to depend.

This approach has been applied to even the most hallowed example of media independence: Vietnam. In his detailed account of media coverage of the war, Daniel Hallin (1986) challenges the myth that a proactive and critical media corps deliberately sabotaged US military involvement. In the early days of the war, the US temporarily halted its bombing of North Vietnam in a move designed more to win domestic and international favour than to secure peace. Hallin concludes that reporters abandoned any notion of 'objective journalism' in disseminating the administration's view of events: the 'television journalist presented himself, in this case, not as a disinterested observer, but as a patriot, a partisan of what he frequently referred to as "our" peace offensive' (1986: 116). Even by the end of the war when US society was split over the question of Vietnam, 'for the most part television was a follower rather than a leader: it was not until the collapse of consensus was well under way that television's coverage began to turn around; and when it did turn, it only turned so far' (1986: 163).

This chimes with the claim by Edward Herman and Noam Chomsky (1988) that media reporting of the Vietnam War was defined by what it *excluded*: the voices of the anti-war movement in the US, the motives of the Vietnamese people and the 'inexpressible' notion that the US, not North Vietnam, was the aggressor in the conflict. This argument 'is not present even to be refuted. Rather, the idea is unthinkable' (1988: 252). According to Herman and Chomsky, media coverage of war is notable for the way in which views that run counter to official sources are deemed unacceptable, ideological alternatives are ignored and discussion is 'bounded'. Mainstream media reproduce the frameworks of political and military leaders and in so doing provide propaganda rather than 'disinterested' journalism.

There are a significant number of examples that appear to bear out the argument that, for all the occasional tensions, the relationship between media and military remains a close one that impinges on reporters' ability to speak independently. In March 2000, Alexander Cockburn reported that a handful of military personnel, based in the psychological operations unit at Fort Bragg, were working as 'regular employees' for CNN and that, according to a US Army spokesman, they 'would have worked on stories during the Kosovo war. They helped in the production of news' (quoted in Cockburn, 2000). In the run-up to the planned invasion of Iraq in late 2002 and early 2003, hundreds of US reporters participated in Pentagon-organized programmes that taught journalists basic battlefield survival, military policy and weapons-handling skills (Strupp, 2003). One of the most controversial examples of the convergence between military and media networks was the revelation in November 2002 that Roger Ailes, chairman of the conservative Fox News Channel in the US, had sent a note to President Bush shortly after 9/11 advising him to take 'the harshest measures possible' (quoted in Deans, 2002) in retaliation for the attacks. The intimate relationship between the entertainment industry and the defence establishment is further explored by Jonathan Burston in his chapter in this volume.

The third model of communicating conflict assumes that military and media networks have converged to the point where they are now virtually indistinguishable: that media constitute the spaces in which wars are fought and are the main ways through which populations (or audiences) experience war. The argument here is not whether media promote or oppose particular conflicts but that they are the means by which contemporary conflicts are literally played out. This idea of the media as battleground is related to two somewhat disconnected developments: the postmodernist critique of reality that foregrounds the importance of the spectacle; and technological innovations that have led to a 'revolution in military affairs' (RMA), in which war is increasingly technologized, informatized and mediated. While it is true that the wilder claims of postmodernism – best epitomized by Jean Baudrillard's polemical claim (1995) that the Gulf War was a gigantic simulation in which we were bombarded by TV images rather than missiles – have been discredited following empirical evidence of the existence of thousands of material (not textual) bombs and human (not symbolic) casualties, some of its conclusions are reflected in more mainstream military discourse.

The Pentagon boasts of the 'smart' bombs, computerized surveillance systems and digital simulations that coalesce around the notion of a 'future combat system' (FCS) (Hambling, 2003), a 'network-centric' model of warfare. This is designed to de-humanize war and complements the US military's strategy in recent conflicts to rely on aerial bombing campaigns in which, not surprisingly, there are few American casualties (and, ideally, minimal media interest in civilian casualties). Major innovations in information and communications technology have been eagerly embraced by the military establishment in their PR efforts to present a new and 'bloodless' view of war that looks good on domestic television screens. James Der Derian has described this as 'virtuous war' which combines virtual technologies with a claim to embrace humanitarian motives. This US-led imperial initiative 'relies on computer simulation, media manipulation, global surveillance and networked warfare to deter, discipline and, if need be, destroy potential enemies' (2002: 105).

Underlying these theories of 'virtuous war', FCS and RMA is the notion that something fundamental has changed in the conduct of war: that there are fewer bodies to observe and less mess to clean up. Yet modern conflicts are not 'media wars' or 'screen battles' but encounters in which there are plenty of civilian casualties, horrendous destruction and unimaginable misery for the victims. Reflecting on one of the main soundbites of the 1991 Gulf War, Philip Taylor concludes that, although the war will 'undoubtedly be remembered as CNN's war or television's war, it was no such thing. The conflict belonged to the coalition's armed forces, and to the victors went the spoils of the information war' (1992: 278).

Many of the contributions to this book proceed on the basis of the second model: that, in general, the media are likely to privilege and publicize official versions of conflict. The chapters from both academics and professional journalists attempt to identify the range of constraints – both organizational and ideological – that prevent the media from reporting conflict in a truly critical or independent way.

The conception of a partisan, cheerleading media in Western liberal democracies has been articulated with great clarity and influence by scholars like Robert McChesney, John Nichols and Noam Chomsky. They argue that an increasingly market-led media largely ignores dissenting voices in favour of corporate and government tunes. This has led to a situation today where mainstream media accepts and reproduces dominant definitions of, for example, 'terrorism' (what others do to us) and 'self-defence' (what we do to others) in order to mobilize popular consent for military action against 'rogue states'. Populations have been 'effectively depoliticized with daily infusions of nonsense news' (McChesney and Nichols, 2002: 32) by a media hell-bent on securing maximum profits. Chomsky accuses the media of indoctrinating the public with 'what amounts to a form of self-imposed totalitarianism, with the bewildered herd marginalized, directed elsewhere, terrified, screaming patriotic slogans, fearing for their lives and admiring with awe the leader who saved them from destruction' (Chomsky, 2002: 65).

However, it is important not to exaggerate the ideological grip that the corporate media exert over citizens. In the two countries with perhaps the most extensive 'propaganda' systems, public opinion has proved to be reluctant to endorse the bombing of Iraq. In January 2003, British opposition to war was running at 47 per cent compared to 30 per cent in favour (Travis, 2003) while in the US, despite an overwhelmingly sympathetic media, only a small majority (52 per cent) were prepared to support George Bush's war drive with 43 per cent against (Gallup News Service, 2003).

At a time when consensus starts to break down, sections of the media are forced to respond to major public debates. However, the critical stories that do emerge from mainstream media are not the result of an intrinsic pluralism or a deep-rooted commitment to 'objective journalism' but reflect shifts in consciousness amongst wider layers of the population. The decision, for example, by the mass-circulation newspaper, the British *Daily Mirror*, to campaign against a US/UK attack on Iraq reflects its desire to articulate the views of the anti-war constituency as well as to compete with its main tabloid rival, the *Sun*. It is about politics *and* product differentiation. The stakes in reporting conflict are high but they are far from independent of the tensions that arise out of the struggle of political elites to get their way and the determination of citizens to stop them.

War and the Media – the book

Against this background why is there need for another book on war and the media? This collection aims to provide a framework for analysing the interplay between the media and its representations of war and conflict in an era of sophisticated information warfare and news management. In doing this it integrates both media theory and journalistic practice, with essays from leading scholars and observations from well-known journalists from the front-line of reporting conflict. The volume offers a range of critical perspectives and a transnational approach, with contributions from three continents.

The book is divided into five parts. Part 1 is context-setting, with Aijaz Ahmad, one of India's best-known critical scholars, providing a political framework for analysing the US 'war on terrorism'. Ted Magder examines the impact of 9/11 on communications in the US and globally, while Jean Seaton emphasises the importance of understanding the nature of the audience response to the tragedy of conflict presented in the news.

Part 2 focuses on new dimensions of information warfare. Frank Webster discusses the shift from industrial to information warfare and how the discourse of human rights has come to take the centre stage in describing conflict in terms of humanitarian interventions. John Downey and Graham Murdock critique the notions of 'new wars' and the Revolution in Military Affairs (RMA) and argue that hi-tech war has its own limitations and low-tech guerrilla actions, driven by political motives, may sometimes be more effective. Robin Brown looks at media management in the wake of 9/11, while Philip Taylor, one of Britain's leading authorities on propaganda, analyses the role of psychological operations (PSYOPS) during the war in Afghanistan, with examples from radio broadcasts and propaganda leaflets.

Chapters in Part 3 focus on the impact of the shift to rolling, 24/7 television news. Daya Kishan Thussu argues that the competition for ratings and profits is forcing television journalism towards infotainment, projecting war as a bloodless virtual conflict. This part also includes a report on the findings of a study of television news conducted by the Glasgow University Media Group, on how the framing of the news on Israel/Palestine influences audience perceptions of one of the world's most protracted conflicts. Media researcher Noureddine Miladi examines the origins and evaluates the growing influence of the pan-Arabic news network, Al-Jazeera, whose coverage of the war in Afghanistan in 2001 received international attention.

Part 4 is concerned with the representations of the 'war on terrorism'. Jonathan Burston explores the creative links between Hollywood and the Pentagon – the military-entertainment complex – and stresses the need to rethink media research agendas to incorporate a hidden aspect of entertainment. The chapter by Bruce Williams is based on an ongoing project about the role of on-line communications in a conflict situation. Williams examines how internet chatrooms became sites of heated debates and contestation, only minutes after the destruction of the twin towers. In her contribution, Cynthia Weber juxtaposes the Pearl Harbor and Palm Harbor events to discuss the US response to external and internal security threats, while Jayne Rodgers makes a case for a more gender-sensitive analysis of conflict, taking her examples from the media portrayals of 9/11.

Contributors to the final part examine the changing cultures of journalism. In their chapter, Howard Tumber and Marina Prentoulis focus on the journalistic subculture of foreign corresponding. Following the events of September 11, they argue, an already occurring cultural shift in war reporting has been accelerated and amplified, bringing the concept of attachment and emotional literacy to the centre of attention. The final four contributions are based on journalists writing about their first-hand experiences of covering conflict. Nik Gowing, who has extensive experience of television journalism having worked for both ITN and the BBC, enumerates the problems and challenges faced by television reporters operating under the pressure of the 24/7 news cycle. Kieran Baker, who covered the war in Afghanistan in 2001 for CNN and now works for Fox News, discusses the perils of reporting from a country with little communication infrastructure. Yvonne Ridley, who herself became a story for the media when she was arrested by the Taliban in September 2001, recounts her experiences as a witness to news management during the war in Afghanistan, while the BBC's Gordon Corera emphasizes the need for journalists to provide context and to be more culturally sensitive in their overseas reporting.

Earlier versions of many of the chapters that constitute this volume were first presented at a joint symposium organized in May 2002 by New York University in London, the Department of Media and Communications of Goldsmiths College, University of London, and the Institute of Communications Studies, University of Leeds. We are grateful to all the speakers and other participants for making the symposium an intellectually stimulating experience. We are especially indebted to Professor David-Hillel Ruben, Director of NYU in London, for hosting the event and for his constant encouragement and generosity of spirit. The symposium would not have succeeded without the excellent organizational support from staff at NYUL, particularly Yvonne Hunkin, Louisa Ellis and Pete Campion-Smith. We would also like to record our appreciation for Jayne Rodgers of the Institute of Communications Studies, University of Leeds for her help in organizing the event. Our thanks are also due to colleagues at the Department of Media and Communications at Goldsmiths College, especially James Curran, Ivor Gaber, David Morley and Angela Phillips, for their support. Julia Hall at Sage deserves our grateful thanks for backing the project from an early stage and seeing it through within a remarkably short period of time. Last but not least, the book would not be in the shape it is without the invaluable editorial contribution of Liz Thussu.

References

Ajami, Fouad (2003) 'Iraq and the Arabs' Future', *Foreign Affairs*. 82 (1).

Ali, Tariq (2001) *The Clash of Fundamentalisms: Crusades, Jihads and Modernity*. London: Verso.

Baudrillard, Jean (1995) *The Gulf War Did Not Take Place*. Bloomington: Indiana University Press.

Chesterman, Simon (2001) *Just War or Just Peace? Humanitarian Intervention and International Law*. Oxford: Oxford University Press.

Chomsky, Noam (2002) *Media Control: The Spectacular Achievements of Propaganda*. 2nd edn. New York: Seven Stories Press.

Cockburn, Alexander (2000) 'CNN and Psyops', 26 March, available at http://www.counterpunch.org/cnnpsyops.html

Deans, Jason (2002) 'Fox News chief at centre of political storm', *Guardian Unlimited*, 19 November, available at http://media.guardian.co.uk/broadcast/story/0,7493,843179,00.html

Der Derian, James (2002) '*In Terror*: Before and After 9/11' in K. Booth and T. Dunne (eds) *Worlds in Collision: Terror and the Future of Global Order*. Basingstoke: Palgrave, 101–117.

Gallup News Service (2003) 'Americans Distrust Iraq but Favor Giving U.N. Inspectors More Time', Gallup Poll, 27 January, available at http://www.gallup.com/poll/releases/pr030127.asp.

Haass, Richard (1999) *Intervention: The Uses of Military Force in the Post-Cold War World*. 2nd edn. Washington: Brookings Institution Press.

Hallin, Daniel (1986) *The Uncensored War: The Media and Vietnam*. Oxford: Oxford University Press.

Hambling, David (2003) 'The war after next', *The Guardian*, online section, 23 January, 1–2.

Herman, Edward and Chomsky, Noam (1988) *Manufacturing Consent – the Political Economy of the Mass Media*. New York: Pantheon Books.

Herman, Edward and McChesney, Robert (1997) *The Global Media – The New Missionaries of Corporate Capitalism*. London: Cassell.

Hoge, James and Rose, Gideon (eds) (2002) *America and the World: Debating the New Shape of International Politics*. Washington: Council of Foreign Relations.

Ikenberry, John (2002) 'America's Imperial Ambition', *Foreign Affairs*. 81 (5).

International Organization (2000) 'Legalization and World Politics', *International Organization*. Special issue, 54 (3).

International Security (2001) 'The Threat of Terrorism: U.S. Policy after September 11,' *International Security*. Special issue, 26 (3).

Karim, H. (2002) *The Islamic Peril – Media and Global Violence*. 2nd edn. Montreal: Black Rose Books.

Kaufman, Edward (2002) 'A Broadcasting Strategy to Win Media Wars', *The Washington Quarterly*. 25 (2): 115–127.

Knightley, Philip (1989) *The First Casualty – From the Crimea to Vietnam: The War Correspondent as Hero, Propagandist and Myth Maker.* London: Pan Books.

McChesney, Robert and Nichols, John (2002) *Our Media, Not Theirs: The Democratic Struggle against Corporate Media.* New York: Seven Stories Press.

Mermin, Jonathan (1999) *Debating War and Peace – Media Coverage of US Intervention in the Post-Vietnam Era.* Princeton: Princeton University Press.

Metzl, Jamie (1997) 'International Intervention: When Switching Channels isn't Enough', *Foreign Affairs.* 76 (6): 15–20.

Orbis (2001) 'A Decade of Humanitarian Intervention', *Orbis.* Special issue, 45 (4).

Pike, John (2002) 'The military uses of outer space,' pp. 613–64 in *SIPRI Yearbook 2002: Armaments, Disarmament and International Security.* Oxford: Oxford University Press.

Price, Monroe and Thompson, Mark (eds) (2002) *Forging Peace – Intervention, Human Rights and the Management of Media Space.* Edinburgh: Edinburgh University Press.

Ranney, Austin (1983) *Channels of Power: The Impact of Television on American Politics.* New York: Basic Books.

SIPRI (2002) *SIPRI Yearbook 2002: Armaments, Disarmament and International Security.* Oxford: Oxford University Press.

Strupp, Joe (2003) 'U.S Military Tries to Make Peace With Press', *Editor & Publisher*, 7 January, available at http://www.editorandpublisher.com/editor andpublisher/headlines/article_display.jsp?vnu_content_id=1788729

Taylor, Philip (1992) *War and the Media: Propaganda and Persuasion in the Gulf War.* Manchester: Manchester University Press.

Thussu, Daya Kishan (ed.) (1998) *Electronic Empires – Global Media and Local Resistance.* London: Arnold

Thussu, Daya Kishan (2000) *International Communication – Continuity and Change.* London: Arnold.

Travis, Alan (2003) 'Support for war falls to new low', *Guardian Unlimited*, 21 January, available at http://www.guardian.co.uk/Iraq/Story/0,2763,879104, 00.html.

US Government (2002) Annual Report To The President And The Congress by Donald H. Rumsfeld, Secretary of Defense, available at http://www. defenselink.mil/execsec/adr2002/index.htm

Von Hippel, Karin (2000) *Democracy by Force: U.S. Military Intervention in the Post-Cold War World.* New York: Cambridge University Press.

Part 1

COMMUNICATING CONFLICT IN A GLOBAL WORLD

1

CONTEXTUALIZING CONFLICT: THE US 'WAR ON TERRORISM'*

Aijaz Ahmad

The date of September 11 has a powerful resonance in the annals of modern history. In 1973, on this day, the Central Intelligence Agency-sponsored coup of General Augusto Pinochet overthrew the democratically elected socialist government of President Salvadore Allende in Chile and established a regime of terror which killed an estimated 35,000 people in the first few weeks and continued to brutalize Chilean society for some two decades. September 11 was also the date of the Camp David Accords (1978), which signalled Egypt's final surrender to US imperialism and Israeli Zionism, leaving the Palestinians at the mercy of the latter. And, September 11, 1990 was the day when George H. Bush, father of the current President of the United States, made his fateful speech to the US Congress announcing the war against Iraq – that supreme act of terror which killed an estimated 200,000 people in the course of that brief assault and which has led to the death of at least half a million Iraqi children over the next decade, thanks to the US-dictated blockade of their country.

Betrayal of the Palestinians, the destruction of Iraq. One can reasonably assume that these two great devastations of the Arab-Muslim world were vivid in the memory of those 19 hijackers on 11 September 2001, when they commandeered four civilian aircraft owned by two major US airlines, and smashed three of them into the World Trade Center and the Pentagon – nerve centres of US financial and military power – while committing collective suicide in the process. The White House – the seat of US political power – was probably to be struck by the fourth aircraft but something in the hijackers' plan went awry. More than 3,000 innocent civilians from 60 countries – some 500 of them from South Asia alone, including the son of a close friend of mine – died within a couple of hours in a calculated and hideous act of terrorism carried out with stunning technical precision.

The deaths in New York pale in comparison with Hiroshima and Nagasaki, which claimed 220,000 lives – the most famous of the numerous cities that the US destroyed in the 'long' and violent twentieth century. This was the first time the Americans came to experience what it means for cities to be at the receiving end of such destructive force. This hijacking operation, carried out by less than two dozen individuals, was the largest attack on mainland United States in its history, larger than Pearl Harbor, while American armies, assassins and covert operators of all kinds have been active around the globe for well over a century.

Being at the receiving end of violence on their own soil was such a novel experience for the US centres of power, that this attack on a couple of buildings at the heart of the imperial centre produced effects that no amount of terror and destruction in the outposts – or even the secondary and tertiary centres – of the empire could have produced. An economy that was already slowing down went into a fully-fledged downturn, and the week following the hijackers' attack proved to be the worst in the history of US finance since 1933.

What happened was unspeakably hideous, cruel and senseless. The loss of thousands of precious lives, many of them cut down in the flower of their youth, has neither a moral nor a political justification. For once, President Bush's speechwriter was right: those who carry out such acts in the name of Allah blaspheme the name of Allah; they hijack Islam in the name of Islam; in the larger, largely humane world of Islam, they are a dangerous, fringe element.

The new global militarism

George Bush first called it a 'crusade', then a 'War for Civilization', then 'A Task that Never Ends', then a 'War against Global Terror', then a 'Titanic War on Terror'. The rhetorical inflation and the fudging of facts is infinite. It is supposed to be all about September 11 and Al-Qaeda, but senior officials of the Federal Bureau of Investigation (FBI) have been quoted as saying that 'Al-Qaeda itself, we know, is less than 200' (*Palm Beach Post*, 27 July 2002): two hundred members, including those held by the Americans at Guantanamo Bay in Cuba. Undeterred by facts asserted by his own officials, Bush claimed at just about the same time: 'We know that thousands of trained killers are plotting to attack us.' Vice-president Dick Cheney continues to speak of a war against '40 to 50 countries'; down from 60 or so that Bush had estimated in September 2001. Defense secretary Donald Rumsfeld intones that he has instructed the Pentagon to 'think the unthinkable', that is, the actual use of nuclear weapons.

The US has a long history of overt and covert interventions around the globe with the explicit aim of overthrowing existing governments. The Islamicist jihad in Afghanistan, which eventually gave rise to the Taliban, was itself the product of such a policy, which was aimed at overthrowing the government of the People's Democratic Party of Afghanistan, and the policy had come into force well before the Soviet Union had intervened militarily to defend that government. In more recent years, such a policy was implemented successfully in Yugoslavia and unsuccessfully in Somalia. What is new is a certain globalization of this policy, a declaration that the US has the unique right to make war against any and all governments that it considers inimical to its interests, and the notice that has been served upon the world to either support this policy or face retribution. Kofi Annan, the United Nations secretary general, who does the US bidding in such matters, has even been awarded a Nobel Prize for his efforts.

With dozens of new military bases and facilities established from Turkmenistan to the Philippines, the occupation of Afghanistan accomplished, the destruction of Palestinians going on and on, and a full-scale war against Iraq being planned by the US administration, attention has been focused quite rightly on the global nature of this perpetual war.

Taking advantage of the anger and the human anguish arising from the September 11 tragedy, the US administration moved quickly to plan a new, globalized, permanent war; to expound what amounts to a new doctrine of America's right to use its might as it pleases; to expand the war-making powers of the Presidency; to put in place a new regime of infinite surveillance; and to demolish whatever restraints had been introduced after the Vietnam War on America's right to undertake assassinations and covert actions across the globe. All this was accompanied with hair-raising rhetoric, which tended at times to portray the war as a clash between the Judeo-Christian and Muslim civilizations.

Bush called his 'war on terrorism' a 'crusade' early on, with no sense of the historical meaning of that word. Only opposition from a wide spectrum of opinion in the Muslim world made him retract that stance and start saying that the war was not against Islam as such but only against certain Muslims. Not to be outdone, the Pentagon named its planned operation 'Infinite Justice', a phrase not even from the Bible but from the lexicon of Christian fundamentalism. Not only Muslims but even liberal Christians were outraged, and Protestant pastors themselves pointed out that 'Infinite Justice' referred to God's own divine justice, an attribute that no human power ought to claim for itself, America's vision of its own omnipotence notwithstanding. The Pentagon sheepishly promised to reconsider the code name.

Congress swiftly passed a resolution authorizing Bush to use wide powers in pursuit of this war on terrorism, asserting that 'all necessary and appropriate force' could be used against nations, organizations and individuals. No nations or organizations were named, let alone individuals; the President could determine which one was to be attacked as he went along. Nor was there a time limit; he was authorized to act against present danger as well as in anticipation of 'future attacks'. The powers were in some ways wider than a mere declaration of war could have bestowed, since such a declaration would name the country against which the war was to be waged.

Echoing John Foster Dulles, the rabid foreign secretary of the Eisenhower years, who said that non-alignment – the path of some Third World countries like India during the Cold War – was 'immoral', Bush too has put the whole world on notice: if you do not explicitly join us in this global crusade, we shall treat you as a hostile country! Enemies are lurking in thousands of little corners, in dozens of countries across the globe, and America will choose its targets as well as its methods and timing of dealing with them as it goes along, according to its own convenience; every country must join up each time, or else it too becomes an enemy and perhaps the next target. This war, 'unlike any we have ever seen,' he said, shall be perpetual but largely secret. Some of it shall be seen on television, he said, but much shall go unrevealed – even in success, he emphasized. Congressional leaders in Washington are now talking of putting the CIA 'on a war footing' and cite with admiration the Israeli example of an open policy of assassinations without regard to legal niceties.

It is quite astonishing, though predictable, how quickly one government after another has fallen in line. India of course joined the crusade and offered its airspace and naval facilities with shameless alacrity. Pakistan President Parvez Musharraf then cited India's pre-emptive oath of allegiance as his reason for offering the same to the US; India would otherwise have a strategic edge, he reasoned. Competitive servilities, one might say.

Tony Blair, who acts as Washington's agent while doubling as the British prime minister, flew across the Atlantic to register his presence at the moment of birth of this new era of perpetual war. The European Commission has been scurrying around formulating new policies of cooperation over the question of terrorism, urging individual members of the European Union to allocate more funds and build new systems of surveillance. The Russian parliament has passed a bill to create an international body to fight terrorism and, aping the US president, calls for the elimination of terrorists as well as the governments which are said to finance them.

China has been more shrewd, somewhat more independent; it urges a policy that involves presentation of concrete evidence, does not involve sacrifice of innocent civilians and is within the bounds of international law, but it also promises cooperation if the US was more receptive to its interests in Tibet, Taiwan and Xinjiang – and on the issue of National Missile Defence. The US, in turn, moved quickly and put in place a new deal facilitating China's entry into the World Trade Organization.

The less powerful, many of whom also happen to be directly involved – in some cases even directly targeted – are of course treated differently. On 14 September 2001, William Burns, Assistant Secretary of State for Near Eastern Affairs, called in the ambassadors of 15 Arab countries, including Syria, which is otherwise one of the 'target' states, as well as the PLO, and imperiously read out to them a list of actions they were to undertake, including the arrest and prosecution of those on their soil who the US designates as 'terrorists'. Everyone seems to have fallen in line, including Yasser Arafat, who has extended 'full cooperation'. Even President Mohammed Khatami of Iran has made sympathetic noises and expressed the wish to use the occasion to draw closer to the US.

Terrorism and the emerging neo-imperialism

Such is the asymmetry of power in our time: those who rule the universe shall be victorious against the poorest and the most wretched of this earth; those who refuse subjugation shall be made to suffer miseries that no previous period in human history inflicted on the powerless. War shall be permanent because the war cannot end without justice and justice is what the US has set out to deny, permanently. The war shall be globalized because in this period of globalization there is a singular power whose task it is to guarantee regimes of injustice throughout the world. And much of this war shall be secret, like much of the movements of finance capital because finance capital is what this war serves and therefore imitates. Bush is right: this is truly 'a task that has no end' – until someone rises to end it.

A brief word about this particular form of fighting which is called 'terrorism'. Bush was careful enough to say that America's enemy was a particular 'terrorism' which 'has global reach'. In other words, he is not particularly concerned with the great many varieties, which include the Roman Catholic Irish Republican Army (IRA) in Ireland and the largely Hindu Liberation Tigers of Tamil Eelam (LTTE) in Sri Lanka. Nor is 'fundamentalism' the issue: Taliban fundamentalism is bad but Saudi fundamentalism is good, and Bush himself of course speaks the language of that Christian fundamentalism which defines the far-right in contemporary United States. 'Terrorism with global reach,' the designated enemy, is the one that can challenge American power.

This is a complex and important subject. Briefly put, 'terrorism' is what comes when the Communist left and anti-colonial nationalism have both been defeated while the issue of imperialism remains unresolved and more important than ever. Hatred takes the place of revolutionary ideology. Privatized, retail violence takes the place of revolutionary warfare and national liberation struggles. Millenarian and freelance seekers of religious martyrdom replace the defeated phalanx of disciplined revolutionaries. Unreason arises where reason is appropriated by imperialism and is eliminated in its revolutionary form.

There were no Islamic terrorists in Afghanistan before the Americans created them as a counterweight against the secular left. Islamism arose in Iran to fill that space which had been left vacant with the elimination of the secular, revolutionary left by the CIA-sponsored regime of the Shah. Islamic secret societies arose in Egypt after imperialism and Zionism combined to defeat Gamal Abdel Nasser's secular nationalist project. The Hamas arose in Palestine because the cosmopolitan Palestinian nationalism was denied its dream of a secular state in the historic land of Palestine where Jew and Arab could live as equals. What gets called 'terrorism with global reach' today is a mirror of defeat but also the monster that imperialism's Faustian success made possible and which now haunts its own creator. The loss of over 3,000 lives in the blaze and collapse of the World Trade Center is the price the victims and their families paid for the victory of imperialism.

America can never defeat 'terrorism with a global reach' because for all its barbarity and irrationality, religiously motivated 'terrorism' is also a 'sigh of the oppressed', and if some Palestinians cheered it, that too was owed to the fact that even an 'opiate of the people' is sometimes mistaken for the medicine itself. The only way to end this 'terrorism' is to rebuild that revolutionary movement of the left whose place it occupies and with whose mantle it masquerades.

Authoritarianism at home

The 'war on terrorism' has a significant domestic dimension. Bush was always a candidate of what is the ultra-right wing even within the Republican Party. However, the constraint on his ability to act on their agenda came from the fact that even his election was barely legal and his popularity ratings, low to start with, had kept declining. At the time of the September 11 events, that rating stood at 40 per cent. Popularity soared with his speech declaring a global 'war on terror' and rose to over 90 per cent after the bombing of Afghanistan began on 7 October 2001. Permanent war hysteria has been used to maintain exceedingly high popularity ratings, which in turn have been used to implement that agenda. Alain Joxe, head of CIRPES (the Paris-based centre for inter-disciplinary research in areas of peace and strategic studies) wrote in *Le Monde* on 17 December 2001 that 'the American leadership is presently shaped by dangerous right wing Southern extremists'. These 'extremists' are connected, in turn, with the fact that the American South is home both to a hard core of the evangelical Christian fundamentalist constituency which is represented by the Republican right and the core of the military-industrial complex comprising the oil interests and the war industries.

Bush is connected with that whole constituency. He was governor of the oil-rich southern state of Texas and his family has been closely associated with the oil interests. As for the military significance of the South, *CounterPunch* (20 June 2002) summarized it as follows: 'The South represents only a third of the nation's population, but supplies 42 per cent of the country's enlisted soldiers. . . . Southern politicians are Congress's biggest hawks, tilting US foreign policy away from peace and diplomacy. 62 per cent of southern senators scored in the bottom fifth of the legislative scorecard for Peace Action, a non-profit watchdog. Anchored by defence boom centres in Virginia, Texas and Florida, the South produces more weapons than any other region, landing 43 per cent of US arms contracts in 2001.' Significantly, over two-thirds of the arms used by Israel come from southern arms corporations. These realities play an important role in the current drift into greater militarism and authoritarianism.

Congress itself gave Bush the authority to concentrate extraordinary powers in the office of the President, more or less indefinitely. Gore Vidal, the 77-year-old novelist and veteran commentator, described the US legislature most aptly as 'a supine Congress, the best that corporate money can buy.' Immediately after September 11 this 'supine Congress' passed a Bill, 420–1 in the House and 80–0 in the Senate, stating that 'the President is authorised to use all necessary and appropriate force against those nations, organizations, or persons he determines planned, authorised, committed, or aided the terrorist attacks that occurred on September 11, 2001, or harbored such organizations or persons.' This was a licence to wage war against not only Afghanistan but also any other nation that Bush saw fit to invade, but in bestowing such vast authority against even unnamed 'organizations' and 'persons' who even 'harbored' the suspects, it also opened the floodgates for infinite surveillance and repression at home and abroad.

The draconian Act, which Bush signed into law on 26 October 2001, was the direct result of this absolutist authority. It was expansively, and absurdly, called 'Uniting and Strengthening America by Providing Tools Required to Intercept and Obstruct Terrorism' for the sole reason that the name could then be shortened as 'USA Patriot Act'. It gave the intelligence agencies unlimited powers to tap any telephone. The agencies have also been given the power to gather a broad range of information from various public institutions – schools, hospitals, credit and other financial agencies, Internet communications, commercial establishments, and so on – without having to reveal to any court of law either a criminal charge or the purpose and scope of the investigation, so long as it has to do with the vaguest suspicion of 'terrorism'.

This is of course surveillance of the old, familiar kind, though taken now to new extremes in an otherwise democratic country. As for the truly high-tech, New Age techniques of surveillance, an Associated Press report of 21 November 2001, for example, had this to say: 'The FBI is going to new lengths to eavesdrop, building software to monitor computer use and urging phone companies to help make wiretaps more reliable. The FBI's "Magic Lantern" technology would allow investigators, via the Internet, to secretly install powerful software that records every keystroke on a person's computer, according to people familiar with the effort.'

The CIA itself has been given wide powers in domestic intelligence gathering since it is now empowered to designate persons who would be objects of surveillance. The FBI, which was established as a strictly domestic intelligence agency, is now active worldwide and maintains offices in numerous capitals, including New Delhi. The US attorney general and the secretary of state now have the power to designate any domestic group as a terrorist organization and belonging to it would be considered a crime, even retroactively. The Act invents a new term, 'domestic terrorism', which is so broadly defined as to include the use of a 'firearm, weapon or other dangerous device. . . to cause substantial damage to property'. Defence of all kinds of property thus becomes part of a fight against 'terrorism', and a 'dangerous device' could be just a brick that hits a parked car. Riot control thus becomes part of 'war against terrorism'.

Thus, the meaning of 'terrorism' was now squarely broadened to cover the 'economy' and any conflict of interest between 'citizen' and 'non-citizen'; in principle, any non-citizen who successfully competed in business against a citizen, with 'adverse effects' for the latter, could be dragged before such a tribunal, tried as a 'terrorist' and summarily executed. Thus, the US arrogates to itself the unilateral right to impose the death penalty on a non-citizen without due judicial process and without the government of that person's own country having the right to try its citizens in its own court and under its own laws. The 'kangaroo court' thus arrogates to itself a global jurisdiction.

These examples are cited merely to illustrate the manner in which the events of September 11 have been used to strengthen greatly the regime of surveillance within the US, as an integral feature of enhanced authoritarianism. Those events were also a boon for the war industries, as corporate America understood immediately. The day the Wall Street stock market opened after the destruction of the Twin Towers, the share value of Lockheed Martin, the US military's biggest supplier, rose by a staggering 30 per cent. Within six weeks of the tragedy of September 11, the company (with its main plant in Texas, Bush's home state) had secured the biggest military order in history: a $200 billion contract to develop a new fighter aircraft. The 'war on terrorism' was used to push through the National Missile Defence (NMD) programme and then the largest military budget in history, of close to $400 billion, the increase alone amounting to $50 billion and with clear allocations to inaugurate NMD-related research.

US military technology is already a decade or so ahead of what is available elsewhere in the world. What is planned now is a new generation of weapon systems in view of the projected permanence of global war. The US is currently developing an array of radar, imaging, vehicle and computer technologies that will afford its military the ability not only to find enemy armies in darkness, fog, dust, inside buildings and beneath foliage, but also to strike within minutes of detecting and identifying them. An enemy will find it more difficult each passing year to hide from spy planes and satellites and a host of airborne and land-based robotic vehicles. Within ten years, the US arsenal will be equipped with sensors and weapons far more rapid, more precise and more lethal than what we see today. Even existing weapons are being improved. The B-2 Stealth bomber, for example, will by 2004 be able to carry 80 500-pound JDAM (Joint Direct Attack Munition) precision bombs that will be independently targetable so that 80 different targets may be struck on a single silent pass at 50,000 feet. All this – and much more besides – is then capped by a whole array of policy statements and documents, such as the 'Nuclear Posture Review', which call for developing small nuclear devices for such purposes as deep earth penetration and smaller nuclear weapons that may be used against non-nuclear states.

A 'MacArthurian regency in Baghdad'?

At the beginning of 2003, this formidable military power was arrayed against Iraq, a country under constant attack for 12 years – both covert and overt – from the US and its closest ally, Britain. An opinion piece that Victor Marshall contributed to *Los Angeles Times* on 5 January 2003, reminds us of the damage inflicted upon the 22 million suffering Iraqis by the Anglo-American axis: 145,000 dead – 40,000 military and 5,000 civilian deaths during the war and 100,000 post-war deaths because of violence and health conditions; sanctions claiming an estimated half a million Iraqi children, according to the UN Food and Agriculture Organization and other international bodies; and the destruction of Iraq infrastructure – petrochemical complexes, telecommunications centres, bridges, highways, railroads (the losses estimated by the Arab Monetary Fund to be $190 billion). The Anglo-American bombardment of Iraq had lasted longer than the US war on Vietnam, indeed longer than the combined duration of the two world wars. US officials have owned up to seven coup attempts that they have instigated.

All of Iraq initially, and much of it subsequently, has been declared a 'no-fly zone' where the Anglo-American axis powers do not allow the government of the country to fly its own aircraft, in flagrant violation of Iraq's sovereignty and without any basis in international law or a Security Council resolution; they have bombed most of the country at will, again without any sanction from the Security Council. Indeed, the conversion of the Security Council into a tool to implement its own designs has been a singular achievement of the United States and its supine allies during this period, with respect to Iraq and Palestine as much as the various parts of the former Yugoslavia.

The focus on Iraq has taken remarkable turns. We now know that on the morning of 12 September 2001, the day after the destruction of World Trade Center, Defense Secretary Rumsfeld argued vigorously in favour of invading Iraq as the first target and was only dissuaded by Secretary of State Colin Powell's argument that Al-Qaeda was more clearly connected with Afghanistan, that Afghanistan was an easier country to invade and conquer, and that the US should not be engaged in two theatres of war simultaneously. A month later, on 13 October 2001, *The International Herald Tribune* revealed that the Pentagon-based Defence Policy Board, a powerful bipartisan group of national security experts, met for 19 hours on 19 and 20 September, and members of the board agreed 'on the need to turn to Iraq *as soon as the initial phase* of the war against Afghanistan and Mr. bin Laden's organization was over' (emphasis added). The dates of the meeting (19/20 September) are significant: this was before Bush famously declared his 'global war on terrorism.'

Deputy Secretary of State Paul Wolfowitz and Chairman of the Defense Policy Board Richard Perle, along with Vice-President Dick Cheney, were prominent figures at the Pentagon during Bush senior's administration and were then – along with Rumsfeld, Lewis Libby (Cheney's chief of staff), William Bennet (Reagan's education secretary) and Zalmay Khalilzad (Bush's ambassador to Afghanistan) founders of the key think-tank 'Project for the New American Century' (PNAC). Jason Vest of *The Village Voice* (21–27 November 2001) and John Pilger in *New Statesman* (16 December 2002) are among journalists who have drawn our attention to the PNAC's seminal report, *Rebuilding America's Defences: Strategy, Forces and Resources for a New Century*, drafted as a blueprint of US aims for Bush junior before he actually won – rather, stole – the presidential election. As Pilger phrases it, 'Two years ago it recommended an increase in arms-spending by $48 billion so that Washington could "fight and win multiple, simultaneous major theatre wars". This has happened. It said the United States should develop "bunker-buster" nuclear weapons and make "star wars" a national priority. This is happening. It said that, in the event of Bush taking power, Iraq should be a target. And so it is.'

That report described the global spread of the US military forces as 'the cavalry on the new American frontier.' It recommends that the US replace the United Nations in 'peacekeeping' projects; that bases in Saudi Arabia, Kuwait and elsewhere in the Gulf be maintained even after Saddam's overthrow; that the US encourage 'regime change' in China and undertake 'increase of American forces in Southeast Asia'; that 'US Space Forces' be created to ensure supremacy in space and total control of cyberspace; that the US consider developing 'advanced forms of biological warfare; and that North Korea, Libya, Syria and Iran are among the states that require the US to establish a 'world-wide command-&-control system.'

After September 11, 2001, it is rather eerie and astonishing that this report, drafted a year before those events, actually suggested that what the US needed as justification for putting in place its global design for the twenty-first century was 'some catastrophic and catalysing event – like a new Pearl Harbor.' As images of the World Trade Center tragedy were flashed across the world, incessantly, day in and day out, dozens of commentators indeed compared that event to Pearl Harbor again and again, until the analogy – the two great and evil attacks on America – were indelibly inscribed in the minds of viewers, especially within the United States. And, the tragedy of thousands of grieving families was soon turned into the empire's golden opportunity. Nicholas Lemann revealed in the *New Yorker* in April 2002 that Condoleeza Rice, Bush's National Security Advisor, told him she had called her senior officers and asked them 'to think about "how do you capitalise on these opportunities."'

As regards the military design, that thinking has centered essentially on one question: should the US fight several wars at the same time or should it go after its designated enemies around the globe one by one? According to James Webb, a former Assistant Secretary of Defence and Secretary of Navy in the Reagan administration, this debate as well as the unwavering focus on Iraq has been going on for over a decade. As he puts it, it is 'a rift that goes back to the Gulf War itself, when neo-conservatives were vocal in their calls for "a MacArthurian regency in Baghdad"' (*Washington Post*, 4 September 2002). In other words, they have been arguing for all these years in favour of a full-scale US occupation which would last long enough to re-make the Iraqi state much as the US re-made Japanese state after World War Two. Webb, a former Marine officer and an abiding Republican, offers unanswerable arguments as to why this is pure fantasy. However, that kind of argument gained great momentum after September 11, especially because those who represented that view were now in control of the US military policy at the Pentagon.

In a broader geo-political perspective, complete monopoly over oil, the world's most strategic commodity, not only in the Gulf region and the Caspian Sea basin but also all the way from Venezuela to Indonesia, is also seen by these 'neo-conservative American nationalists' as a major weapon for coercion and manipulation in their relations with secondary powers in the advanced industrialized world itself, Western Europe and Japan surely but also, increasingly, China. The weapondollar-petrodollar connection in the US military-industrial complex is the driving force impelling the imperial authority toward permanent war.

A relatively brief chapter such as this one does not permit the space to develop a detailed examination of this new phase of enhanced globalized militarism. Two points may be made in closing, however. One is that authoritarianism is not an incidental but a necessary consequence of this kind of militarism. As the US makes war against country after country, across the developing world, the immigrant populations within the US, which are drawn from those countries, are bound to get restive at the thought of the destruction of societies in what were their countries of origin, and new forms of racism, surveillance and repression shall be required to contain their dissent. This need will be aggravated by the anti-war sentiment that is bound to arise, especially if the growth in authoritarianism and militarism coincides with economic stagnation and bust, which current trends in the stock market, in corporate scandals and even currency valuations seem to presage. For example, at least some of the laws and actual acts of surveillance and repression, which are being legitimized by an ideological offensive against Muslims in general and Arabs in particular, seem designed to contain anti-globalization protests and the growing dissent on elite campuses.

Second, the kind of military technology that already exists and which is sought to be made so very much more advanced and overwhelming, makes a military response to US aggression so very difficult and even virtually unthinkable that desperate and unconventional methods of fighting back – in short acts of what is called 'terrorism' – are likely to increase. There shall undoubtedly be numerous countries, the largest among them being India, which will seek refuge in US patronage itself. For the host of weaker countries that are currently targeted, especially in the vast regions of Central Asia, the Middle East and North Africa, the military prospects are bleak.

Armies shall become increasingly superfluous in the targeted countries, even where there is a will to fight back, and the burden of fighting may well shift to small, scattered groups of desperados which will be, in their own way, just as lawless and frightening as the US war machine itself is. A barbaric civilization that struts across the globe with such technological superiority in its killing machines is bound to increase the quantum of barbarism on the opposing side as well, at least in the foreseeable future.

Note

* This chapter is compiled from three recent essays by the author which appeared in the Indian magazine *Frontline*, published in Volume 18, Issue 22,

October 27–November 9, 2001; Volume 19, Issue 17, August 17–30, 2002 and Volume 20, Issue 2, January 18–31, 2003, reproduced with the kind permission of the author, who is also a senior editorial consultant for *Frontline*. (www.frontlineonnet.com)

WATCHING WHAT WE SAY: GLOBAL COMMUNICATION IN A TIME OF FEAR

Ted Magder

'Here speaks a voice from America. Every day at this time we will bring you the news of the war. The news may be good. The news may be bad. We shall tell you the truth.' *First broadcast of the Voice of America. February 24, 1942 – transmitted in German.*

From UNESCO to the clash of civilizations – the conundrum of global communication

We live in a time of empire, a time when the military and economic prowess of one nation has no parallel in the course of human history. We live too in a time of globalization, when the density of networks crossing borders leaves no place unexposed to forces – economic, political, social, cultural, and environmental – that emanate from afar. This is also a time when the idea of human rights has taken its place among the principles that claim standing in the affairs between states and peoples. Not least, we live in a time of conflict and terror, when even the empire's capital is open to attack and the prospect of mass violence perpetrated by small bands of individuals or states is real.

And all of this takes place in an age of near instantaneous communication across borders, a time of information and media abundance, a time when the prospect of a global conversation, directly and indirectly, by the second and by the hour, is palpable. It is incumbent on those of us who study communication to make better sense of the role it plays in global politics and, more importantly, to be responsible in the claims we make about the relationship between communication and conflict. For almost a generation, most especially in the fields of cultural studies and media studies, much of the scholarship in the discipline of communication has steered clear of this terrain: cynicism of all things political and a reluctance to use the language of values, morals, or ethics, have compromised our ability to speak responsibly and prescriptively about how we should do global communication, especially in a world full of fear.

This is not an entirely new challenge. After World War Two, the search for a lasting peace included a new set of international institutions designed to nurture tolerance and understanding through communication. Alongside the traditional military and political apparatuses – foreign occupation, overseas bases, and alliances such as NATO – a small parcel of land on the east side of Manhattan became home to the United Nations. At the same time, the United Nations Educational, Scientific and Cultural Organization (UNESCO) was established to articulate, and give substance to, a broad set of values and priorities tied directly to global communication and world cultures. As we struggle to find the language and principles that might help lay the foundation for global communication, the preamble of UNESCO's constitution, adopted in November 1945, is worth quoting at length:

> That since wars begin in the minds of men, it is in the minds of men that the defenses of peace must be constructed;
>
> That ignorance of each other's ways and lives has been a common cause, throughout the history of mankind, of that suspicion and mistrust between peoples of the world through which their differences have all too often broken down into war;
>
> That the great and terrible war which has now ended was a war made possible by the denial of democratic principles of dignity, equality and mutual respect of men, and by the propagation, in their place, through ignorance and prejudice, of the doctrine of inequality of men and races;
>
> That the wide diffusion of culture, and the education of humanity for justice and liberty and peace are indispensable to the dignity of man and constitute a sacred duty which all the nations must fulfil in a spirit of mutual assistance and concern; . . .
>
> For these reasons, the States Parties to this Constitution, believing in full and equal opportunities for education for all, in the unrestricted pursuit of objective truth, and in the free exchange of ideas and knowledge, are agreed and determined to develop and to increase the means of communication between their peoples and to employ these means for the purposes of mutual understanding and a truer and more perfect knowledge of each other's lives . . .
>
> (UNESCO, 1945)

It would be easy enough to judge the language of UNESCO as hopelessly idealistic. Some have even suggested that it represents the slippery rhetoric of the US and its allies eager to ensure that foreign markets remain open to Western media products and to place a moral code over the practices of empire (Preston *et al.*, 1989). To be sure, UNESCO's history is awash with controversy and flawed ventures. But failed ventures have their purposes, and the language of the UNESCO charter does two things: it reminds us that the stakes involved in doing global communication are high; and it offers a set of principles that should provide the foundation for global communication. Utopian though it may seem, the constitution of UNESCO gives substance to a profound belief: that communication can promote tolerance and provide the foundation for a politics that makes it possible to change peacefully (without violence and social turmoil) the rules we live by.

Easier said than done. Conflict in the world is not merely a function of miscommunication and misunderstanding. It can, and does, reflect trenchant disagreement over the allocation of scarce resources and the core habits and rules that shape communities and societies. In fact, easy and frequent communication across borders may be a source of conflict as much as a means to resolve it. In this sense, Samuel Huntington (1996) was right: as the interactions between different civilizations increase, so to does the prospect for animosity and violence. It would seem, at least since September 11, 2001, that the 'clash of civilizations' now dominates world politics.

What we face is the challenge of global citizenship and the question of global governance. Citizens participate in the public affairs that bear on their lives. Citizens must be able to speak or, at the very least, they must be represented by credible and responsible agents who speak on their behalf. Citizenship implies democratic practices, both in the articulation of those things that matter to many and in their resolution through practice and law. Citizenship requires dialogue and communication and vigilant attention. None of these are easy, not even on a national scale; on a global scale the challenge may seem insurmountable.

Communication at a distance: from cultural imperialism to media worlds

Communication scholars like to say that mediated forms of communication – everything from smoke signals to the internet – reduce space as a barrier to communication. One of the great advantages of mediated communication over face-to-face conversation is that it can take place over distances much greater than the unaided human voice can be heard. But only in the last 150 years, has it become relatively easy to send messages across vast distances at superhuman velocities. Electricity made it possible to send signals at speeds faster than any mode of human transportation, whether horse, boat, or plane. Considerable barriers to global communication still exist: borders remain closed; gatekeepers control access to technologies and sometimes monitor the flow of messages; the resources necessary to join the conversation are costly to many and, in certain cases, virtually unavailable. But there is no denying these simple facts: communication across great distances is commonplace; the quantity of messages is unparalleled; and the speeds can be nearly instantaneous. In this sense, Marshall McLuhan is surely right: the world has become a 'global village.'

One way to make sense of the vastness of this daily symbolic traffic is to measure the flow of messages across borders and to identify the main interlocutors – those people or institutions who speak most frequently across vast distances. The tallies should come as no surprise. In the aggregate, Western countries predominate in the flow of news and information as well as entertainment. They dominate too in the production and management of the cross-border flow of computer data and the use of surveillance technologies, such as remote sensing satellites, to gather and disseminate information for commercial and political purposes. And of the Western countries, the United States is easily the most dominant entity in every facet of the world communication system.

Among scholars of foreign policy and international relations, US dominance in the international flow of media and information is now identified as a strategic asset. Joseph Nye, in particular, has given it a name: 'soft power.' For Nye, 'soft power' is the ability to get 'others to want what you want' through the expression and demonstration of values that others find worthy of emulation. 'Hard power can rest on inducements (carrots) or (threats),' writes Nye, while soft power 'co-opts people rather than coerces them. . . . Soft power is more than persuasion or the ability to move people by argument. It is the ability to entice and attract. And attraction often leads to acquiescence or imitation' (2002: 8–9). The point is simple: power is a function of many variables, some of which exist in the realm of ideas and values and culture[1].

Nye's distinction between hard and soft power has made an impression on the foreign policy community, but it is old-hat for most scholars of communication. At least since the late 1960s, when the collection of data on cross-border flows of media became commonplace, the term cultural imperialism – and its implications of dominance and coercion – has been commonly applied to describe the consequences of the Western edge in the flow of media across borders. The culmination of this argument envisions drastic consequences: a transformation in the core habits of thought and action that define social orders, cultural practices and collective identities, summed up in terms such as Americanization, Westernization, or the more colloquial McDonaldization, Coca-Colanization, or Disneyfication.

The rhetorical appeal of these terms is undeniable. But their scholarly value is limited, especially if they are used to short-circuit analysis of how media and information flows work and how cultures change. These terms rightly draw our attention to the inequalities of power that typify international communication, but they do not adequately describe the nature or the consequences of the flow of media across borders. Taken at face value they imply that collective identities are easily transformed, and further, that we are living in an age of cultural convergence or homogenization, that the media globalization is leading to the formation of a singular global culture. But as Ulf Hannerz (1991) and John Tomlinson (1990; 1999), among many others, have argued, the evidence of global media flows and the manner in which media are interpreted and used suggest a far more nuanced and complex picture of cultural interaction than can be inferred from the master term imperialism.

One place to look more clearly for evidence is in the area of international or global news. On the face of it, the language of imperialism seems appropriate. News that crosses borders, assembled and distributed by a few, large transnational companies, has been a core feature of international communication since at least the late nineteenth century. Three European news agencies, Reuters (UK), Havas, which became *Agence France Presse* (France), and Wolff (Germany), led the way, mirroring and aiding the expansion of European colonialism. In 1870 they signed a treaty to divide between them the global market for the provision of news across borders, with Reuters, by virtue of the British empire's reach, the dominate partner in what became known as the 'ring combination' (Boyd-Barrett, 1980). The Associated Press (AP), and later United Press International (UPI), became prominent players after World War One, paralleling the rise of the US as a superpower. If the 'ring combination' dominated the supply of international print news in the latter half of the nineteenth and first part of the twentieth century, it is the Anglo-American connection that dominates the supply of global TV news today. AP and Reuters are the two biggest wholesalers of raw audio-visual news material. CNN and the BBC are the two most formidable international sources of packaged TV news delivered to viewers.

At this level of analysis, the dominance of Western news agencies seems unassailable. In fact, by the early 1970s, UNESCO itself became embroiled in a dispute over its consequences, with the majority of its members arguing that the news agencies in particular, and the media more generally, had either become agents for 'the domination of world public opinion or a source of moral and cultural pollution' (Tracey, 1985: 28). CNN's coverage of the 1991 Gulf War, when it became the world's only instant chronicler of a major conflict, seemed only to confirm the formidable role played by Western news agencies in covering and framing international events. Indeed, by the mid-1990s, some scholars and certain policymakers had come to the conclusion that CNN in particular was having a measurable impact on the way governments conduct world politics (cf. Robinson, 2002).

But the international clout of CNN, the BBC, Reuters and AP in the aggregate do not tell the tale if we want to fully understand the story of global news in the 1990s. Surveys of global news reveal similar patterns throughout the world. On any given day, there is no such thing as a common international news agenda. Instead, foreign news has a regional or continental quality: European news agencies focus on things European, while news agencies in South-East Asia focus their international news on South-East Asia. Summarizing one of the most detailed surveys of the main evening news programmes in countries from every region of the world, Graham Chapman had this to say: 'What comes out of this analysis is that the world is not really next door. Some major stories come from one side of the globe to the other, but seem of interest only to Western networks and agencies. The rest? Local concerns predominate. What it is the world chose about itself on this night is myriad, diffuse, disconnected. It seems there are many worlds on this one earth − and that mostly they stay next door, minding their own business.' (Chapman, 1992: 33). We may live in the age of globalization, but we do not yet live in the age of global news per se, either in the sense that audiences the world over pay attention to the same international stories on an everyday basis or even in the sense that audiences get more global (or foreign) news than in the past.

This is certainly true in the US where, by virtually every measure, foreign news as a percentage of total news has shrunk since the end of the Cold War. A variety of surveys reveal a similar pattern. In 1998, only two per cent of total newspaper coverage focused on international news, a drop from ten per cent in 1983 (Shaw, 2001: 27). The amount of time that network TV devotes to international news shrank from 45 per cent of total coverage in the 1970s to 13.5 per cent in 1995 (a decline of more than 70 per cent) (Moisey, 1996: 09; cf. Utley, 1997; Hoge, 1997; Lang and Lang, 2000). *Time* magazine covers devoted to foreign affairs dropped from 11 in 1987 to zero in 1997, and foreign reports in *Time* between 1985 and 1995 dropped from 24 per cent to 12 per cent. *Newsweek*'s coverage of foreign affairs shows a similar decline (Randal, 2000: 32).

Part of the explanation for this general reduction in foreign coverage is cost or, to be far more precise, revenue. Even as the costs of gathering and assembling news from afar have declined because of advances in technology, newsrooms and news divisions have fallen under the general directive to turn a profit. Relative to other news items, foreign stories are still expensive and they rarely generate a higher audience or readership than domestic news or 'soft-news.' Maintaining a full-time foreign correspondent and bureau is an expensive proposition − upwards of $150,000 a year. Instead, networks and major daily newspapers have adopted a just-in-time approach to foreign news, dropping journalists and (sometimes) anchors into a hot-zone for a breaking story. Not surprisingly, the stories that merit this kind of coverage are major crises and conflicts, especially those that might involve the use of armed forces or those that signal a threat to established 'national interest.' In general, foreign news is 'domesticated': it is less about the world than about America in the world (Lang and Lang, 2000). The one exception may be global business or economic news, where there has been an increase in overall coverage over the past decade. According to one industry survey, The *Wall Street Journal* alone now accounts for one-third of US foreign newspaper correspondents (Shaw, 2001; cf. Hoge, 1997). The growth in specialized economic and financial news is also evident at Reuters, where general interest foreign news now represents less than 10 per cent of its revenue (Moisy, 1996: 5). We have come to know a lot about the price of oil, but little of the politics or the culture of the places from which most of it comes.

In the place where most of the oil comes from, the private satellite news channel, Al-Jazeera, operated out of Qatar, is more than a match for CNN or the BBC. Since its inception in 1996, Al-Jazeera, which translates as 'the Peninsula,' has made a name for itself by offending Arab governments that routinely treat the notion of a free press with contempt and by scooping all TV news networks with its broadcasts of interviews and tapes of Osama bin Laden[2]. But what is most important, in the current context, is that it offers Arab households a close visual encounter with the Israeli-Palestinian conflict on a daily basis unfiltered by Western agencies. A decade ago, the conflict would not have received the same airing on television – the means were not yet available. But in the last ten years, the use of direct broadcast satellites (Arabsat, in particular) has dramatically altered the audio-visual space of the Arab world, creating a rich mixture of private and state-owned channels that Tourya Guaaybess calls an 'Arab broadcasting space' (2002; see also Ayish, 2002). Those familiar with this new televisual landscape caution against overestimating the level of uniformity and consensus within it. The Arab world may speak with nearly one voice on the matter of the Israeli-Palestinian conflict, but there remain significant political and cultural differences between broadcasters and the publics they address (cf. Golden, 2002). With that said, it is still an environment where state-owned broadcasters routinely work at the behest of their paymasters, and where states can exercise a chilling degree of scrutiny and coercion over private broadcasters. And though it is true that many of the private pan-Arab broadcasters have adopted some of the idioms and formats of Western broadcasters, it would be hard to claim that the system is in the process of being Westernized. Nor is it a space free of controversy: in November 2002, during Ramadan, Egypt's first private satellite station, Dream TV, broadcast a 41-part mini-series, *Fares Bela Gawaad* (Horseman Without a Horse), that raised hackles among the Western press and the US State Department. As part of its history of the Arab struggle against European colonialism, *Fares Bela Gawaad* tells the story of a Hafez Maguib, an Egyptian journalist in the late nineteenth century, who sets out to prove the Zionist plot to control Palestine by demonstrating the validity of the *Protocols of the Elders of Zion*, a document fabricated by the Russian czar's secret police in the nineteenth century (Howeidy, 2002; Jacinto, 2002)[3].

No country has a monopoly on the retelling of history. Certainly, the impact of *Fares Bela Gawaad* has to be measured against Hollywood's remarkable presence in virtually every overseas market and its recent penchant for Arab bad guys amidst a long-standing tradition of foreign villains. But even Hollywood does not entirely control the afterlife of the stories it tells. In the days and weeks after the attacks of September 11, 2001, three videos were widely available for sale in Wenzhou, China, a city that makes 60 per cent of the world's supply of disposable lighters. *Surprise Attack on America, America's Disaster: Pearl Harbor of the 21st century*, and *The Century's Great Catastrophe*, interlace American news footage with shots from Hollywood movies – such as *Wall Street, The Rock, Pearl Harbor* – and soundtracks, such as *Jaws* (Hessler, 2001). Godzilla makes an appearance in *Surprise Attack*. On one cover Osama bin Laden and President George Bush flank each side of the flaming towers. The back cover of *The Century's Greatest Catastrophe* rattles off credits to Touchstone Pictures, Jerry Bruckheimer and Tom Hanks, and Columbia Pictures. Osama bin Laden is featured on *Century*'s front cover and Chen Xioanan, well known in China as a newscaster for the News Corporation's Hong Kong-based Phoenix TV, does the voice-over.

The challenge that we face may have less to do with cultural homogenization than parochialism. While it may be impossible to hold the whole world in one's head, somehow the knowledge deficits and stereotypes and Manichean imagery that characterize much of the media landscape must be overcome. We live, to a large extent, in media worlds (Ginsburg *et al.*, 2002; cf. Smith, 1990). Not one world but many, where the production and reception of media is shaped as much by local and regional forces as by the macro-economics of the media industries. And while we have managed technically to overcome space as a barrier to communication, we have not accomplished the art and practice of a global dialogue.

The press, the state, freedom of information, and public diplomacy

Shortly after the attacks of September 11, 2001, the White House Press Secretary stood in front of a room crowded with reporters and gave an indication that the bedrock was shifting: 'people have to watch what they say and what they do' (Carter and Barringer, 2001a). Ari Fleischer was commenting on a remark by Bill Maher, host of ABC's *Politically Incorrect*, to the effect that flying a plane into a building may take more courage than firing a cruise missile at an unseen target. Fleischer's new-fangled version of 'loose lips sink ships' was enough of a departure from the prevailing assumptions about latitudes of public speech by government officials to be stricken for a time from the official White House transcripts. In the land where the First Amendment is the First Amendment, it is presumed to be offensive for a White House spokesperson to push the press around or, at least, to be seen doing so. But in the aftermath of 9/11,we would do well to refocus our attention on the resources that states can wield, and the tactics they employ, to influence the process of international communication both by limiting access to information and by managing the public perception of events.

There is substantial evidence that media coverage of foreign events closely follows the interpretative frames offered by political elites. Once the phrase 'national security' can be uttered with some degree of legitimacy, the mainstream press is likely to adopt a patriotic pose. In the strong version of this thesis, state actors have an unassailable ability to 'manufacture consent' (Herman and Chomsky, 1988). In the more nuanced version of this thesis, the press gains a measure of relative autonomy to the extent that there is some dissent or disagreement among political elites themselves (Hallin, 1997). Piers Robinson (2002), in his recent examination of 'the CNN effect', suggests that in times of policy uncertainty and elite dissensus there may be considerable space for typically marginal actors to influence the framing and interpretation of international events. But, as Robinson and others indicate, during a foreign conflict, moments of serious policy disagreement are rare: in a conflict elite opinion tends to 'rally' around the executive branch of government (cf. Lang and Lang, 2000). All of this literature directs us toward one broad conclusion: that in matters of foreign policy state actors have the upper-hand in setting and framing the news-agenda.

In the aftermath of 9/11, the rally effect was ever present. Political elites and the American public lined up quickly behind the White House in a moment of intense patriotism. The press went along. TV news networks branded their coverage of 9/11 with screen crawls such as 'America Fights Back' (CBS), 'America's New War' (CNN), and 'America United' (Fox). Anchors and reporters wore flag pins and red, white and blue ribbons, and the cable news networks, Fox, CNN, and MSNBC, projected a US flag onto the corner of the screen. Shortly after the attack, CBS anchor Dan Rather made an emotional appearance on the *Late Show with David Letterman*. 'George Bush is the President,' said Rather, 'he makes the decisions, and, you know, as just one American, if he wants me to line up, just tell me where' (Rutenberg and Carter, 2001; cf Cohen, 2001). No channel has been more outspokenly patriotic and vehemently in favor of a war effort than Fox News and viewers have responded favorably: its audience is up over 40 per cent in the past year and it now routinely beats CNN for total viewership[4].

As the 'war on terrorism' has escalated and has come to include war on Iraq, the press has remained generally in the thrall of the executive branch. What has made news are minor disagreements within the executive branch over tactics, such as the dispute between Secretary of State Colin Powell and Secretary of Defense Donald Rumsfeld over the role of the United Nations in the build-up to war on Iraq. But the idea of war itself and considerable public opposition to it has gone under-reported. In late October 2002, an anti-war rally in Washington DC drew at least 100,000 people, according to police estimates at the time, the largest anti-war demonstration, to that date, since the Vietnam War. But according to the *New York Times*, in an article headlined 'Thousands March in Washington Against Going to War in Iraq,' even though the sun had come out after days of rain 'fewer people attended than organizers had said they hoped for' (Clemetson, 2002). Flooded with protests and mounting evidence to the contrary, the *Times* published a new version of the event three days later with the headline 'Rally in Washington Is Said to Invigorate the Antiwar Movement,' noting that though organizers had expected about 30 bus loads of demonstrators, over 650 arrived from as far away as Nebraska and Florida (Zernike, 2002). Now, according to the *Times*, as many as 200,000 people may have joined the protest 'forming a two-mile wall of marchers around the White House' (Zernike, 2002: A17).

But The White House has done much more than rely on the apparent complicity of news agencies to ensure that its message gets through. In the period since 9/11, the White House has been remarkably bold in its effort to manage the flow of news and information. In early October 1991, Condoleezza Rice, President Bush's National Security Advisor told television network executives to exercise caution in broadcasting videotapes from Osama bin Laden because they could be a signal to terrorists to attack, this despite the fact that Al-Jazeera itself reaches close to 150,000 US households by satellite or cable (Carter and Barringer, 2001b). Rice's remonstration was part of a sequence of events to curtail access to information (RCFP, 2002; Clymer, 2003). Earlier that week members of Congress were shut out of intelligence briefings they normally attend and the daily Pentagon press briefings were cancelled. Three days after the attacks on the World Trade Center and the Pentagon, the Federal Aviation Administration removed information concerning 'enforcement actions' against security violators, including commercial airlines that flout safety rules; on 2 October, the Internal Revenue Service reading room eliminated public access except with an escort; by 7 October, the day the attacks on Afghanistan began, the Bureau of Transportation Statistics had removed the National Transportation Atlas Databases and the North American Transportation Atlas (which environmentalists often use to assess the potential impact of new highway construction), and the US Geological Service asked libraries to destroy all CD-ROM charting surface water supplies in the US. Two days after Rice's conference call to network executives, Attorney General John Ashcroft signed a memorandum that effectively reduced access to government documents under the Freedom of Information Act. On

1 November, President Bush issued Executive Order 13233 restricting public access to the papers of former presidents. Not least, as the number of detainees in the 'war on terrorism' multiplies, their names are withheld and the White House indicates that some may be tried by military tribunals with no public access. Even the President himself is less accessible: after his first 21 months in office, President Bush had held 36 news conferences, less than half the number held by President Clinton over the same period, and substantially less than the 61 held by his father over the same period (Rutenberg, 2002).

While access to information was being restricted on the home front, American journalists overseas were denied access to the Afghanistan battlefield, in spite of a 1992 agreement that reaffirmed the Pentagon's commitment to open press coverage of military campaigns. Updated in September 2000, the 'Statement of Principles: News Coverage of Combat' declares that 'open and independent reporting will be the principal means of coverage of US military operations,' and that 'pools are not to serve as the standard' for coverage (Aukofer and Lawrence, 1995: 197). But the first group of reporters to join US troops did not do so until 26 November – six weeks into the war. Even after, access was limited at best. The low point came on 6 December 2001, when Marines locked reporters and journalists in a warehouse to prevent coverage of American soldiers killed or injured by a stray bomb near Kandahar (RCFP, 2002; Hickey, 2002). The Pentagon apologized for the incident, but the orchestration of news continued, primarily through Secretary of Defense Rumsfeld's press briefing in Washington, a masterful display of minimalism dressed in congenial contempt for probing questions.

Each war presents its own logistical challenges. While the Pentagon – by way of Grenada, Panama, and the Persian Gulf – has virtually perfected the pooling of American journalists, new technologies conspire to make the job of controlling press coverage even more difficult. The most noteworthy of these is the commercial availability of detailed satellite imagery. In 1999, Space Imaging, a Colorado-based company, launched Ikonos, the first civilian satellite capable of rendering clear images of human bodies on the ground. As an end run around battlefield access, the press might have made use of Ikonos, but they could not. As the war began, the Pentagon bought exclusive rights to all Ikonos pictures of Afghanistan, though it already had six imaging satellites in orbit, four of them Keyhole satellites, capable of rendering images estimated to be six to ten times greater than Ikonos (Cochran, 1999; Campbell, 2001; Gordon, 2001). The decision to purchase the images was shrewd, not only because it denied the pictures to the press (and other would-be purchasers), but because it allowed the US government to avoid a riskier avenue of containment and control. The sale of satellite images are governed by US laws similar to those which govern the sale of weapons and other high-technology products. The Defense Department has the ability to exercise 'shutter control' over civilian satellites during times of war. However, the legality of 'shutter control' has never been tested in the courts. It is entirely possible that had the US government invoked it, one or more news organizations may have challenged shutter control as a violation of the First Amendment. Purchasing the Ikonos images was a way to avoid possible legal entanglement.

All of this takes place in a country where the legal tradition of freedom of the press has a long and, relatively, progressive history (Smolla, 1992). The legal history of the First Amendment as it applies to the activities and privileges of the press makes one thing clear: the defense (and extension) of press freedom depends on the willingness of news agencies to challenge government restrictions. A free press is a press willing to go to court to protect and defend its freedoms under difficult circumstances (Lewis, 1992). But since the publication of the Pentagon Papers in 1971 by the *Washington Post* and the *New York Times*, and the successful defense of their publication in court, press challenges have been few and victories fewer still[5]. During the Gulf War, it was *The Nation, Harper's, The Village Voice*, and 12 other small publications and individuals (including E. L. Doctorow) that carried the First Amendment case against press pooling into court. The case was deemed moot after the war ended and the pools were disbanded, but the presiding judge did add that 'the issues raised by the challenge present profound and novel challenges as to the existence of the scope of a First Amendment right of access in the context of military operations and national security concerns' (RCFP, 2002: 9; Smolla, 1992: 296). Afterward the major news agencies made noises that they should have joined that court challenge, and with the signing of the 1992 agreement with the Pentagon on press coverage they indicated that, at the very least, future attempts by the Pentagon to impose security review procedures would be challenged (Aukofer and Lawrence, 1995: 198). But the mainstream press took no legal action during the first six weeks of the war in Afghanistan when the Pentagon did not activate the press pools. It was left to *Hustler* magazine publisher Larry Flynt to carry the case to court. Flynt, who also challenged the use of press pools during the 1984 invasion of Grenada, filed suit on the grounds that journalists' access to the battlefield is a First Amendment right. Once again, the case was deemed moot: by the time it was heard, open coverage in Afghanistan had been restored and, for all intents and purposes, the war was over (RCFP, 2002: 10).

There is at least one other visible element to the state's information arsenal. Within the State Department, under the umbrella of the International Broadcasting Bureau, the US government owns and operates broadcasting services aimed at foreign audiences: Voice of America (VOA), Radio and TV Marti, WORLDNET TV, Radio Free Europe/Radio Liberty, and Radio Free Asia. The oldest of these, VOA, was born during World War Two and became a vital player in Cold War propaganda. It broadcasts in 53 languages worldwide. Together with cultural and educational programmes and exchanges, the broadcasters comprise what is termed 'the public diplomacy' arm of the US government (US Government, 2002). Since 9/11, public diplomacy has a new lease on life and a newly-minted Undersecretary of State for Public Diplomacy and Public Affairs, Charlotte Beers. Ms Beers has run two of the world's top advertising agencies, Ogilvy and Mather and J. Walter Thompson. Credited with changing the hearts and minds of Americans on everything from Uncle Ben's Rice to Campbell's Soup, Ms Beers reportedly said of her new job: 'This is the most sophisticated brand assignment I have ever had' (Carlson, 2001: C1). Public diplomacy may never be the same again. Beers has created a series of TV advertisements that have played in Indonesia and other South-East Asian countries that depict the lives of five American Muslims and the tolerant and open communities in which they live (Perlez, 2002). She has also spearheaded Radio Sawa (Radio Together). Now available throughout the Middle East, Radio Sawa features a blend of American and Arabic pop music with brief news segments twice an hour. Its objective: to reach the younger generation of Arabic-speakers with a hip dose of soft power, something the staid VOA was unable to do (Soskis, 2002; cf. Peterson, 2002). It is available at www.ibb.gov/radiosawa

4CISR and fear

For a short time in the autumn of 2002, at the entrance way to the Children's Aid Society's pre-school in Greenwich Village there was a poster with an anonymous quotation from one of the children. It read: 'something bad happened and then the flags came out'. How do we live in a time of fear? The answer from the White House seems to be that we should adopt a permanent state of national security exceptionalism. So far, domestic resistance to this information strategy has been meek and muted. A recent survey indicates that almost 50 per cent of Americans think that the First Amendment goes too far in the rights it guarantees and a similar number believe that the press has gone too far in criticizing the 'war on terrorism' (Paulson, 2002). As the White House extends its reach and closes its doors, it is adopting a military approach to civilian government and especially to the management of public information. In the early 1990s, the US military redesigned its information management strategic plan and introduced the label 4CISR. It means Command, Control, Communication, Computers, Intelligence, Surveillance, and Reconnaissance (Department of Defense, 1999). 4CISR may be an excellent model for military coordination. In some cases, it may even reduce the level of fear. But to live in a globalized world and to do global communication that will increase tolerance and make democratic governance possible will take more than militarized information management systems and flags. We need to talk.

Notes

1 Nye is keenly aware that soft power is a double-edged sword and that 'ambivalence about American culture' may limit its effectiveness. See Nye, 2002, especially, pp. 69–76.

2 Al-Jazeera maintains over 25 bureaus. It has had numerous run-ins with Arab governments that, historically, have shown little respect for freedom of the press. Saudi Arabia bars Al- Jazeera from its territory, except to cover special events (a recent talk show with Saudi dissidents was the last straw); Algeria cut its signal after a programme probed Algeria's civil war; Egypt's state media have campaigned against its 'sinister salad of sex, religion, and politics;' Bahrain has banned it for being 'pro-Israel;' and the Palestinian Authority has attempted to have unflattering images of Arafat removed from the air. After 9/11, Secretary of State Colin Powell asked Qatar to quell the station's enthusiasm for airing its exclusive 1998 interview with Osama bin Laden and what the US embassy in Qatar regarded as anti-American bias. Despite ranking as the region's most watched pan-Arab news network, Al-Jazeera does not attract as much advertising revenue as its competitors. Advertising accounts for only about 40 per cent of its revenues (Zednick, 2002; Simon, 2002).

3 It would appear that the use of the Protocols was a minor subplot of the broadcast and perhaps an attempt to boost ratings. Dream TV has flirted with controversy before. In the month before airing *Fares*, it annoyed Egyptian leaders by broadcasting criticisms of the government and a talk-show exploring the sexual angst of Egypt's young adults (Howeidy, 2002; Postelwaite, 2002).

4 Roger Ailes, the chairman of Fox News, part of Rupert Murdoch's News Corporation, has made no apologies for his network's tone. Nor has the former republican strategist, who helped George H. Bush reach the White House in 1988, apologized for the recent revelation that after the attacks of 9/11 he advised President Bush on how to cope with its aftermath (Woodward, 2002: 207; cf. Rutenberg, 2001).

5 The Pentagon Papers case, *New York Times vs. United States*, concerned prior restraint, not the right of access. The *Washington Post* and the *New York Times* had received copies of Defense Department documents detailing the history of US military strategy in Vietnam and began publishing them in serial form. The government sought and gained an injunction against further publication, but the Supreme Court ruled, by a bare majority, that the government could not prove a compelling threat to national security if publication continued. Later that year, in *Pell* v. *Procunier*, the Supreme Court said: 'It is one thing to say that the government cannot restrain the publication of news emanating from certain sources. It is quite another to suggest that the Constitution imposes upon the government the affirmative duty to make available to journalists sources of information not available to members of the public generally' (RCFP, 2002: 10). See also, Smolla (1992) and Levinson (2001).

References

Aukofer, F. and Lawrence, W. (1995) *America's Team: the Odd Couple: A Report on the Relationship Between the Media and the Military*. Nashville: The Freedom Forum First Amendment Center. Available at www.fac.org

Ayish, M. (2002) 'The Impact of Arab Satellite Television on Culture and Value Systems in Arab Countries: Perspectives and Issues', *Transnational Broadcasting Studies*. Vol. 9, Fall–Winter. Available at http://www.tbsjournal.com/Ayish.html

Boyd-Barrett, O. (1980) *The International News Agencies*. London: Constable.

Campbell, D. (2001) 'US Buys Up All Satellite War Images', *The Guardian*, 17 October, p. 1.

Carlson, P. (2001) 'The USA Account; Ad Woman Charlotte Beers' New Campaign: Getting the World to Buy America', *Washington Post*, 31 December, p. C1.

Carter, B. and Barringer, F. (2001a) 'In Patriotic Time, Dissent is Muted', *New York Times*. 28 September, p. A1.

Carter, B. and Barringer, F. (2001b) 'Networks Agree to U.S. Request to Edit Future bin Laden Tapes', *New York Times*, 11 October, p. A1.

Chapman, G. (1992) 'TV: The World Next Door?' *Intermedia*. 20 (1): 30–3.

Clemetson, L. (2002) 'Thousands March in Washington Against Going to War in Iraq', *New York Times*, 27 October, p. 8.

Clymer, A. (2003) 'Government Openness at Issue as Bush Holds On to Records', *New York Times*, 3 January, p. A1.

Cochran, B. (1999) 'Freedom of Information: Fighting the Feds Over Shutter Control', *Communicator*, December. Available at www.rtnda.org/foi/si.shtml

Cohen, L. (2001) 'Sticker Shock: Who Brands America 'United', 'On Alert' and in a 'New War'', *[Inside]*, 24 September www.inside.com

Department of Defense (1999) Information Management (IM) Strategic Plan: Information Superiority, version 2. October. Available at www.defenselink.mil/dodreform/briefs/itmstpln.doc

Ginsburg, F., Abu-Lughod, L. and Larkin, B. (eds) (2002) *Media Worlds: anthropology on a new terrain*. Berkeley: University of California Press.

Golden, T. (2002) 'Crisis Deepens Impact of Arab TV News', *New York Times*, 16 April, p. A16.

Gordon, M. (2001) 'Pentagon Corners Output of Special Afghan Images', *New York Times*, 19 October, p. B2.

Guaaybess, T. (2002) 'A New Order of Information in the Arab Broadcasting System', *Transnational Broadcasting Studies*, Vol. 9, Fall–Winter. Available at www.tbsjournal.com/Guaaybess.html

Hallin, D. (1997) 'The Media and War', in J. Corner, P. Schlesinger and R. Silverstone (eds) *International Media Research: A Critical Survey*. London: Routledge.

Hannerz, U. (1991) 'Scenarios for Peripheral Cultures', in A.D. King (ed.) *Culture, Globalization and the World-System*. London: Macmillan.

Herman, E. and Chomsky, N. (1988) *Manufacturing Consent – The Political Economy of the Mass Media*. New York: Pantheon.

Hessler, P. (2001) 'Straight To Video', *The New Yorker*, 15 October, pp. 83–7.

Hickey, N. (2002) 'Access denied: Pentagon's War Reporting Rules Are Toughest Ever', *Columbia Journalism Review*. 40 (5): 26–31.

Hoge, J. (1997) 'Foreign News: Who Gives a Damn?' *Columbia Journalism Review*, Vol. 36, November/December: 48–52.

Howeidy, A. (2002) 'Protocols, Politics and Palestine', *Al-Ahram* (weekly on-line). 7–13 November. Available at http://weekly.ahram.org.eg/2002//611/eg7.htm

Huntington, S. (1996) *The Clash of Civilizations and the Remaking of World Order*. New York: Simon and Schuster.

Jacinto, L. (2002) 'Pandora's Box: The Battle Lines are Drawn Over A Controversial Egyptian TV Series', *ABCNews.com*, 21 November. Available at http://abcnews.go.com/sections/world/DailyNews/egypt021121_TV.html

Lang, K. and Lang, G.E. (2000) 'How Americans View the World: Media Images and Public Knowledge', in H. Tumber (ed.) *Media Power, Professionals and Policies*. London: Routledge.

Levinson, S. (1991) 'What is the Constitution's Role During Wartime? Why Free Speech and Other Rights are Not as Safe as You Think', *Findlaw's Legal Commentary*. http://writ.news.findlaw.com/commentary/2001/1107-levinson.htm

Lewis, A. (1992) *Make No Law: the Sullivan case and the First Amendment*. New York: Vintage.

Moisy, C. (1996) *The Foreign News Flow in the Information Age*. Joan Shorenstein Center on the Press, Politics, and Public Policy: Harvard University. Discussion Paper D-23, November.

Nye, J. (2002) *The Paradox of American Power: Why the World's Only Superpower Can't Go it Alone*. New York: Oxford University Press.

Paulson, K. (2002) 'We Lose Sight of Our Rights When Freedom and Fear Collide,' Freedom Forum, 8 September. Available at www.freedomforum.org/templates/document.asp?documentID=16915

Perlez, J. (2002) 'Muslim-as-Apple-Pie Videos are Greeted With Skepticism', *New York Times*, 30 October, p. A1.

Peterson, P. (2002) 'Public Diplomacy and The War on Terrorism', *Foreign Affairs*. 81 (5): 75–94.

Postlewaite, S. (2002) 'A Mideast Media Revolution', *Business Week*, 23 December, p. 45.

Preston, W., Herman., E. and Schiller, H. (1989) *Hope and Folly: the United States and UNESCO, 1945–85*. Minneapolis: University of Minnesota Press.

Randal, J. (2000) *The Decline, But Not Yet Total Fall, of Foreign News in the U.S. Media*. Joan Shorenstein Center on the Press, Politics, and Public Policy: Harvard University, Working Paper Series.

RCFP (2002) *Homefront Confidential: How the War on Terrorism Affects Access to Information and the Public's Right to Know*. Reporters Committee for Freedom of the Press, 2nd ed., September. Available at www.rcfp.org/homefrontconfidential

Robinson, P. (2002) *The CNN Effect: The myth of news, foreign policy, and intervention*. London: Routledge.

Rutenberg, J. (2001) 'Fox portrays a War of Good and Evil, and Many Applaud', *New York Times*, 3 December, p. C1.

Rutenberg, J. (2002) 'White House Keeps a Grip on Its News', *New York Times*, 14 October, p. C1.

Rutenberg, J. and Carter, B. (2001) 'Draping Newscasts with the Flag', *New York Times*, 20 September, p. C8.

Shaw, D. (2001) 'Foreign News Shrinks in Era of Globalization', *Los Angeles Times*, 27 September.

Simon, J. (2002) 'Look Who's Inspiring Global Censorship', *Columbia Journalism Review*. 40 (5): 64–5.

Smith, A. (1990) 'Towards a Global Culture?' *Theory, Culture & Society*. Vol. 7: 171–91.

Smolla, R. (1992) *Free Speech in an Open Society*. New York: Vintage.

Soskis B. (2002) 'Weapons of Mass Diplomacy', *Shout*, October/November, pp. 54–7.

Tomlinson, J. (1990) *Cultural Imperialism: A Critical Introduction*. London: Pinter.

Tomlinson, J. (1999) *Globalization and Culture*. Chicago: University of Chicago Press.

Tracey, M. (1985) 'The Poisoned Chalice? International TV and the Idea of Dominance', *Daedalus*. 114 (4): 17–56.

UNESCO (United Nations, Educational, Scientific and Cultural Organization) (1945). *UNESCO Constitution*. Available at www.unesco.org/education/pdf/UNESCO_E.PDF

US Government (2002) *2002 Report: Building America's Public Diplomacy through Reformed Structure and Additional Resources*. U.S. Advisory Commission on Public Diplomacy. Available at www.state.gov/r/adcompd

Utley, G. (1997) 'The Shrinking of Foreign News: From Broadcast to Narrowcast,' *Foreign Affairs*. 76 (2): 2–10.

Woodward, B. (2002) *Bush at War*. New York: Simon and Schuster.

Zednik, R. (2002) 'Inside Al-Jazeera', *Columbia Journalism Review*. 40 (6): 44–7.

Zernike, K. (2002) 'Rally in Washington Is Said to Invigorate the Antiwar Movement', *New York Times*, 30 October, p. A17.

UNDERSTANDING NOT EMPATHY

Jean Seaton

News is one of the great political and artistic forms animating contemporary collective and private lives – and it deals with how we understand our condition. Violent news can be awesome and its bitter sights addictive. Yet at times we read and watch events comparable to the fall of Troy or the sack of Constantinople with casual indifference – or prefer other sillier, lighter, things.

News is often still treated as little more than either a mirror of reality or as something which is compromised by the habits which assist in its construction. There is far less concern with the way in which news has changed. Yet all news is not the same and we need to consider how one terrible and politically crucial kind of news is handled and consumed: news of hideous events that are important. This distinction already involves a media dimension – for political weight is attributed to events, partly at least, by the media. As Tim Allen has suggested, a modern definition of war might well be that of a conflict named as such by the media (Allen and Seaton, 1998). Yet although the news is often relentlessly preoccupied with the bizarre and unimportant, and journalists frenziedly sate themselves and their journals on events which are of no significance, nevertheless they do sometimes deal with terrifying and critical issues. Although these happenings and how they are displayed have a complicated relationship with history, as well as fiction and fantasy, the key to their unique authority is that they really did occur.

Nevertheless, of course, news does not merely happen. Even 'breaking news', apparently unfolding as it happens in front of our eyes requires tremendous efforts of organization and discrimination in order to create and present a vivid and convincing reality. Paddy Scannell's concern with 'liveness' as a long-term and fundamental aspect of the very nature of broadcasting is important here. Real-time news is as much a product of broadcasting practices as it is a consequence of the compulsion to present news, any news, faster and 'hotter' than previously (Scannell, 2000). Indeed, news reality is now so sophisticated and so much part of our experience that its capacity to weave together the components of an event into a single account is barely appreciated.

Thus we need to consider a particular kind of news – those stories that are about horrifying misfortunes, and especially those that have, or seek to claim political weight. News brings us, as spectators, into the direct apprehension of the tragic disruption of everyday lives. The sight of the contrast between quotidian normality broken by violence is always poignant. Yet we routinely watch events of overwhelming magnitude and importance to other people while we remain safe. It is into this world of casual and comfortable spectatorship that the news seeks to infiltrate and command attention. Of course, the contrast between comfort and horror is not new. In Homer's *Iliad*, the horror of such a contradiction is used to make audiences acutely sensitive to the fragility of normal life. It makes audiences appreciate the consolations of their own comfort more intensely. Andromache, Hector's young wife prepares for her husband's expected return from battle. In this passage, Hector the warrior is also described in his civilian aspect, sweetly and decorously as 'the guardian of chaste wives and little children'. Andromache does not yet know what we the audience already know – that Achilles has killed Hector and is desecrating the body outside the city walls of Troy. Busy in wifely concern, she dashes around the palace. She is dealing with emotional and material things – still in her everyday life, reminding spectators of the vulnerability of the private, tender world where individuals matter most to each other:

> Her voice rang through the house calling her bright-haired maidens
> To draw the great tripod to the fire that there might be
> A hot bath for Hector upon his return from combat.
> Foolish one! She knew not yet how far from hot baths
> The arm of Achilles had felled him – Because of the green-eyed Athena.
> (Homer, 1984: 393)

It is such a fracture of ordinariness that spectators of modern disasters are encouraged to observe in others while still themselves remaining close to their own hot baths. Perhaps it is illuminating to contrast the purposes of the construction of audience feelings in this moment with how the news is consumed. This episode comes in the greatest book of the *Iliad*, when the long drawn-out war around Troy has been going on for a decade, and the readers are intimately aware of the characters and fate of the protagonists. The *Iliad* shapes feelings so that audiences pity and hope for all of the characters in this moment, understanding but by no means condoning what has occurred, while prompted to reflect on their own condition. It is terrible but it is also engrossing and beautiful. Sometimes, the contemporary witnessing of catastrophe is grand and eloquent in a similar way, and widens our understanding of what drives other people and our own position, but at other times the media merely exploit suffering for sensation.

The witnessing of distress on a previously unimagined scale, often making of us unwittingly the spectators of violent death, may have many social effects. The journalism that presents us with the suffering of others is already a more complete act of witnessing (Durham Peters, 2001), as it both observes and articulates the condition of distant victims. Thus many of the processes of news-making are really concerned to secure the trust of the audience in its accounts – and this is important because of how unreliable we all know witnesses can be, motivated by their own interests or simply confused about what they have seen. The issue is partly how much of our passive witnessing of the news translates into an understanding that is useful – either for those that suffer misfortune, or indeed for ourselves.

News is how we know ourselves and the world. It can be ruthless in pursuit of a story. When a news 'feeding frenzy' is running it can seem to bystanders, or those subject to its attentions, more like a mob. To be on the inside of a news-hunt is appalling. News has become more savage over the last twenty years. Newsrooms and journalists construct stories that may be completely misleading – may in fact be lies – out of fragments of verifiable fact. Most news is about destruction, assassinating character, undermining futures. News is also a commodity, subject to market pressures, and always changing. The fact that there is a public interest in news being well made – that the realism of political estimates depends, at least in part, on its comprehensiveness and accuracy – is only one, increasingly weak element in the manufacture of news.

News is often routine and weary, repeating and inventing stories rather than finding and showing us what we need to understand. Some news is well made, curious and full of integrity. Other news is badly, lazily or corruptly made, while much is technically proficient but panders to what we would like the world to be like, or what the newsmakers would like the world to be like. Such news comforts us and confirms our complacent prejudices rather than alerting us to our conditions or that of others. Much of the time this does not matter, but sometimes it can be dangerous. When news only tells us what we want to hear, it displays a contempt for audiences, and when we collude with it we display a kind of contempt for our own possibilities. But in order for news to do either its fruitful, alerting work or its numbing, malevolent work, it has also to entertain us. At the very least it has to attract our attention. In this way the political explanation of the role of news in democracies as mobilizing publics around their own interests ought never be opposed, as it often is, to a quite different tradition: that of public amusement. Entertaining audiences is not a bad thing. Indeed, democracy requires news to be popular and good. But in any case entertainment and political expression are not antithetical; they simply cannot be separated. This is particularly true in the contemporary reporting of dreadful and compelling events.

The reality is that we appreciate – or even enjoy – thrillingly disturbing news. News is so incestuously inbred with democratic life that it responds to and helps shape every nuance of how parties, electorates, demographies, and political processes develop. Styles of news, attitudes towards politics and politicians, the political formation of generations of journalists, the political movements not folded into traditional parties, all set the increasingly difficult terms of trade between the media and politics. You do not 'reach' democracy and own it, nor do the media remain in a stable relationship with political forms. Partly we still need to ask crude questions about the purposes and effects that drive this particular kind of news-making. While this is ultimately an argument about politics, and teases at some of the pressures on news, and how audiences and stories develop, it is not about how the news has allegedly been 'dumbed down.' Such a view depends on what the historian Michael Schudson (1995: 3) has called 'retrospective wishful thinking', summing up visions of a mythic golden age of journalism which never existed. News is as disconcertingly volatile as democratic forms themselves. Arguably the news we get is faster, slicker, better informed and more popular than ever before. There is certainly more of it available – although perhaps only in the sense that there are more hours and more pages of it, and not always in the sense that news values have become deeper. Perhaps most importantly of all, live news, unfolding before our eyes on television as it happens, now exerts a seductive dominance. It has always been one goal of news to carry events to audiences as swiftly as possible, and the enchantment of seeing things as they happen are great. Yet other goals of journalism – to produce understanding, to produce reliable information, when rumours may sell as profitably as sourced information – have to accommodate to the new chemistry of time.

Journalists at different times, working in different periods of history when world events moved in different ways, with different ambitions, employed in brutally evolving industries are an important – but certainly not the sole – determinant of the news we get. It is also the product of how it is sold, what audiences appear to want, technological innovation, who owns the media, how they are regulated, social change together with developments in other competing sources of information and amusement. The potentially disturbing, untidy, irresolvable realities of the news vie increasingly directly with the cheaper, more predictable, more gratifying, less anxiety-provoking patterns of fictions and other realities – trials by ordeal for example – more susceptible to predictable or insignificant outcomes. News is under pressure and not all of those pressures are healthy, healthy neither for democracies nor for our realistic apprehension of what is happening. Broadcast news is losing its privileged positions in the schedules while news budgets get cut, not by accident but because all over the world there has been a long after-effect of so called 'deregulatory' policies that has stripped news of audiences. At the same time there have been changes in politics and the authority of politicians has been eroded. News is above all a business, and one that not only sells audiences but also one that is often increasingly a small part of wider commercial conglomerations with little interest in the product but a lot of interest in profit.

However, news and politics both act in the ever-shifting theatre of social values. At its very simplest, we need to consider how radically our expectations of what is acceptable evolve – and how this has influenced how we consume important and dreadful news. There is always a tension between what could be called a 'Whig' theory of values, in which we believe our contemporary preferences to be superior to those held in the past, and the competing narrative of moral decline. (Actually such views are central to news reporting.) Contemporary values seem to indicate that we now believe ourselves simultaneously more refined and delicate, more tender-hearted than our cruel predecessors, and more robust, liberal and prepared to face up to the horrid brutality than our squeamish recent ancestors. Thus we could set out to assess the real movement of values, say since World War Two, and there is no doubt that there is a determinate history to such things. The historian Mark Mazower has recently argued that the commitment to 'Human Rights' embodied in the United Nations Charter of 1947 – often seen as a transforming moment in international history – was a product of the impossibility in the post-war world of implementing the previous ideal: that of the integration of minorities (Mazower, 2002). The belief in the 'improvability' of the post-war world was in turn shattered by media representation of the conflicts in Biafra. Indeed, representing misery certainly has its own history which is disconcertingly independent of the history of misery itself.

We need a sceptical questioning of how we in the comfortable West recognize and deal with the things that happen to people. Values swirl in bewildering directions, and it is important to at least appreciate the speed of change and the ways in which this influences, and is influenced by, news and the practices of producing it. Does what we once found horrid no longer worry us or are we more fastidious than we were? In many ways the media are indeed far less influential than they appear, yet how the news seeks to bring us to understanding is not just an issue of survival, but a creative and cultural product as well.

One aspect of this sceptical questioning is to recognize that the ways in which news about savage events is constructed, and the ways in which we consume it, owe much to traditions that few practitioners or audiences are aware of. In this way news is part of a great tradition of representing torment in order to make claims on spectators. But representing pain is also always political. Conflict over the interpretation of pain has always been highly charged, and of real consequence to those in conflict. Martyrs need a theatre and an audience – otherwise they are merely victims. It may be that we can understand something of the role of the news by looking at the way in which arguments developed in the past about depicting suffering. In this way it uses analogy to help dissolve accustomed acceptances. The history of the representation of suffering has never been that of a simple reflection of events. We always distrust the pain of others and organizations as disparate as the Royal Society of Anaesthetists, Amnesty International and the Hospice movement share a focus on diminishing our suspicions. In such a process the media are key agents of change, bringing to our attention, ranking and focusing concern on legitimated suffering. But showing pain always denotes an argument and interest. This does not diminish its hold over us or our obligations to those in difficulty (whether we act to help them or not). But the political and argumentative nature of such news is an uncomfortable but stark reality. It is also related to the various ways in which we enjoy being spectators of harsh events.

Thus we also believe that our witnessing of the endurance of others speaks well of us. It is not merely that our knowledge may be useful to subjects, but also there is virtue in frankly recognizing the suffering of others. News comes at the end of a long, deeply embedded belief in the value of witnessing suffering. Being a spectator may sometimes bring out the best in us – we might be ashamed of not responding to what we see in a way that we would be prepared to defend in front of others. Of course being a spectator can also bring out the worst aspects of collective sentiment, calling up irrational and frequently punishing frenzies. But in either case the first task of the news is to catch, and to hold our attention when there is so much competition for it. In this way news of terrible events have a particular value because they can make large claims to be worthy of attention.

Indeed, news practices now bear a great weight of common experience and provide rhetorically ubiquitous ways of dealing with crises in our collective and personal lives. Thus, to take one example in the past, historians like Phillipe Aries (1977) have claimed everyone was familiar with the 'good' quiet death of the private citizen but went on to suggest that modern practices had become impoverished. On the contrary, now it is the 'bad' death of news disaster whose rituals we all understand. News which tells the story of the unjust violent death is our key way of resolving, in contemporary terms, the age-old problem of the proper dispatch of the lingering but not yet re-socialized person of those who have died. Modern, mass-consumed news has also, in an important way democratized age-old issues about the transfer of power embodied in funeral rights. Great state funerals developed in order to stabilize and legitimate transfers of power; now news accounts of the undeserved death of humble commoners can carry huge emotional and, even more critically, political weight.

But are these rituals and habits producing a common, even global, way of experiencing the world? There has been a huge spread in the interest in arguments about human rights. Has this been influenced by spectatorship? Does the ubiquity of news rituals produce common feelings? All over the world news looks the same, so do we all share a sentimental education? There have been many arguments about the role of feeling in contemporary life, but any empathy we might feel for the situation of others is now mediated through the media. The media are not an optional add-on extra to how we understand the world; we all see things through their eyes, and the habits of emotional argument are shaped through public taste. Thus do we all feel the same now? Surely feelings are in fact always processed through any public's sense of its own interests. Feelings are modulated by circumstances. This may be unfashionable but sentiments are still refracted through how people grasp their own interests and situations. Political calculation still calibrates feeling. This is not merely to say that audience members 'interpret' what they consume differently – of course they do. The point is different. It is about the intimate relationship between keenly felt individual feelings and the larger political calculations that drive the sentiments of whole audiences. The news media are often vital to this relationship. Surely I am not alone in being at times disconcerted by how vividly I 'feel' about events? Or indeed the disconcertingly similar nature of the feelings to those of everyone else? Recognizing the politics of sensibility is an important step to putting volatile (and frequently unpleasant and punishing) sentiment into perspective. Thus just as news may 'heat' up feelings, the rational 'chilling' of feeling by information has trad. 'on-ally been a key democratic role of the news. Yet, it is one which commercial interests militate increasingly against. Indeed, as Schudson has shown, news mutates. And the contemporary combination of declining press circulations together with a still powerful press domination over the news agenda makes the pressures on news ever more heated. News is changing but there are few institutions or authorities that hold the news itself to be accountable.

News has to simplify things while not trivializing them (if they are not trivial). It is a tough challenge. In order to do this it shapes events into stories and attracts our attention to things that matter (as well as diverting us with things that hardly matter that we all enjoy, some of which profoundly form and express values and expectations). The fierce discipline of producing stories, some of which are very hard to write or make, is central to news. The competition in the market for readers' and viewers' attention is desperate and the source of such independent power that the media exercise. So the pressure to fit events into well-understood frameworks is intense. Yet history and our condition is disturbingly manifold. Sometimes the shaping of stories makes them more like dramas with resolutions satisfyingly predictable (even if horrible) rather than the tragedies that they really are. As risky conflict is exciting and the news has to gain attention, genuine causes go unexplored in comparison to the thrillingly familiar horrors of well-recognized genres of violence, disaster and catastrophe. There are many pressures on news-making that push it towards pleasing us rather than illuminating the anxious variety of what is happening. Thus on 11 September 2001 CNN was running the unfolding story under the headline *America Under Attack!* By the second day this had changed to *America Strikes Back!* – as if what we were seeing were episodes in a familiar blockbuster called *War*. It is not only that all wars are distinct, but that news remains one of our key ways of recognizing these important differences. Of course, audiences are sometimes difficult, bored, uninterested and lazy, and sometimes the news-making media have to act as substitutes for the ideal alert citizen, standing in their stead. But leading audiences to the understanding of real difference and real change is what we all most need from the news. The really viscerally shocking thing is the novel and the unexpected and the congealed difficulty of knowing what is to be done with obdurate events.

Thus how journalists make news, and the institutions they work in that shape it, are changing. How together they reflect and manage audience attention is also altering. Sometimes, though not always, this is done in the interest of the journey of the story about things people might also prefer not to know about. It is, of course, possible to distinguish between the well informed, principled journalism produced by responsible and ambitious journalists working for good outfits, and the terrible depressing, enervating, vicious and demeaning stuff that also goes under the name of news. Such differences are very important to the quality of our public lives – and indeed to our safety and health. Some journalists working in some organizations reporting on some stories are models of a kind of propriety. Scrupulous, principled and quite often brave. But much journalism survives on an exposed precipice that the public and consumers barely begin to appreciate – poised between the glamour of the stories and the squalor of journalism. News stories, the actors in public imaginative life are always glamorous because they matter. But journalists survive unsteadily from one story to the next in the fairly brutal world of news-making in which the real world outcomes of stories are not the responsibility of journalists or the news. Concern for the quality of news institutions is a matter of real public concern, yet there is barely a discussion of how the news might at least be made a little more accountable.

Yet distinguishing between good and irresponsible, venal, malignant journalism is only partly the issue. For both kinds are dominated by the demands of the form that news has become. News is a collective transitory efflorescence that as a form changes over time. As such it is a revealing and a powerful contemporary collective cultural product. One whose condition we ought always to be concerned about. Oddly enough, however, the argument is not about how powerful the media are and they are often invested with a modern witchcraft and ascribed the magic power of alchemy (this is certainly how they feel if you are in the uncomfortable needy world of the news subject rather than the cosy safety of observing). But it is rather about how much news is part of other social structures, and also about how really subject to change it is.

Journalists do not trust what other people write about their business (just like academics and doctors and people who work in the Treasury would be equally uncomfortable with the views of outsiders about what they do.) News-making can be a peculiarly engrossing, high-octane and competitive industry, and people in it feel, understandably, that they know more about it than mere observers. Good journalists bear the scars of battles for things that matter. It is important to recognize this as well as asking some rather obvious questions about the role of news because how we apprehend very important, very unpleasant things often feels rather distant – though it may, of course, at any moment become a more intimate and direct problem.

News has a difficult job here: helping us sympathize with people by elucidating how like us they are, is one aspect of what it has to do. Partly because it may make audiences understand what is going on better, as it makes the appeal of the story directly relevant to something they already understand. It is a common and proper complaint that all too often the news makes people in different circumstances to us dismissible because they are portrayed as 'other' and not quite human in the same way that we the consumers are. This eliciting of empathy is also a good way of selling the news because it involves using our feelings about ourselves, which tend to be strongly held and vivid, in order to construe how someone else responds to the worst things that can happen to people. It is also usually celebrated as the basis for wanting remedies to be supplied. According to the influential political philosopher John Rawls: 'With justice, we require not only common principles, but sufficient ways of applying them in particular cases so that the final ordering of conflicting claims can be defined . . . we do this by seeing *others* and ourselves in the same way.' Such a view, he argues, means that 'the perspective of eternity is not a perspective from a certain place beyond the world . . . rather it is a certain form of thought and feeling that rational persons can adopt within the world' (Rawls, 1999: 514). But however attractive empathy is, there is something self-reflective about it and it runs the danger of telling us about ourselves and not about the difficult things we need to know.

Empathy makes us feel good, which is, after all, very easy to bear. News ought to deal in the real world of grey confused reality, when the actions of good people may have dire effects and unattractive people be the only ones you have to work with. We need news to elucidate the reality that compromise means giving up things you really care about and that compromise is not 'sell-out' but, perhaps uncomfortably, the very stuff of the only way we have of managing the world: politics. At the same time, in a harsh commercial climate, press, broadcast and online news may be too anxious about our sensibilities because they underestimate public appetite for reality or are worried about the market consequences of unpalatability.

Of course, the news also demonizes some actors, implying that those who are our enemies are not at all normal, and that empathy is tantamount to approval. At the same time it canonizes other groups as innocent victims. The reality is frequently more disturbing. Indeed, arguably, the other real job for the news, one in sharp tension with empathy, is that of describing the real divergences between people. Grasping how other people's interests are really different and even opposed to our own requires realism and sometimes toleration – that most strenuous and unpleasant of tasks. The *Iliad* took its audiences to the heart of painful, bitter events, but although it mobilized sentiment it did so in the service of understanding. It is the most even-handed and scrupulous account of harrowing events. It is never propaganda but it deals in harsh truths. So must news (see Seaton, forthcoming). If the news pleases us too much it may fail to alert us properly and this is not a moral problem, but a hard, practical, self-interested one of survival.

References

Allen, T. and Seaton, J. (1998) 'Introduction' to *The Media of Conflict*. London: Zed Books.

Aries, P. (1977) *The Good Death*. Harmondsworth: Penguin.

Durham Peters, J. (2001) 'Witnessing', *Media Culture and Society*. 23 (6): 707–724.

Homer (1984) *The Iliad*. translated by R. Fitzgerald. Oxford: Oxford University Press. p. 393.

Mazower, M. (2002) 'Hitler and the Creation of Human Rights', Inaugural Lecture, Birkbeck College, University of London, February.

Rawls, J. (1999) *A Theory of Justice*. Oxford: Oxford University Press. (1st edn, 1971.)

Scannell, P. (2000) *Broadcasting and Everyday Life*. Oxford: Blackwell.

Schudson, M. (1995) *The Power of News*. Cambridge, MA: Harvard University Press.

Seaton, J. (forthcoming) *Carnage and the Media*. London: Penguin Press.

Part 2

NEW DIMENSIONS OF MANAGING CONFLICT

INFORMATION WARFARE IN AN AGE OF GLOBALIZATION*

Frank Webster

We live today in an era of 'new wars', which is to say that the circumstances surrounding such conflicts have been radically transformed by the ending of the Cold War, the triumph of neo-liberalism, and the accelerated spread of globalization which is simultaneously integrating and fragmenting the world while radically reducing time and space constraints (Kaldor, 1999). Furthermore, war itself is changing, increasingly being what one might call Information War (for those most able to wage it), by which is broadly meant saturation with information and communications technologies (ICTs), plus a special concern for the media.

In this milieu, media play an integral and vital role both in the conduct and even in the commencement of war. To be sure, there has long been a close association between media and warfare, but as a rule media have been harnessed closely to the war effort, being conscripted (usually willingly) to support the struggle of the motherland. However, in the different circumstances which prevail today – and I shall argue that 'new wars' and 'information warfare' mark a radical change – media may, and indeed generally do, play a different, much more ambiguous and ambivalent role than hitherto.

Globalization

Globalization needs to be placed at the core of the argument. It has been much discussed and debated, particularly at the level of economics and politics (Held *et al.*, 1999). But the symbolic dimensions of globalization ought not to be underestimated. Globalization is having enormous consequences on the cultural level, simultaneously bringing into being a common symbolic environment as well as different outlooks, practices and opinions. Media are to the fore in this, but one ought also to factor in the astonishing growth of migration, travel, cuisine, music and clothing to fully appreciate the simultaneous spread of similarity and difference. It is an extraordinary feature of the world today that there is so much more symbolic content, and that this is available continuously from around the globe. At once this is inflected, being massively disproportionately Western, yet the symbolic environment is also more diverse and differentiated than hitherto (Tomlinson, 1999). The media explosion of recent decades has led to there being staggering amounts of information available today – anywhere, anytime we have 24 hour news services, entertainment, radio talk shows, and internet sites. This is dominated by the West, but there is such a quantity of information, in so many different outlets, coming with such velocity and with such turnover that, in a real sense, it is beyond control.

In this context, with regard to media coverage of warfare, two points may be made. The first is that war is newsworthy and, as such, of compelling interest to media. War is dramatic, attention-grabbing, and played for enormously high stakes and, as such, it is a top priority for news-makers. This does not mean that war is in itself sufficient to gain media attention – there are clearly other factors involved such as the scale and intensity of the conflict, its location, where the participants come from, as well as its strategic implications. However, the inherent newsworthiness of war remains and increases the likelihood of it receiving prominent and sustained attention.

A second feature of media and warfare is paradoxical: one witnesses journalists acting from a deep ethical commitment at the same time as they exude profound cynicism towards sources of information on the conflicts they cover. Amongst the most revered journalists covering war are those with reputations for seeking 'truth', however much that might displease powerful interests. One thinks here, for instance, of exposés from Vietnam by the likes of Seymour Hersh and David Halberstam; of William Shawcross' dispatches from Chile, pointing the finger at US involvement following the Pinochet coup in 1973; of John Pilger's accounts of Cambodian atrocities in the early 1980s; of Robert Fisk's thirty-year record of filing reports from Northern Ireland, Lebanon and Afghanistan; of Maggie O'Kane from the Balkans, and of Suzanne Goldenberg's fearless accounts of the recent situation in Israel for the *Guardian* newspaper. Phillip Knightley (2000) wrote a fine book on war reporting during the 1970s which he titled *The First Casualty*, and it is often so that truth is blurred in the fog of war. But Knightley himself, and many other war journalists, testify to an ethic of resistance to manipulation of news in warfare. This is not to say that it does not happen, but it is to stress that there is an ethic imbued in them that their mission is to 'tell it like it is', no matter how difficult that may be and no matter how unpopular this may make one with the powers that be. War reporting, it might be added, is a dangerous occupation, there being more fatalities amongst journalists in Afghanistan in late 2001 than there were amongst United States troops (Tumber, 2002).

The cynicism comes in large part from the experiences of the reporters in conflict situations, where they are likely to receive sharply conflicting accounts of events. A particular cause is surely the efforts of combatants to 'perception manage'. Since the Vietnam War and the humiliating defeat there of America, the notion that it was an uncontrolled media which led to withdrawal gained ground amongst powerful figures, in military circles especially. Beginning with Robert Elegant's *Encounter* article, 'How to Lose a War' (1981), the conviction that media were important to war, but not to be trusted, informed military and political 'planning for war'. Since then there has been a marked preparedness to 'handle' journalists, with 'minders' allocated, military spokespeople carefully groomed, and 'unfriendly' reporters held at bay. So self-conscious and developed is this process of 'perception management' that it is easy to believe that the outcome in terms of media coverage is a one-way flood of items gathered away from the battlefield, at locations chosen by the military, and from handouts issued by the Ministry of Defence. In certain circumstances, this may indeed be the case – coverage from the Falklands, far away in the South Atlantic, accessible only by military transport, and with the media reliant on military technologies to get their messages through is one such example (Morrison and Tumber, 1988). Against this, however, what the efforts to manage war coverage by those who wage it have done for journalists is to bolster their scepticism. It makes a cynical profession more cynical still when it notes the attempts of the military and official spokespeople to ensure that the media are 'on side'. When one adds to this the fact that journalists nowadays converge on trouble spots from around the globe, then one appreciates how difficult tight control becomes. There were an estimated 2000 journalists in the Kosovo region during 1999; it is simply too complex a situation and they are too variegated a bunch of people to be straightforwardly controlled. Together these factors mean that, however urgent and sustained the efforts to control and contain coverage made by combatants are, there will always be 'seepage' in what gets out.

One needs to factor into the above the important influence of globalization on the nation state. No one thinks that the nation state is set to disappear in the near future. Nevertheless, globalization does mean that nation states are increasingly 'porous'. At the level of the symbolic, globalization means that nations are markedly less self-contained and exclusive than before, less able to contain the information people within receive and give out. On one level, this is a matter of technological change – cable and satellite television, and computer communications facilities, mean that it is increasingly difficult for nations to restrict what their inhabitants watch and send because technologies thwart attempts to do so. At another level, however, there is a worldwide decline of deference, an increased unwillingness to know one's place and not question what one's leaders do, which stimulates the development of information which is challenging and even critical. An important dimension of this tendency is the global development of democracy and the human rights that accompany it. There are many illustrations of this – few more vivid than reportage of the British monarchy. Fifty years ago all was due reverence, the national media leading the way in enhancing the mystique of the Royal Family. For the last decade and more, however, there has been markedly salacious treatment, audacious approaches to the monarchy which stress its 'ordinary' celebrity, even soap opera, status. The marital problems, and extra-marital relations, of Princess Diana and Prince Charles, were given enormous, intrusive and vivid coverage across the globe.

One might add here some observations on globalization's effect on other matters, which are of enormous consequence. An effect of globalization has been the stimulation of what Anthony Giddens has termed 'states without enemies' (Giddens, 1994: 235). The reasoning goes that, if there is large-scale crossover of ownership of capital, real-time decision-making across borders, increasingly open markets and heightened trade around the globe, then there is a declining propensity for nations to go to war with one another over territory. For the last several centuries war has been primarily about precisely this – land and the resources that accompanied its seizure by one side or the other. If it is the case that territory is no longer of such compelling importance in today's world, then logically it follows that states are less likely to have enemies with whom they may fight. The Stockholm International Peace Research Institute gives credence to this view when it reports that, in 2001, there were 24 major armed conflicts, only one of which (between India and Pakistan) was interstate (SIPRI, 2002: 11).

One might suppose that this heralds an era of world peace, but there are more negative effects of globalization which stoke conflict. There is a toxic mix of increased inequalities on a global scale (for instance, the United States, with two per cent of world population, accounts for almost one-third of the world's wealth) and frenetic change induced by heightened competition and technological innovation which exacerbates fragmentation. The advantaged, those with access to capital and possessed of high-level education, may thrive in this world of flexibility, movement and restlessness, but the excluded and marginal find it deeply disconcerting and threatening. This is fertile ground for the strengthening of fundamentalisms of various sorts. Fundamentalism is an expression of certainty in an uncertain world – it is an insistence that some things are not subject to change or challenge, that there are some absolutes of morality, behaviour and belief. It may take many forms, from born-again Christianity to neo-fascism, from an escape into asceticism to embrace of deep ecology – and it may also find outlets in militant zealotry which can feed into terrorist organization and action (for example, the 1995 Oklahoma bombing perpetrated by Timothy McVeigh, a Christian fanatic, and arson attacks on ethnic minorities).

In these circumstances we may experience the emergence of what Giddens (1994) terms 'enemies without states', where fundamentalists combine to resist the 'Great Satan' of globalized and secular capitalism in the name of an absolutist creed which disregards national borders. This is the milieu in which Al-Qaeda and the Osama bin Laden network is situated. Elsewhere we find instances of fundamentalist creeds which urge 'ethnic cleansing' of 'aliens' in the name of a mythic nation – fighting what have been called 'degenerate wars' in regions that have been hard hit by instabilities exacerbated by recent geo-political changes. This reveals an enemy of globalization of which, after 11 September 2001, we are well aware. However, it is a new sort of enemy which poses serious problems for the state's conduct of war which, traditionally, has been conducted against other nations in the name of defence of one's own country.

This is a context in which profound questions are posed for media. If the context is one in which the media are both more pervasive and beyond control by the nation, while national boundaries and reasons for conducting war (and harnessing the media to that end) are diminishing, then what is the motivation for reporting disputes and what might be its consequences? I think we may gain a better perspective on this by drawing a distinction between Industrial and Information Warfare.

Industrial Warfare

Industrial Warfare, which may be said to have characterized the period from around 1914 into the 1970s, includes the following features:

- War was conducted, for the most part, between nation states and chiefly concerned disputes over territory.
- Mobilization of large elements of, and indeed entire, populations was undertaken to support the war effort.
- Sustained efforts to dovetail industrial production and the military struggle, often involving quasi-nationalization, in a strategy of 'total war'.
- Participation of huge numbers of combatants, something generally involving the conscription of a majority of young men. Concomitantly, when these massed forces were put into action, mass casualties were sustained.
- Strenuous efforts to plan the war effort as a whole, something which extended from government take-over of industries such as transport and energy that were deemed essential to the war effort,

through to elaborate and detailed strategies drawn up by military commanders who would decide centrally how best to deploy their forces.

- Harnessing media to assist the war effort by laying emphasis on the national interest, hence nurturing strong media commitment in support of the fighting forces and using, where necessary, national powers to censor and direct information.

Information Warfare

Over the past generation or so we have seen the unravelling of Industrial Warfare, to be replaced, in an incremental but accelerating manner, by what one might term Information Warfare. There is a tendency to conceive this in somewhat narrow technological terms, hence the much discussed Revolution in Military Affairs (RMA). This evokes radical changes in military technologies, from the 'digital soldier' to the latest technologies involving drones, satellites and computer-drenched weapons of bewildering complexity (Cohen, 1996). I conceive Information Warfare in broader terms than the technological. Amongst its other distinguishing features are the following:

- Information Warfare no longer requires the mass mobilization of the population. Conduct of war relies on relatively small numbers of professional soldiers, pilots and support teams. This represents a shift in the military towards what have been called 'knowledge warriors', a term which underscores the centrality of personnel adept in handling complex and computerized tools such as advanced fighter aircraft, surveillance systems, and guidance technologies.
- This changing character of the military machine is consonant with what have been described as 'post-military societies' (Shaw, 1991) where war-fighting institutions have moved to the margins of society and have taken on more specialized and technically demanding roles, as well as with what Edward Luttwak (1996) has called a 'post-heroic' military policy where one's own side brings to bear overwhelming force on an enemy chiefly through bombing while few, if any, casualties are risked from one's own side.
- The expectation is that future conflicts will be what have been termed 'instant wars' (Castells, 1996: 454–61), by which are meant relatively brief encounters, with active operations lasting only for days or a few weeks, in which the US (or NATO and/or UN approved forces) is victorious by virtue of the overwhelming superiority of its military resources. The Persian Gulf War of 1991, the Balkans War

of 1999, and the Afghanistan battles of 2001, each of which lasted between just six and eleven weeks, exemplify this feature. In the Gulf War the Allied Forces were insuperably better equipped than were the Iraqis, and the consequences were evident in the brevity of the campaign and in the respective losses: 300 or so on the American and British side, between 30,000 and 60,000 on the enemy's, the Iraqis having endured 42 days of war in which, it has been estimated, more explosive power was delivered than during the whole of World War Two (Mandeles *et al.*, 1996: 24). The situation in Serbia during 1999 was broadly comparable. There was extreme reluctance to commit ground troops from the NATO alliance for fear of taking casualties against which domestic opinion might rebel. Accordingly, the war was fought by NATO entirely from the air and there were no fatalities inflicted on the allies by the Serbian forces. And in the war against the Taliban in Afghanistan during late 2001, despite the anxieties expressed beforehand (about hardened and zealous warriors, in treacherous terrain and with heavy armaments – much the same fears had been expressed about battle toughened Serbian troops in 1999), the war was rapidly brought to an end with minimal US loss and little soldier-to-soldier combat (air attack dominated and the US enjoyed absolute supremacy).

- Information Warfare requires meticulous planning, but this is planning for flexibility of response, in contrast to the much more elaborate plans of the Industrial Warfare period. Today enormous volumes of information flows, along with the incorporation of software into weapons themselves, feeding into complex planning for war which prioritizes mobility, flexibility, and rapid reaction. A recurrent theme now is that the military should have flexibility to 'swarm' into troubled regions, to converge at speed from various points to attack enemies that are also likely to be dispersed (Arquilla and Ronfeldt, 2001). There are many examples of this 'fusing information with firepower' (IISS, 2002: 235), from the presence of AWACS (Airborne Warning and Control Systems) planes, con-tinuously off the ground, which monitor huge areas in detail, then pin-point targets for precision attacks from backup forces, to the capacity, during the Afghanistan battles, for air command in Saudi Arabia to deliver bomb strikes to Afghanistan within 19 minutes of receiving co-ordinates from special forces on the ground.
- The removal of the civilian population to the margins of the day-to-day conduct of Information Warfare, and the reliance on expert 'knowledge warriors', has profound implications for the experi-ences of war. Without mass mobilization, the general population has little direct involvement with Information War, even when this is undertaken in its name. Against this, however, the general population has a very much expanded second-hand experience of

warfare, in the particular sense of massively increased media coverage of conflicts (of which more below). That is, while in Information Warfare the fighting units are at the margins of society, media coverage is massive and a most important and intrusive dimension of the wider public's experiences of war.

- It follows that Information Warfare must devote great attention to 'perception management' of the population at home and, indeed, round the world. This is especially pressing in democratic nations where public opinion is a vital factor in the war effort and where a nagging fear for military leaders is a concerted domestic reaction against the war since this may seriously impinge on the fighting capability of their forces. Information War relies much less on the public than does Industrial War, since the public is unlikely to be involved or even seriously affected by such war. However, precisely because Information Warfare is typically waged in the name of democracy itself, then public approval is critical to its conduct. A corollary is that, while today the public are no longer mobilized to fight wars as combatants, they are mobilized as spectators of war – and the character of this mobilization is of utmost consequence (Ignatieff, 2000). From the military leadership there is apprehension that the public will react to vivid pictures from the battle zones of the wrong sort, as there is serious domestic opposition to the war being extensively reported and even sympathetically treated. Inevitably, this impels military and political leaders into management of information from and about the war, though at the same time assiduous efforts must be made to avoid the charge of censorship, since this flies in the face of democratic states having a 'free media' and it risks undermining the credibility of what does get reported. Perception management must therefore attempt to combine ways of ensuring a continuous stream of media coverage that is positive and yet ostensibly freely gathered by independent news agencies. This is extraordinarily difficult to achieve in today's complex and variegated information environment.

Information warfare, human rights and media

It is obvious that during conflict combatants desire to have the media on board, so that what happens in war is presented in ways that are acceptable to the wider public. However, 'perception management' is difficult to achieve, chiefly because strict control of the media in an era of globalization is impossible when there are thousands of journalists present, when they define their role primarily as an investigate activity and they are sceptical of news sources, when domestic dissent is sure to get some coverage in democratic regimes, and where technologies, from video cameras to the internet, mean that images, reports and opinions are relatively easily gathered and communicated.

But the media are needed for more than reporting acceptable news from the battlefield. They are also central players in justifying war itself, and again, especially so in democratic regimes. It needs to be held in mind that the late twentieth century witnessed dramatic progress in the expansion of democracies. By the end of the millennium 140 of nearly 200 nations held multi-party elections (Human Development Report, 2002). Democratization, while by no means complete, advanced remarkably around the globe, and with it its close cousin, respect for, and concern about, human rights (Eley, 2002). Accordingly, the public may only be spectators in Information Warfare, but interventions need to be legitimated and, in today's world, this is considerably more difficult than in the period of Industrial Warfare, when the nation at war, for national interests, could harness national media to its war ends. On the one hand, this legitimation is essential because withdrawal of public support means that the fighting forces are weakened in their efforts. On the other hand, this need to gain public support in democratic societies is a key point of entry for consideration of 'human rights regimes'. And this is, necessarily, something in which media are involved, not merely as conduits for opinions of military or government leaders (though this is present), but as agencies which examine and explore the democratic bases for interventions from outside.

Furthermore, media are generally present before actual war starts, and can play a key role in 'shaming' regimes by exposing poor human rights records and even in instigating intervention in certain areas. There were, for instance, alarming reports about the chaotic and murderous situation in Sierra Leone prior to British intervention in 2000 which were quickly amplified as politicians and other concerned parties picked up on the coverage. There has developed an increased sensitivity towards, and awareness of, 'human rights' and their abuses around the world. The spread of news reportage and television documentaries are crucial, but so too is the massive extension of foreign travel, as well as organizations such as Amnesty International, UNICEF, Human Rights Watch, the Red Cross and Médecins Sans Frontiers. The proliferation of non-governmental organizations (the United Nations calculates that in 2000 there were 37,000 recognized NGOs, a 20 per cent growth in a decade) has been an important factor in inculcating sensitivity to one's fellow human beings across national frontiers. Of course NGOs do not act with a single purpose, and neither do they transmit messages of a uniform kind, but they do engender sentiments that human beings have universal rights – of freedom from persecution and torture, of religious toleration, of open elections, of self-determination, of political representation, of suffrage, of access to resources such as food and water, and so forth. It may be objected that this commitment to 'human rights' is vague, but nowadays it has important institutional support and presence.

In addition, accelerated globalization and the collapse of communism have weakened nation states and encouraged a more global orientation in which universal rights are more important than hitherto. This represents a significant break with established practices where emphasis has been placed on the territorial integrity of nations. Appalling things might be happening to citizens inside a nation, but to date it has been exceedingly difficult to envisage other governments, so long as their own borders and/or interests were not threatened, intervening out of concern for victims within another's sovereign territory. Even today it is not easy to get international forces to invade others' national frontiers. It is possible, for instance, that NATO's involvement in Kosovo would not have happened but for the horrific recent history of Bosnia, itself given saturation media coverage, and perhaps most notably the slaughter by the Serbian militia of up to 7,000 Muslim men and adolescent boys who surrendered at Srebrenica in July 1995.

At the same time, neither the NATO involvement in Kosovo during the spring and early summer of 1999, nor the British entry into Sierra Leone in 2000, can be explained satisfactorily in terms of strategic, still less territorial interests that dominated military decision-making in the days of the supreme nation state. Since there has been a recent propensity to suggest that anti-Islamic feeling motivates the Western powers, it is perhaps important to remember that the Kosovo intervention was to assist Muslims who were being attacked and dispossessed by Serb forces. With regard to Sierra Leone, this tiny nation has scarcely any significance on the global stage, but ten years of internecine struggle, the displacement of almost 50 per cent of the 4.5 million population, and the practice of the 'Revolutionary United Front' for using child soldiers and routinely mutilating those who crossed its path, persuaded the Blair government to order troops into the country so that the bloodshed would be stopped. Of course, strategic interests have by no means disappeared, as the 'realist' advice at the time of these interventions testifies: to stay out of areas where ancient ethnic hatreds prevailed and where no direct interest was evident. Nonetheless, they have weakened *vis-à-vis* the pressures of human rights and democratization. Thus the attack on the Taliban forces by the US was presented not only as an assault on forces supporting the terrorists who carried out the bombing of the Twin Towers on 11 September 2001, but also as a rejection of those who denied basic human rights especially to women (girls excluded from school, women excluded from social affairs and forced to wear the *burqa* (Hitchens, 2001)).

The abject circumstances of the Jews inside Nazi Germany, over a period in excess of a decade, seems to me to be an instance of the former extreme unwillingness for outsider nations to become involved in others' internal affairs until their own borders were threatened. And even then, it should be remembered, total war was waged to counter German territorial aggression rather than to resist the genocidal policies that were being implemented inside the Axis nations – the most telling evidence for which being the well-documented reluctance of the Allies to give sanctuary to large numbers of Jewish refugees just before and even during the War, as well as the refusal to bomb extermination camps though the 'final solution' policy was known by the early 1940s and millions of Jews had already been murdered (Lacquer, 1980; London, 2000; Wasserstein, 1979).

Václav Havel (1999) articulated the changed situation when he voiced support for the NATO engagement in Kosovo on the grounds that 'the notion that it is none of our business what happens in another country and whether human rights are violated in that country. . . should . . . vanish down the trapdoor of history'. Tony Blair, more directly involved, made the same case for intervention to bring down the Taliban regime in Afghanistan. He defended intervention on grounds of democracy and human rights:

> . . . When Milosevic embarked on the ethnic cleansing of Muslims in Kosovo, we acted. The sceptics said it was pointless, we'd make matters worse, and we'd make Milosevic stronger. And look what happened: we won, the refugees went home, the policies of ethnic cleansing were reversed and one of the great dictators of the last century will see justice in this century. And I tell you if Rwanda happened again today as it did in 1993, when a million people were slaughtered in cold blood, we would have a moral duty to act there also. We were there in Sierra Leone when a murderous group of gangsters threatened its democratically elected government and people.
>
> (Blair, 2001)

Of course, one cannot be blind to the fact that nation states remain important and that *realpolitik* concerns will continue to tell when it comes to questions of intervention of forces. Nonetheless, it still seems to be the case that Information Warfare must unavoidably be concerned with more than strategic or territorial interests, precisely because the informational elements of organized violence are nowadays critical and hard to contain. And a key feature of these elements is the spread of a universalism which denies the right of nations to do as they will inside their own borders and new media (combined with other agencies and actors) which ensure that nations cannot easily hide from outside scrutiny. As Havel (1999) says, it would 'seem that the . . . efforts of generations of democrats. . . And the evolution of civilization have finally brought humanity to the recognition that human beings are more important than the state'. The pursuit of General Pinochet across Europe during the late 1990s to insist that he answers crimes committed thirty years ago, the arraignment of alleged war criminals, including Slobodan Milosevic himself, at the UN War Crimes tribunal in the Hague, and the foundation of the International Criminal Court in 2002, all support this view.

Note

* This article draws on 'Information Warfare, Surveillance and Human Rights', which appears in Kirstie Ball and Frank Webster (eds) (2003) *The Intensification of Surveillance: crime, terrorism and warfare in the information age*. London: Pluto Press.

References

Arquilla, John and Ronfeldt, David F. (2001) *Networks and Netwars*. Santa Monica, CA: RAND.

Blair, Tony (2001) *Speech to Labour Party Conference*. Brighton: Labour Party. 2 October.

Castells, Manuel (1996) *The Rise of the Network Society*. Oxford: Blackwell.

Cohen, E.A. (1996) 'A Revolution in Warfare', *Foreign Affairs*. 75 (2): 37–54.

Elegant, R. (1981) 'How to Lose a War', *Encounter*. 57 (2): 73–90.

Eley, Geoff (2002) *Forging Democracy: The History of the Left in Europe, 1850–2000*. Oxford: Oxford University Press.

Giddens, Anthony (1994) *Beyond Left and Right*. Cambridge: Polity.

Havel, Václav (1999) 'Kosovo and the End of the Nation-State', *New York Review of Books*. 29 April.

Held, David, McGrew, Anthony, Goldblatt, David and Perraton, Jonathan (1999) *Global Transformations – Politics, Economics and Culture*. Cambridge: Polity.

Hitchens, Christopher (2001) 'Against Rationalization', *The Nation*, 8 October.

Human Development Report (2002) *Deepening Democracy in a Fragmented World*. Oxford: Oxford University Press.

Ignatieff, Michael (2000) *Virtual War: Kosovo and Beyond*. London: Chatto and Windus.

IISS (International Institute for Strategic Studies) (2002) *The Military Balance 2002–3*. Oxford: Oxford University Press.

Kaldor, Mary (1999) *New and Old Wars: Organized Violence in a Global Era*. Cambridge: Polity.

Knightley, Phillip (2000) *The First Casualty: The War Correspondent as Hero and Myth-maker from the Crimea to Kosovo*. London: Prion Books.

Lacquer, Walter (1980) *The Terrible Secret: an investigation into the suppression of information about Hitler's 'Final Solution'*. London: Weidenfeld and Nicolson.

London, Louise (2000) *Whitehall and the Jews, 1933–48: British Immigration Policy and the Holocaust*. Cambridge: Cambridge University Press.

Luttwak, Edward (1996) 'A Post-Heroic Military Policy', *Foreign Affairs*. 75 (4): 33–44.

Mandeles, Mark D., Thomas C. Hone and Sanford S. Terry (1996) *Managing 'Command and Control' in the Persian Gulf War*. Westport, Conn: Praeger.

Morrison, David and Tumber, Howard (1988) *Journalists at War: the dynamics of newsreporting during the Falklands*. London: Constable.

Shaw, Martin (1991) *Post-Military Society: Militarism, Demilitarization and War at the end of the Twentieth Century*. Cambridge: Polity.

SIPRI (2002) *SIPRI Yearbook 2002: Armaments, Disarmament and International Security*. Oxford: Oxford University Press.

Tomlinson, John (1999) *Globalization and Culture*. Cambridge: Polity.

Tumber, Howard (2002) 'Reporting Under Fire: The physical safety and emotional welfare of journalists', in Barbie Zelizer and Stuart Allen (eds) *Journalism after September 11*. London: Routledge, pp. 247–62.

Wasserstein, Bernard (1979) *Britain and the Jews of Europe, 1939–1945*. Oxford: Oxford University Press.

5

THE COUNTER-REVOLUTION IN MILITARY AFFAIRS: THE GLOBALIZATION OF GUERRILLA WARFARE

John Downey and Graham Murdock

The last decade has seen a sustained debate on the future of war, prompted by two major shifts in the military operating environment – the collapse of the Soviet Empire and the growth and convergence of digital information and communications technologies. The end of the Cold War, coupled with the proliferation of regional conflicts in the Balkans and the Horn of Africa, has focused attention on the changing landscape of armed conflict and produced a series of attempts to discern what is distinctive about contemporary patterns of warfare. This re-thinking has centred on the notion of 'New Wars'. Simultaneously and separately, the rapid growth of new, information-processing and communications capacities, built around innovations in the technologies of satellite and computer networks, has stimulated military thinking to follow speculation on change more generally and to see information as the key resource of the future. This assumption underpins the influential argument that we are currently living through a Revolution in Military Affairs (RMA) in which communication and information systems will assume a central role as both essential infrastructural supports for new kinds of network-centric military strategies and primary targets for attack.

Both these frameworks have generated sizeable literatures that have largely ignored each other. Both have serious flaws that systematically disable them from understanding the pattern of conflict signalled by the attacks on the World Trade Centre and the car bombings of tourist centres in Bali and Mombasa. These events are more usefully seen as incidents in the emerging globalization of guerrilla warfare. The New War framework is unable to address this development properly because it downplays the ways in which contemporary conflicts have been shaped by both the consolidation of American global power and popular disillusion with Western oriented national modernization projects. The Revolution in Military Affairs framework, which has gained widespread support within the military and security communities, suffers from a relentless focus on the near technological future and the Cold War past. As a consequence, military spending is still primarily directed to meeting threats constructed on the basis of mistaken assumptions. Because it sees present and up-coming innovations in information technology as 'revolutionary' it misses both the strong continuities with past conditions and the growing mismatch between the military capabilities now being put in place and the nature of the new threat, between low intensity initiatives and high-tech responses. In our view, the events of 11 September 2001 herald a *counter-revolution* in military affairs in which the established weapons of modern guerrilla warfare (hijacking, car bombs, suicide bombers, small arms and portable rocket launchers), coupled with the global dispersal of combatants effectively counteract many of the supposed gains from advanced weapons systems and communications networks.

New wars and old

The most persuasive advocate of the 'New War' thesis is Mary Kaldor who argues that although the period between 1945 and 1991 was dominated by superpower rivalry, underneath the cover of the Cold War other types of conflict were developing (Kaldor, 1999). With the collapse of the Soviet Union, these have come to the fore, particularly in Eastern Europe and Africa. More specifically she argues that wars have changed their character in the following ways:

- political leaders in crumbling states attempt to win popular support by mobilizing forms of identity politics based on exclusive definitions of nations, ethnicities and religious communities, which leads to civil war;
- there is a blurring of the distinction between war, organized crime, and large-scale human rights violations;
- violence is decentralized, carried out by militias and directed primarily towards civilians;
- there is increased involvement by both non-state actors (mercenaries and private armies) and by transnational interests (peacekeepers and NGOs).

In the face of such conflicts, Kaldor argues, the international community should intervene, with the intention of establishing respect for human rights and not turn its back, as occurred in Rwanda and Bosnia.

The North Atlantic Treaty Organization (NATO) involvement in Kosovo and British intervention in Sierra Leone are cited as examples by advocates of new 'just wars'. To claim the mantle of a 'just war,' such interventions need to be part of a cosmopolitan political project, founded upon international law.

In a trenchant critique Paul Hirst takes issue with Kaldor on three counts. Firstly, he notes that 'New' wars are not that new. He points to the bloody Greek-Turkish war of 1921–2 and the Spanish Civil war, but one could also cite the 1948 Israeli-Arab war where hundreds of thousands of Palestinians were forced to leave their homes by Israeli militias. Secondly, he argues that Kaldor underplays the continuing importance of old wars between states in the contemporary period. The Arab-Israeli wars, the Gulf War in 1991, and the Iran-Iraq war are obvious examples. Finally, Hirst argues, since the moral choices posed by contemporary wars tend to be between 'different kinds of bad guys' (Hirst, 2001: 86), left-wing adherents of humanitarian intervention are deluded if they see this as a 'solution', since intervention is equally likely to generate new problems or reactivate old ones.

From the vantage point of 2003, both Kaldor's thesis and Hirst's critique seem dated. The idea that future Western involvement in war will centre around humanitarian interventions backed by international law to settle internal rivalries in damaged 'Third World' states appears now as a mere sideshow in comparison to the main feature – the globalization of guerrilla warfare and the US-led 'war on terrorism'. This emerging conflict is not a 'new war' in Kaldor's sense. Although she sees 'the guerrilla warfare of Mao Tse-Tung and his successors' as representing 'the harbingers of the new forms of warfare' (Kaldor, 1999: 29–30), her own analysis focuses on internal struggles within weak states and not on the globalization of guerrilla warfare. Nor is it an old style war where armies belonging to nation-states line up against each other. Rather it is made up of dispersed attacks by militant Islamic guerrillas against Western interests, particularly those of the US, its most vociferous allies, and Israel. At the same time, Kaldor is right to link new patterns of warfare to the internal politics of developing states. As we shall argue later, the present wave of attacks is intimately bound up with struggles for power within Islamic societies.

The Revolution in Military Affairs

Kaldor's characterization of 'new wars' may be open to criticism but it does acknowledge that contemporary conflicts are messy, dirty, and often involve large-scale civilian casualties. In marked contrast, the Revolution in Military Affairs (RMA) thesis focuses on mean, clean machines capable of delivering clinical strikes with minimal 'collateral damage' to non-combatants.

Despite its clear links with the US defence establishment, elements of the RMA have gained widespread acceptance, even in left-wing circles. Perry Anderson (2002: 13) for example, sees the comprehensive application of electronic advances to weapons and communications systems as one of the main factors permitting a rapid victory in Afghanistan with only minimal American troop casualties. This is altogether too simple. Rather than accepting US military claims that the RMA played a decisive role in the Afghan conflict, we need to focus on the fortuitous political conditions presented by a weak and unpopular regime and the plethora of internal groups ready to oppose the Taliban regime militarily. The US took full advantage of this opportunity by simultaneously mobilizing state-of-the-art technologies and supporting a low-tech civil war on the ground fought largely by proxies drawn from the various warlord groupings that had controlled the country before the rise of the Taliban. As Martin Shaw has argued, this transfer of the risks of war to local allies and civilian populations, is as much a defining characteristic of the 'new Western way of war' as precision air strikes (Shaw, 2002: 4). Anderson's attachment to the RMA rhetoric, however, leads him to underplay the importance of social and political dynamics and overestimate the importance of technological superiority.

Among the swelling ranks of celebratory commentary on the RMA, Kevin Robins and Frank Webster stand out for the clarity of their critique. Their argument centres around the assertion that the 1960s and 1970s saw a paradigm shift in the nature of armed conflict, as the system of Industrial Warfare, that had remained dominant since its consolidation in the Great War of 1914–1918, was displaced by a new system of Information Warfare. As with all models that posit a decisive break between one condition and another, this conception over-simplifies a highly complex and uneven process.

Two major reservations can be lodged against Robins and Webster's account of Industrial Warfare. Firstly, by concentrating on the twentieth century they present a historically truncated account of a process that was already well underway by the second half of the nineteenth century. William McNeill, for example, has argued persuasively that the American Civil War was the 'first full fledged example of an industrialised war' and provided important models for World War One (McNeill, 1982: 242). Secondly, while they concede that information has long been important for the conduct of war, they focus on forms of human intelligence rather than on intelligence mediated by technology (writing, telegraphy, photography, radio, radar) (Robins and Webster, 1999: 154). By largely ignoring the substantial impact that developments in mediated information and communication had on the organization of warfare before the 1970s, they misrepresent the newness of 'Information Warfare'. The mass mobilization of Napoleon's *levée en masse* which put well over a million men into the field in 1793 would have been impossible without the increasing military use of maps, written orders and strategic planning. Similarly, the expanding transcontinental telegraph network played a central role in military command and control in a situation where, by the end of nineteenth century, 80 per cent of the globe was controlled by a European imperial power, and Britain alone had fought 50 colonial wars. The strategic importance of the telegraph system was firmly established by the outbreak of World War One. This led to the cutting off of the German cables linking Germany to the US within hours of the expiry of the British ultimatum in 1914, as the first manoeuvre in the battle to win American support (Taylor, 1995: 177). By the time World War Two started, the kind of complex distanciated command and control systems associated with the arrival of Information Warfare were fully operational, permitting the rise of *Blitzkrieg* – rapid, co-ordinated air and land attack – as a form of war.

The historical evidence then, strongly suggests that Industrial War was always also Information War. But are they nevertheless right to claim that the contemporary situation represents a step-change in the organization of warfare? The 1991 Gulf War, which they nominate as 'the first Information War' provides an instructive test case.

The Gulf War involved the largest US mobilization since World War Two, half a million full-time and reservist personnel and, in its later assessment, the US Department of Defense pointed to serious deficiencies in logistic support of a decidedly mundane industrial character. There were not enough roll-on roll-off ships to transport heavy equipment, for example. While precision-guided munitions and stealth fighters were important in disabling Iraqi command and control capabilities, the vast majority of sorties were undertaken against traditional targets (airfields, troop placements) using 'dumb' bombs. Altogether, the tonnage dropped per month was 40,416 compared to 47,777 in World War Two and 44,014 in Vietnam (Federation of American Scientists, 2002).

On the other hand, the Gulf War did see a notable intensification in the use of satellite technology for surveillance and communication. The range of satellite systems deployed was unprecedented. They included: a Lacrosse radar satellite that could penetrate cloud and was thus unaffected by the bad weather that hampered the observational capabilities of the three Kennan digital imaging satellites; around 20 signal satellites; three defence weather satellites, and over a dozen Navstar GPS (global positioning systems) satellites. Even so, the information acquired by satellites, for the purposes of Battle Damage Assessment for example, often proved inadequate because of adverse weather conditions. Similarly, commercial GPS costing a few thousand dollars and commonly used on small boats had been bought off the shelf, bypassing the normal military procurement process, but did not find their way below brigade level. Nor were ground forces the only participants to encounter information and communication failures. The Daily Air Tasking Order for US aircraft carriers had to be delivered by hand because the communications systems used by the Navy and Army were incompatible. Added to which, the vast majority of military communication used insecure commercial telephone lines and exchanges (Aspin, 1992: 23).

Rather than confirming the Gulf War as an Information War then, the evidence points to the stubborn persistence of core features, and failures, of Industrial Warfare. This in turn suggests that rather than trying to locate a decisive rupture in the organization of warfare we need to have a longer duration – longer-term view, looking for evolutions, transitions and continuities, and to the co-existing and mutually reinforcing character of industrial and information capabilities.

In arguing for a paradigmatic shift from one condition to another Robins and Webster, who elsewhere in their work pursue an avowedly anti-deterministic and 'neo-Luddite' approach to understanding the role of technology in driving change (1986), concede too much ground to the technological determinism that characterizes mainstream writing on the Revolution in Military Affairs and pay less attention than they should to the social, political and ideological dynamics currently reshaping the conduct of war. In the course of the 1990s, US military thinking gradually began to move beyond the Cold War and consider the new asymmetric geopolitical environment, but this thinking remained strongly influenced by technological determinism.

Re-assessing the enemy

This assumption informs every page of the first quadrennial defence review of the George W. Bush Presidency, published on 30 September 2001, but largely conceived and written before the events of September 11. Recognizing that the US is now without a conventional military rival and that its interests are global in scope it 'focuses more on how an adversary might fight than who the adversary might be and where a war might occur' (Department of Defense, 2001: 22). This sense that the US military needs to prepare for multiple scenarios leads the Review's authors to supplement conventional threat-based analysis, where the enemy can be readily identified, with a capability model, where the precise enemy is unknown and risk assessment is based on the capabilities of weapons systems thought to be at hand or potentially at hand in the near future. Three specific dangers are noted: the proliferation of chemical, biological, nuclear, and ballistic capacities, popularly known as 'weapons of mass destruction'; information warfare, and mass casualty terrorism.

Combating these threats is seen to require a range of responses, from old style wars involving the territorial invasion of states hostile to its interests, to more limited military interventions to effect regime changes and install friendly governments, and low intensity guerrilla warfare against elusive enemies targeting civilians. These strategies in turn are seen to require a new infrastructure capable of supporting effective, flexible action within a global theatre of conflict.

To this end the US network of military bases is being extended to more regions of the world, focusing particularly on areas of political instability, regions of strategic economic importance in ensuring supplies of energy and essential raw materials, and emerging competitors. As well as continuing to station forces in Europe and North East Asia, bases will be established in South West Asia and the East Asian littoral, which covers the area from the Bay of Bengal to the Sea of Japan. These installations will also include missile defence capabilities to protect US forces, allies and friends. The aim is to become a global military presence capable of safeguarding US interests around the world without the need for large reinforcements from traditional bases. It is important, however, to see this development not as a radical break but as the adaptation of a strategy that has been consistently pursued since 1945 (Anderson, 2002). Securing this goal is even more urgent now. The world's gross domestic product is predicted to double over the next 20 years leading to an increased demand for oil. At the same time, oil reserves will begin to dwindle by three per cent every year by 2005. Assuming no short-term development of major new fields or alternative fuel sources, control over remaining reserves inevitably becomes a core strategic issue. It is clearly in the interests of the US and its allies to secure access to these stocks by ensuring that 'friendly' regimes are established in oil-rich countries and countries vital to the security of oil pipelines. In some situations this may require a full-scale military assault. Elsewhere, as in Afghanistan, it can be accomplished through limited intervention and the deployment of local proxies. US Special Forces in Afghanistan did carry sophisticated global positioning equipment but they also asked to be supplied with boots, ammunition and horse feed and led a cavalry charge at Mazar-e-Sharif before engaging in close quarter combat. As the US Secretary of Defense, Donald Rumsfeld noted, 'the nineteenth century met the twenty-first' in Afghanistan (Rumsfeld, 2002).

Information, information, information

Command, control and communications (C3) systems have been central to military strategy and tactics since the arrival of mass armies and dispersed theatres of conflict in the nineteenth century. However, the increasing reliance on computer networks to coordinate these functions has been widely hailed in military circles as paving the way for new kinds of network-centric warfare systems. The thinking around these emerging systems sees military force as made up of four overlapping grids; a sensor grid composed of terrestrial, cyber and space based surveillance systems providing raw intelligence; a communications grid that collects, processes and distributes this material; a command grid that formulates responses; and an engagement grid that acts on these decisions by activating weapons systems (or 'shooters' as they are dubbed in the military jargon) (see Layton, 2002). Military proponents of this model envision an integrated system which will allow 'all warfighting systems to plug into a common battlespace picture, or Battlespace Wide Web' and permit 'every combat system to push and pull from this web the information it gathers or needs' (Colella, 2002: 1). In this conception 'Network forces will not mobilize, march to the front, conduct mass frontal assaults [they] will swarm . . . gather and disperse in different volumes and formations, combinations and directions' (Dillon, 2002: 74). Recent experience however suggests that present arrangements fall a long way short of this ideal of flexible coordination and that there are serious flaws in the way both sensor and communications grids currently operate in relation to the globalization of guerrilla warfare.

The 17 October 2002 written statement of by the Director of the CIA before the Congressional Joint Inquiry Committee on 9/11 provides a fascinating insight into what Clausewitz called the 'friction' of warfare. The Director notes that in aftermath of the Cold War the number of CIA personnel was cut by nearly 25 per cent, seriously depleting the scope of human source intelligence on the ground and forcing the Agency to rely more heavily on technologically gathered data. At the same time, most of that technologically mediated intelligence was focused on supporting military operations rather than on intelligence gathering per se because of Department of Defense cutbacks. As a result, despite the increase in funding since 9/11, he is forced to concede that 'we have hardly scratched the surface in our efforts to recover from the manpower reductions, and we cannot reconstitute overnight the cadre of seasoned case officers and assets overseas, or the expert team of analysts we've lost' (Tenet, 2002: 17). According to a former senior Near East Division operative for example, 'the CIA probably doesn't have a single truly qualified Arabic-speaking officer of Middle Eastern background who can play a believable Muslim fundamentalist' (Gerecht, 2001). There could hardly be a more candid admission that as far as intelligence gathering on guerrilla operations is concerned, technology is relatively insignificant in comparison to numbers and quality of personnel.

Alongside these sensor grid failures, 9/11 also revealed serious deficiencies in the information flows on which network centric operations depend. Crucial mistakes were made by both the CIA and FBI in the handling of information that might have prevented the attacks on the World Trade Centre and the Pentagon. For example, FBI whistleblower Colleen Rowley has argued that field officers in Minneapolis had enough grounds to search the personal effects of one of the leaders but were hampered by the failure of FBI Headquarters to respond to locally gathered information.

Similarly, the CIA obtained a copy of the passport belonging to one of the leading hijackers in January 2000 (20 months before the attack) but failed to place him on the US State Department's Watchlist, which is used when granting visas and allowing entry to the US.

These instances of friction within key agencies and lack of cooperation between them suggest that the possibility of constructing a coordinated, network-centred response, seamlessly linking comprehensive intelligence gathering to effectively targeted action, remains for the moment in the realm of science fiction where many of its favoured metaphors and scenarios originated. Once again, however, the response to these gaps and deficiencies is to rely on technological solutions and to construct an ever-more complex and comprehensive apparatus of computer-mediated surveillance and analysis.

In November 2002 the US Government launched its Total Information Awareness Project (TIA) with the aim of trying to locate potential 'terrorists' by tracking their patterns of movement through the myriad locations of everyday activity, using the widest possible range of databases, from telephone calls, parking permits, academic transcripts, drug prescriptions, emails, bank records, credit card slips to website visits. The guiding assumption, that 'terrorists' can be identified by the distinctive behavioural patterns revealed by comprehensive data mining is highly questionable, since it presupposes that they constitute a distinctive and coherent category, when the available evidence suggests that they are successful precisely because they have learnt to be inconspicuous. In an ironic twist, the project is directed by John Poindexter who was found guilty of conspiracy and obstruction of justice in 1990 in connection with the Iran-Contra affair, a covert operation in which funds from illegal arms sales to Teheran were secretly funnelled to support the right-wing Contra guerrillas in Nicaragua.

The TIA project is currently in the pilot stage and faces formidable logistical and software problems before it is fully operational. Even so, the concept is 'dazzling in its obtrusiveness' and would impose 'a level of surveillance and monitoring of ordinary Americans that is unprecedented in peacetime' (Goldenberg, 2002: 7). At one level it is a rational response to the globalization of a guerrilla war whose combatants can move easily across borders and within multi-cultural Western states without arousing undue suspicion. 17 of the 19 hijackers involved in the 9/11 attacks had no police or security record. While in the US they dressed in Western clothes, remained clean-shaven, avoided mosques, and were indistinguishable from the millions of Muslims who live, study and travel in the United States, Europe and Australasia. At the same time, attempting to locate them by tracking their movements across the full range of electronic webs poses profound threats to civil liberties.

The TIA project's central aim of developing techniques for identifying, classifying, and managing groups sorted by levels of dangerousness replaces individualized suspicion with categorical suspicion in which whole classes of people may be detained for questioning and required to demonstrate that they do not pose a threat. In these circumstances 'it is hard to see how the presumption of innocence could be maintained' (Stadler and Lyon, 2003: 89). The Anti-Terrorism, Crime and Security Act 2001 has already gone a considerable way to abandoning this tenet in Britain by sanctioning the detention without charge of foreign nationals whose presence in the UK is deemed 'not conducive to the public good'. At the time of writing, 14 people have been detained under this provision. Two have agreed to return to their countries, 12 are still being held indefinitely. However even this draconian reaction is likely to prove ineffective in countering global guerrilla warfare since it only applies to non-UK citizens. Even if adequate intelligence had been available, the young British supporter of Osama bin Laden who attempted to detonate a bomb hidden in his shoe on an airliner in midflight would not have been covered by its provisions.

It is precisely because the new guerrilla campaign is being waged by nationals as well as by migrants and visitors that the new surveillance assemblage now being put in place requires information to be gathered from every available location. In the process it further dismantles the protective walls that have separated the military from civil society and assigned internal policing and military intelligence to separate spheres. By promoting the primacy of military objectives across the whole span of civilian life it marks a decisive shift towards a more militarized society. This increasing blurring is given a further push by the explosion of speculation around Information Warfare.

As Terry Eagleton has argued: 'If terrorism finds strength in its own weakness, it does so by sniffing out the weakness latent in the enemy's strength' (Eagleton, 2002: 24). The military's growing reliance on new information and communication technologies is a double-edged sword. It increases the potential speed and flexibility of response but it also creates new vulnerabilities. Information Warfare, aimed at corrupting or destroying an adversary's information sources and computer networks, offers the weaker side in asymmetric conflicts a powerful weapon of mass disruption which can be launched remotely in the form of computer viruses or hacker attacks (Eriksson 1999: 57). Although key military systems are generally well protected and not accessible through the internet, the systems regulating the infrastructures at the centre of civilian life – heat, power, lighting, water, and telephony – are much more open to penetration and manipulation and present enticing targets to guerrilla groups intent on instilling a permanent sense of vulnerability in the general population. This has led military commentators to conjure up images of highly trained 'network ninjas', working for the enemy, 'inserting the latest virus into the internet' in much the same way as guerrillas on the ground may attempt to poison the water system or leave packages containing toxic chemicals on the subway system (Stein, 2002: 7). The plausibility of these scenarios however, depends on how one characterizes the groups at the centre of the global resurgence of guerrilla warfare.

Old terrorists, new guerrillas

It is commonplace to find Al-Qaeda described as a terrorist network. However, this tells us more about the popularity of the network metaphor in contemporary public debate in the West than about the organization of Al-Qaeda. When Yosri Fouda, the London bureau chief of the Arabic language Al-Jazeera television channel, went to interview one of Al-Qaeda's leading figures, Khalid Al-Sheikh, he was surprised to find that he introduced himself as head of the organization's Military Committee and went on to outline how the Department of Martyrs had hand-picked the men who would accompany the 9/11 hijackers. As he later recounted, 'I hadn't thought of Al-Qaeda as a formal organization' (quoted in Fouda, 2002: 3). However, Osama bin Laden's reported account of the preparations for 9/11 suggests that some members of his inner circle were not aware of the plan and that some of the hijackers did not know what targets they were to attack. This points to a highly secretive organization where individuals only receive information on a need-to-know basis and where there is little contact or exchange between dispersed cells. It certainly does not suggest a formally constituted global network. On the contrary, as Yossef Bodansky, director of the US Congressional Task Force on Terrorism has argued, it is more accurate to characterize Al-Qaeda as 'a wide tent without walls that serves as an umbrella for all the like-minded' in which action is 'locally adapted to fit prevailing conditions at each and every locale,' adding that it is precisely because of this that the US and its allies are facing 'endemic problems in rolling them back' (quoted in Foden, 2002: 3). 'This is not,' therefore, 'the old terrorism of the IRA or ETA, with structures, doctrines and pseudo-military organization . . . it is the *idea* of al-Qaeda [sic], not its physical reality, that is the key'. It is 'less a hierarchical organization . . . than a dynamic dialogue between like-minded radicals conducted via mosques, radical publications and the internet. A specific order is almost redundant as individual groups know exactly what must be done and when, adapting themselves to new security constraints and to new targets' (Beaumont, 2002: 29). But what are the shared experiences and common ideas that knit this dispersed coalition together?

The call to arms

Although President Bush's 'axis of evil' includes states like North Korea and Iraq, deemed capable of launching attacks on US interests using 'weapons of mass destruction' (chemical, biological and nuclear), the main arena of conflict is now seen as 'war on terrorism' and the enemy is firmly identified with various factions within fundamentalist Islam. For a number of commentators these groups are simply 'anti-American', envious of the US's affluence and power and opposed to its core democratic ideals. This characterization has the attractions of simplicity but by conflating two separate processes, each with their own distinctive histories and trajectories, it actively misrepresents the situation. The globalization of guerrilla warfare is fuelled not only by opposition to American and, more generally, Western imperialism but also by a renunciation of the Western models of modernization and 'development' pursued by many post-colonial states (Venn, 2002: 132).

The first current has a long history in Islamic societies. In the 1920s, for example, Hasan al-Banna, founder of the Muslim Brotherhood, launched an influential rhetorical attack on the wave of Westernization he saw sweeping across his native Egypt, denouncing Westerners for, 'their liquors, their theatres, their dance halls, their amusements, their stories, their newspapers, their novels' (Barber, 1996: 210). His principal targets were the European empires that still occupied large tracts of territory in Islamic North Africa and the Middle East. Swimming beneath his sentences, however, it is already possible to glimpse the outlines of a new US-centred imperialism, based on growing globalization of American popular media and consumer culture. The 1920s saw a significant expansion in US global cultural reach, with the increasing export of Hollywood films, jazz, and New York advertising styles. As the American theologian, Reinhold Niebuhr, noted in 1931, 'We are the first empire in the world to establish our sway without legions' (quoted in Colley, 2002: 378). This pronouncement conveniently forgets that America's imperial 'sway' was supported and often secured by extensive armed intervention but it does point to the centrality of ideas, beliefs and cultural forms as key battlegrounds. In analyzing recent reactions to this perceived cultural 'invasion' we need to follow Olivier Roy (2002) in distinguishing carefully between Islamicist and neo-fundamentalist movements.

The Islamicist movement developed in the 1970s and 1980s in response to the growth of monarchical and military regimes that sought to develop secular societies that excluded Islam from political power. They rejected both Western models of modernization and the Soviet system's marginalization of religion and sought to build modern societies grounded in the basic tenets of Islam. While rhetorically still invoking the Ummah, the notion of a pan-Islamic state, these movements have now largely given up the supranational agenda that was originally part of their ideology. Thus, Islamicists in Iran, Algeria, Palestine, Lebanon, Turkey and Egypt are better described as Islamo-nationalists, seeking to establish *national* Islamic states.

In contrast, neo-fundamentalists consider themselves to be Muslims first and foremost and remain bound to the notion of the *Ummah*. Neo-fundamentalism as a socio-cultural phenomenon developed in response not only to the perceived threats posed by Western imperialism but also to the political and economic problems of autocratic rule, corruption, and inequality within Islamic societies. It promotes a conservative interpretation of Islam that seeks the strict imposition of Sharia law and the expulsion of Western influence in all societies with substantial Muslim populations. Unlike Islamo-nationalism therefore, its ambitions are global in their reach. Groups such as Al-Qaeda are the armed expression of neo-fundamentalism as a socio-cultural movement.

In order to understand both Islamo-nationalism and neo-fundamentalism's capacity to act effectively and their choice of targets however, we need to take account of the key role played by the guerrilla war against the Soviet occupation of Afghanistan and the 1991 Gulf War.

The initial development of armed neo-fundamentalism was largely bankrolled by Saudi Arabia and armed by the US. They, together with Pakistan, encouraged Islamic radicals from a number of Asian and African countries to assist the guerrilla war in Afghanistan in the 1980s as part of a policy of building opposition to the Soviet Union in the central Asian republics. Between 1982 and 1992, more than 35,000 Islamic radicals from 43 countries would fight with the Afghan mujaheddin and some 100,000 radicals altogether would come into contact with Afghan and Pakistani radicals either through involvement in the conflict or by studying in a *madrassa* (Rashid, 2001: 130). After the Soviet withdrawal from Afghanistan many of these radicals returned home to lead Islamo-nationalist movements. Afghan veterans, for example, led the GIA (*Groupe Islamique Arme*) guerrilla war against the military regime in Algeria largely taking over leadership of the radical Islamic movement there from the FIS (*Front Islamique du Salut*).

The other turning point in shifting attention away from the Soviet Union and towards the US was the Gulf War when the US deployed over 500,000 troops in Saudi Arabia, leaving 20,000 stationed there after the defeat of Iraq. For many devout Muslims, such a substantial American military presence in a country charged with protecting Islam's holiest sites was the ultimate sacrilege and strengthened neo-fundamentalist opposition to both the US and the Saudi regime. The 1990s saw the establishment of bin Laden-financed camps in Somalia, Egypt, Sudan, Yemen, and Afghanistan and a number of attacks against US interests.

These incursions hardened American attitudes and confirmed neo-fundamentalism as a significant threat. The shooting down of two Black Hawk helicopters and the killing of 18 US soldiers in fighting in the Somali capital of Mogadishu in 1993 left a particularly vivid impression of threat and vulnerability.

Captives

The 9/11 attacks were the most significant manifestations to date of the globalized guerrilla war that has emerged over the last decade. They herald a *counter-revolution* in military affairs in which low-tech weaponry has demonstrated its capacity to by-pass current weapons systems and communications networks. In response, the US military have used the shock of September 11 to write a long wish-list of ever smarter and more sophisticated surveillance, information and armament systems. The 2003 US defense budget stands at $379 billion, $50 billion up on the figure for 2002 which itself represents a seven per cent increase in real terms over 2001, Clinton's last year in the White House. But it is hard to imagine the 'war on terrorism' ever being won by these means, if 'winning' is defined as an end to attacks on civilians. There are two reasons for this. Firstly, the high-tech systems currently in development are designed primarily for conventional wars not for low intensity global guerrilla conflict. Secondly, an escalating armed response does nothing to address the historical and political roots of the present conflict.

Throughout this chapter we have employed the term 'guerrilla' rather than 'terrorist'. This is deliberate. To label an act of violence as an instance of 'terrorism' is not simply to condemn it for its callousness and disregard of life but to detach it from the historical and political contexts that have shaped it. The language of 'terrorism' inhabits the mental no-man's land of absolute evil. It refuses to acknowledge that an appalling act may have an intelligible social and political rationale and defines any attempt to find one as a gesture of support for the 'enemy'. It systematically conflates explanation with excuse. In addition, by applying the term 'terrorist' exclusively to the actions of the other side it silences all attempts to suggest that the state's draconian responses to threat, involving saturation surveillance and the suspension of historic civil liberties, can, with some justification, be labelled as 'state terrorism' designed to deter by instilling a pervasive fear of arbitrary punishment.

In her provocative re-reading of British colonial history, Linda Colley draws attention to the many instances when British nationals were held physically captive by the peoples they sought to subjugate. She presents these defeats as a potent metaphor for the inherent fragility of Britain's imperial project, 'always overstretched, often superficial, and likely to be limited in duration' and contrasts it with the current reach of American empire which she sees as 'likely to prove far more enduring' (Colley 2002: 378). But here too we see a landscape filled with captives, confined by the pervasive fear of attack at home and abroad. It is no accident that tourist destinations have been prime targets for guerrilla assaults, most notably in Luxor, Egypt in 1997 and in Bali and Mombasa in 2002. Tourists are Western development and modernization made flesh, potent embodiments of the arrogance of affluence, able to purchase at will and translate locally rooted practices into entertaining and exotic spectacles (see Nicholson-Lord, 2002).

As a first step towards lifting the fear of threat and liberating newly re-colonized peoples from the inequalities and humiliations that currently imprison them, we need to re-read the history of empire and trace the complex chains of consequence that have shaped current conditions and responses. Failure will condemn us to remain prisoners of our own misunderstandings and consign large swathes of the world's population to lifetimes of servitude in the shadow of a new imperial system supported by the largest arsenal ever seen. Niebuhr may have been right to claim that America's most powerful 'legions are dollars' but, as Linda Colley notes, although 'the dollar still rules now there are legions too' (Colley, 2002: 378).

These legions cannot 'win' the current global guerrilla war. This is not only because they are pursuing it with weapons designed for other forms of combat.

> By their nature . . . guerrilla campaigns which have deep social roots and draw on a widespread sense of injustice . . . cannot be defeated militarily. And as the war on terror has increasingly become a war to enforce US global power, it has only intensified the appeal of 'asymmetric warfare' to the powerless.
>
> (Milne, 2002: 21)

The eventual solutions are political and economic. Their durability will rest not on advances in information and communication technologies but on a deeper understanding of how past actions and injustices have shaped present conditions and reactions coupled with the determination to act on these insights.

References

Anderson, Perry (2002) 'Force and consent', *New Left Review*. 17, Sep/Oct: 5–30.
Aspin Report (1992) Interim Report of the US House of Representatives Committee On Armed Services on the conduct of the Persian Gulf War. Available at http://es.rice.edu/projects/Poli378/Gulf/aspin_rpt.html consulted March 2002.

Barber, Benjamin R. (1996) *Jihad vs. McWorld: How Globalism and Tribalism are Reshaping the World*. New York: Ballantine Books.

Beaumont, Peter (2002) 'Why we are losing the war', *The Observer*, 1 December, p 29.

Colella, Lt. Col. Robert A (2002) 'Building a Battlespace Wide Web', *Air and Space Power Chronicles*. Available at http://www.airpower.maxwell.af.mil/airchronicles/cc/colella.html accessed 5 November 2002.

Colley, Linda (2002) *Captives: Britain, Empire and the World 1600–1850*. London: Jonathan Cape.

Department of Defense (2001) Quadrennial Defense Review Report. Available at http://www.defenselink.mil/pubs/qdr2001.pdf

Dillon, Michael (2002) 'Network Society, Network-Centric Warfare and the State of Emergency', *Theory, Culture and Society*. 19 (4): 71–79.

Eagleton, Terry (2002) 'The art of terror', *The Guardian*, 30 November, p. 24.

Eriksson, E. Anders (1999) 'Information warfare: hype or reality?' *The Nonproliferation Review*. Spring/Summer, pp. 57–64.

Federation of American Scientists (2002) Available at www.fas.org/man/dod-101/ops/desert_storm.htm accessed March 2002.

Foden, Giles (2002) 'Not again', *The Guardian G2*, 29 November, pp. 2–3.

Fouda, Yosri (2002) 'Covering Al-Qaeda, Covering Saddam', *Transnational Broadcasting Studies*. Available at http://www.tbsjournal.com/Fouda.html accessed 2 December 2002.

Gerecht, Marc (2001) 'The Counterterrorist Myth', *The Atlantic Quarterly*. 288 (1): 38–42.

Goldenberg, Susan (2002) 'Big Brother will be watching America', *The Guardian*, 23 November, p. 7.

Hirst, Paul (2001) *War and Power in the 21st Century*. Cambridge: Polity.

Kaldor, Mary (1999) *New and Old Wars: Organized Violence in a Global Era*. Cambridge: Polity.

Layton, Group Captain Peter (2002) '*Network-Centric Warfare: A Place in our Future,*' Aerospace Centre Working Papers, Number 74. Available at http://www.defence.gov.au/aerospacecentre/publish/paper74.htm accessed 5 November 2002.

McNeill, William (1982) *The Pursuit of Power: Technology, Armed Force, and Society*. Chicago: University of Chicago Press.

Milne, Seumas (2002) 'A war that can't be won', *The Guardian*, 21 November, p. 21.

Nicholson-Lord, David (2002) 'Against the Western invaders', *New Statesman*, 9 December, pp. 22–24.

Rashid, Ahmad (2001) *Taliban: the Story of the Afghan Warlords*. London: Pan.

Robins, Kevin and Webster, Frank (1986) *Information technology: a Luddite Analysis*. Norwood, NJ: Ablex.

Robins, Kevin and Webster, Frank (1999) 'Cyberwars: the military information revolution,' in Kevin Robins and Frank Webster, *Times of the Technoculture: From the Information Society to the Virtual Life*. London: Routledge: 149–167.

Roy, Olivier (2002) 'Neo-fundamentalism'. Available at http://www.ssrc.org/sept11/essays/roy.htm

Rumsfeld, Donald (2002) '21st Century Transformation of the US Armed Forces' National Defense University, Fort McNair, Washington DC. Available at http://www.defenselink.mil/speeches/2002/s20020131-secdef.html

Shaw, Martin (2002) 'Risk-transfer militarism, small massacres and the historic legitimacy of war'. Available at http://www.theglobalsite.ac.uk/press/205shaw.htm accessed 16 May 2002.

Stadler, Felix and Lyon, David (2003) 'Electronic identity cards and social classification' in David Lyon (ed.) *Surveillance as Social Sorting: Privacy, Risk and Digital Discrimination*. London: Routledge: pp. 77–93.

Stein, George J (2002) 'Information War-Cyberwar-Netwar' in *Battlefield of the Future: 21st Century Warfare Issues*, Aerospace Power Chronicles Home page. Available at http://www.airpower.maxwell.af.mil/airchroncles/battle/bftoc.html accessed 4 November 2002.

Taylor, Philip (1995) *Munitions of the Mind – A History of Propaganda from the Ancient World to the Present Era*. Manchester: Manchester University Press.

Tenet, George (2002) Unclassified version of Director of CIA's Testimony before the Joint Inquiry into Terrorist Attacks against the United States. Available at http://www.cia.gov/cia/public_affairs/speeches/speeches.html accessed October 2002

Venn, Couze (2002) 'World Dis/Order: On Some Fundamental Questions', *Theory, Culture and Society*. 19 (4): 121–136.

SPINNING THE WAR: POLITICAL COMMUNICATIONS, INFORMATION OPERATIONS AND PUBLIC DIPLOMACY IN THE WAR ON TERRORISM

Robin Brown

'War', observed the eighteenth-century Prussian military strategist, Karl von Clausewitz, 'is nothing more than the continuation of politics by other means'. As politics and society change so does the nature of war. In the twenty-first century politics is conducted via the mass media with the result that the 'war on terrorism' is a war that is also waged through the media. The way in which the mass media represent the conflict is part of the conflict. Media coverage has effects not simply on 'the audience' understood as a set of passive bystanders, but on those actually and potentially involved in the conflict. Shaping the perceptions of opponents, supporters and neutral groups influences whether they will become involved and how they will participate. Mobilizing, informing and persuading are integral to the conduct of war. The result is that attempting to shape the representation of the conflict becomes more important for the belligerents even as it becomes harder to do.

There are volumes to be written on this topic and this chapter does not pretend to offer a comprehensive discussion. Instead the chapter sets out to do two things: firstly to explore why the presentation of international events has become so important and secondly to examine the ways in which the 'informational instrument' has been employed.

The mediatization of international politics

Over the past century politics has increasingly come to be played out through the media. This is not a narrow claim about the internet or satellite television but rather a claim about the way that modern society has been transformed (and indeed constituted) by changing forms of mediation (Innis, 1951; McLuhan, 1964). Over the course of the twentieth century, politics has been transformed by the increasing involvement of the public and of interest groups linked, informed and mobilized by the media of communication.

The development of a mass economy and mass society gave a greater role for government and in consequence greater incentives to influence the workings of government. While it is television that gave rise to the most visible, and most documented political transformations, these transformations were already well advanced by the time that it appeared on the scene (Donovan and Scherer, 1992; Scammell, 1995). These broad patterns of social change triggered changes in the strategies of political actors, so that, by the end of the twentieth century, political consultant Philip Gould could write that in 'a modern media environment, competence and good communications are inseparable: you cannot have one without the other' (Gould, 1998: 334). The impact of this process on election campaigning has been subject to exhaustive discussion but there is a much less developed strand of writing that argues that this mediatization has changed the nature of governing: that publicity has become an integral part of governance. Government leaders and civil servants have come to understand that in order to achieve their objectives they need to make active use of the media to mobilize support and defuse criticism (Cook, 1998).

This transformation of political life as a result of changes in the pattern of mediation is much more advanced in the domestic politics of the advanced countries than in international politics, but is happening just the same. Historically, diplomacy has been a closed activity, limited to small groups of people, but over the past century, with increasing pace over the last two decades, developments in both politics and communications are opening up this sphere (Eban, 1998: chapter 5).

This mediatization reflects political changes as well as changes in the media sphere. At a political level, international governance is changing. The number of international organizations has increased dramatically. A growing range of issues are subject to 'international regimes', agreements that regulate aspects of international affairs, transnational relationships and domestic society even in the absence of formal international organizations. There has been growth in multilateralism as a mode of governance, addressing international problems through action by groups of states. Even in spheres that involve national security issues, responses are normally mounted by coalitions. International governance increasingly involves large numbers of states, multiple ministries and explicit sets of rules that often mandate the release of information and external review of actions (*International Organization*, 2000; Keohane and Nye, 1977; Murphy, 1994; Rosenau and Czempiel, 1992). These developments have encouraged the creation of groups that seek to influence decisions on international governance or to use them to advance their domestic political positions, for instance by enlisting international support against oppressive governments, their endeavours facilitated by the diffusion of communications technologies, from the telephone to the internet (Deibert, 2000; Florini, 2000; Keck and Sikkink, 1998; Price, 1998).

In parallel with these political shifts, the global media field is changing. There is an expansion in the number of sources of information to which people have access. On a global level, access to the telephone and the internet are becoming more common. With very few exceptions, people have access to more radio channels and more television services than a decade ago. As the access to communications increases, so does the nature of the media sources that are available. Media organizations are less likely to be state controlled. Relatively speaking the media are more commercial and more driven by the need to secure audiences. This reduces the influence of the state and gives more scope for content to be shaped by 'professional' ideas of what makes a story. These changes are driven by increasing competition in the media. Professionalization implies a willingness to report 'both' sides of the story and less willingness for reporting to be shaped by the direct demands of government.

Another element of change is the transnationalization of media organizations. Across large swathes of the planet, media transformation is being driven by the emergence of satellite broadcasting operations that cross borders. This challenges the ability of states to control information flows but forces domestic broadcasters to offer a product that is attractive to audiences (Entman, 2000; Shaw, 2000). Technological changes make it easier for the media to report from anywhere on the planet. Satellite phones and videophones give a new reach for reporters and, although their full impact has yet to be felt, the expansion of private satellite surveillance opens new possibilities for media organizations (Livingston, 2000).

These political and communication changes are mutually reinforcing and have consequences for the dynamics of political issues. Political conflicts can rapidly have repercussions on the other side of the world; different groups can choose to become involved. These technological and political transformations are creating a situation in which the potential visibility of conflicts is dramatically enhanced. Information allows action (Brown, 2002b; Schattschneider, 1960). In this context 'perception management' becomes an increasingly important instrument of political conflict through encouraging the involvement of new groups or attempting to win over hostile groups.

In the United States, in particular, a number of reports on the future of diplomacy have probed the implications of these changes (for example, Advisory Commission on Public Diplomacy, 1998; Centre for Strategic and International Studies, 1998; Project on the Advocacy of US

Interests, 1998). This new environment is seen as underlining the limits of 'hard power' resources, that is sticks and carrots, in achieving international goals. In a multilateral environment greater weight must be given to persuasion, social pressure, framing and agenda-setting as ways of exerting influence; all of these 'soft' strategies depend on communication (Keohane and Nye, 1998; Nye, 1990; Nye, 2002; Nye and Owens, 1996).

Despite a growing volume of research the implications of this more complex policy environment are yet to be fully worked out, both theoretically and in practical terms. What is clear in the US response to the 'war on terrorism' is the way in which the campaign has been shaped by three different responses to this new environment.

The communications armoury: information operations, public diplomacy and spin

In waging the war on terrorism, the United States has made use of three different paradigms of communications as a tool of influence: military concepts of information warfare, foreign policy concepts of public diplomacy, and approaches to media management drawn from domestic politics (Brown, 2002a). All of these approaches are seen as responses to the challenges of this war but all emerge from different institutional contexts and draw on different intellectual paradigms in ways that tend to hamper their effectiveness.

The first of these paradigms is the Information Operations (IO) doctrine. This can be seen as a systematic attempt to make sense of warfare as an exercise in information processing. While popular conceptions of information warfare focus on computers, military thinking has taken the idea a step further. Computer systems are simply tools to gather, process and disseminate information so that IO can be understood more broadly to encompass any effort to attack or defend the information necessary for the conduct of operations (Summe, 2000). This provides a coherent framework to bring together existing activities: psychological operations (PSYOPS), deception, public affairs – that is the military-press interface – and civil military affairs with computer network operations. However logical this may seem, integrating all of these activities has been controversial. The key problem here has been the yoking together of public affairs with activities such as PSYOPs and deception. While military press officers insist that they will not deceive the media, the doctrinal relationship between their work and other elements of IO inevitably creates suspicions. Further, the increasingly seamless global information environment makes it harder to separate what is done in one part of the world from another. Deception efforts in one area may rapidly be exposed by broader reporting or end up with false reports in the US and global media (Defense Science Board, 2000: 9–10).

The second paradigm is public diplomacy. This draws together international broadcasting, cultural diplomacy, educational exchanges and overseas information activities. Public diplomacy has its own complex history. In the decade after World War Two civilian PSYOPS was seen as the key weapon in waging the Cold War against the Soviet Union and the Eastern bloc. After the 1956 Hungarian uprising this instrumental approach was downgraded in favour of what might be termed a milieu approach. Rather than focussing on discrediting the communist authorities and triggering uprisings, the aim of these civilian information operations was to advance American interests through the creation of a positive image of the US by fostering knowledge and understanding about the country. By presenting the truth, including negative stories, the US would build trust and credibility.

This type of activity would contribute to creating the kind of international milieu where American values would flourish. The milieu and the instrumental approaches have coexisted. Milieu goals have been enthusiastically adopted by practitioners within organizations such as the Voice of America but periodically critics, particularly on the right, have demanded a more aggressive approach (Hixson, 1997; Lord, 2000). Although study groups have argued for the growing importance of public diplomacy activities it has been a poor relation, starved of funds, especially since 1999 when the US Information Agency was absorbed into the State Department (Advisory Commission on Public Diplomacy 2000; Keith, 2002).

The third paradigm, that of political news management or 'spin', is, in institutional terms, a newcomer to the international arena. Democratic politicians live and die by the media and have come to develop elaborate mechanisms to secure and control media coverage. This machinery takes in press offices that focus narrowly on short-term media coverage and a strategic communications function that develops proactive communications strategies, for instance by using the activities of leaders to communicate key messages. While these activities have been most obvious in the prominence of political communications in the political strategies of leaders, such as the former US President Bill Clinton and British Prime Minister Tony Blair, they reflect long-term responses to the mediation of political life by television (Cook 1998; Maltese, 1994). Given the way in which spin has become a reflex and the fact that the most prominent spokespersons for any country are its political leaders, it is not surprising that political communications techniques are being imported into international politics. The techniques of the spin doctors stand between the manipulation implied in IO Doctrine and the 'objectivity' advocated by public diplomacy practitioners. On one hand, spin doctors insist that they deal in truth because the mass media are their channel for reaching their target audiences and the loss of credibility with journalists will prevent them from doing this (Fitzwater, 1995: 198–201; Ingham, 1991: 159–60; Speakes, 1989: 279–80). On the other hand they see 'truth' as plural. Their job is to persuade their media that one version of reality rather than another is the 'real' story and that the way that they tell it is the correct one. This approach seeks to balance an active approach to shaping the media environment with a broader commitment to some rules of the game.

All three of these activities have been deployed in the war on terrorism but the differing assumptions that underpin them have undermined their effectiveness. As might be expected, the military paradigm was evident in the dispatch of PSYOP forces to conduct operations over Afghanistan in order to stimulate defections from the Taliban, and to publicize the nature of US objectives, rewards, and food drops (Clandestine Radio, 2001). However, there have been other manifestations of this mindset. One consequence of the IO paradigm has been a growing emphasis on the targeting of the communications infrastructure. 'Physical destruction' is taken to be another weapon in the armoury of information warfare. From the IO perspective the operations of media organizations may appear to be aspects of an opponent's military effort. Taliban Radio was subject to jamming and air attack, knocking it off the air for a period (Clandestine Radio, 2001). More controversially, the Kabul office of Al-Jazeera – the main conduit for the release of Al-Qaeda material – was destroyed by an air strike on 12 November 2001. The US government has claimed that it was being used by Al-Qaeda but the nature of that activity remains ambiguous (Gowing, 2002). Similarly, the narrowly instrumental vision of IO was consistent with the diplomatic pressure applied to the government of Qatar to rein in the activities of Al-Jazeera. Yet this action was seen as suggesting American double standards: supporting press freedom in the Arab world until it was in their interests to suppress it.

The influence of IO doctrine was also apparent in the fiasco of the Office of Strategic Influence. During the autumn of 2001 this was created within the Department of Defense (DoD) in order to 'roll up all the instruments within DoD to influence foreign audiences' including those in neutral and allied countries. It would be permitted to use all instruments including deception and 'truth projection'. Although references to the Office had appeared earlier in the media, word of the Office was leaked to the press in February 2002 apparently by DoD Public Affairs staff (Dao and Schmitt, 2002; Kaufman and Svitak, 2001). This resulted in a storm of criticism from the press, who feared that they were going to be the targets of false information. This in turn drew in the presidential communications staff who were concerned about the risk to their own credibility if the US was seen to be in the business of deceiving media organizations. The result was that within a week Defense Secretary, Donald Rumsfeld announced the closure of the operation (Allen, 2002; Ricks, 2002).

One of the immediate consequences of the attacks of 9/11 was an outpouring of agonizing in the United States about 'why do they hate us?' One explanation that was soon put forward was that cutbacks in public diplomacy had robbed the US of the ability to convey its message in the Middle East (Broder, 2001; Muravchik, 2002; Shadid, 2001). In response there was an expansion of broadcasting operations into the region: the *Voice of America*'s hours in the region were increased and *Radio Liberty* began broadcasts in Dari and Pashto to Afghanistan. A longer-term response was an effort to create the Middle East Radio Network (MERN). Broadcasting under the name of Radio Sawa (Together) it sought to replace short-wave broadcasting with FM rebroadcasting and satellite audio in an effort to reach younger audiences with the American message (Broadcasting Board of Governors, 2002). In the early days of the war the objective-reporting model preferred by broadcasters came under criticism. Conservatives criticized *Voice of America* and demanded the bombing of *Taliban Radio* and the employment of *Radio Liberty* (Safire, 2001).

The third strand of the response was an effort to coordinate coalition communications efforts both across the member countries and across government departments. The initiative here appears to have come from Alastair Campbell, Blair's Director of Communications and Strategy, who identified the difficulties created by the time difference between Islamabad and London and Washington. Given that Pakistan is 10.5 hours ahead of Washington, British and American media efforts were too slow to rebut Taliban statements and claims. His solution was to create Coalition Information Centres (CICs) in Washington, London and Islamabad that would coordinate the release of information, attempt to control the news agenda and rebut opposition claims in exactly the way that the Clinton–Blair 'war room' model operated in domestic politics (DeYoung, 2001). Among the activities of the CICs were the production of a daily briefing sheet listing media appearances by officials and the message of the day, press conferences and the production of briefing materials. Particularly in Islamabad, the press conference allowed a daily opportunity to rebut Taliban claims about civilian and military casualties.

The day after the *New York Times* carried the leak about the Office of Strategic Influence, it carried a story that the Administration had decided to make the US end of the CIC a permanent part of the national security organization of the White House. Initially dubbed the Office of Global Diplomacy this would seek to coordinate foreign information activities across the entire government (Becker and Dao, 2002). Now christened the Office of Global Communications, the convergence between the needs of domestic and international political communications was made clear in a recent report: 'the White House already coordinates communications across agency lines to reach a number of large domestic audiences. The same attention should now be given to international audiences' (Advisory Commission on Public Diplomacy, 2002: 6). The US administration has sought to use the Defense Secretary, Rumsfeld as its chief spokesperson on the war but the ability to communicate effectively has been hampered by differences within the Administration over policy and by the inevitable tendency for elected political leaders to be more sensitive to their domestic constituencies even as these statements are visible to audiences abroad.

Framing the war

How have the protagonists sought to frame the war on terrorism within these channels of communication? The war involves a great many actors. Most prominently it involves the United States. It involves its partners in a shifting coalition that has its disagreements. Then there are the domestic political actors who argue in support of policy or for different ones. On the other side there are Al-Qaeda and its leaders and Taliban and Islamist sympathisers. There are governments and other groups in countries that are not directly involved or which might become involved. Each of these groups seeks to use the media to frame agendas and mobilize opinion. These battles take place in multiple media fields aimed at multiple audiences. In some parts of the world it makes little sense to talk of a battle because one side or the other dominates media agendas, while in others there is a greater degree of contestation.

We have already cited Philip Gould's comment on the relationship between communication and competence. Projecting a coherent message is dependent on reaching a consensus about what is to be done. The communication of military campaigns, just as with political or marketing campaigns, will become incoherent if there is argument over the correct strategy. So far we can see four stages in the presentation of the conflict. Firstly, groping to find a way to present it. Secondly, a period of relative focus and coherence around operations in Afghanistan and thirdly a renewed period of uncertainty as the battle over what to do next was fought out within the US government and the coalition. This has shaded into a fourth phase over the confrontation with Iraq. Each of these phases deserves an extended study in its own right but in this section we look at the fundamental issues concerning the framing of the conflict.

A central question in the presentation of the conflict was the very name that it has acquired. In the wake of 11 September 2001, the US had a choice of language to use. It could portray the attacks as a criminal or terrorist action that would be primarily handled by law enforcement and intelligence agencies or it could use the language of war. In most cases governments faced with armed insurgent groups choose not to use that discourse because the language of war applies equally to both sides. Instead the usual preference is to treat the opponents as criminals (Miller, 1994: 91). Although critics such as Michael Howard have made the case for a primarily law-enforcement response, the war frame emerged rapidly and possibly without a conscious decision (Howard, 2002).

One routinely talks about 'terrorist attacks' and, given the scale of the attacks on the US, its leaders had to grope for a language to encompass them. In his address to the nation on the evening of 11 September 2001, the US President referred to 'winning the war against terrorism' in an abstract sense (Bush, 2001a). On 12 September, newspaper headlines were already using the language of attack and declaration of war. The President talked of 'acts of war' attracting the interest of journalists who had failed to spot the language in his earlier remarks and, by the time of his radio address on Saturday, he was referring to 'battlefields', 'beachheads' and 'assaults' (Bush, 2001b; Bush, 2001c; Fleischer, 2001a). The following day Rumsfeld toured the Sunday-morning chat shows and talked about 'a new kind of war,' although his war on terrorism seemed to be aimed more at the specific organizations that had attacked the US rather than at a mode of behaviour in general (Rumsfeld, 2001). By Monday, the President's spokesman, Ari Fleischer, could refer to a 'war on terrorism' unproblematically. The space in between had been marked by a rhetorical slide. Once the President referred to the attacks as 'acts of war', the Administration found itself entrapped as the media sought to work out what the consequences of this language were. To escape from this, the Administration would have had to have been able to present a counter-definition but in the absence of a coherent response to a complex situation the language of war was probably inevitable once the finger of suspicion pointed at Osama bin Laden.

If the choice of the language of war has attracted some criticism in the West, Al-Qaeda had no such doubt about the nature of the conflict as war and demonstrated the importance of framing for mobilizing support. The Al-Qaeda line was straightforward and unproblematic, while the American response had to steer a more ambiguous line. From Al-Qaeda's perspective the US, in conjunction with its puppet states in the region and Israel, was waging a war against Islam, particularly through its policies in the Israeli-Palestinian conflict, its support for sanctions on Iraq and its military presence in the Gulf region. Given that the US was already at war with Islam the attacks on the US should be seen as part of that struggle. While the basic disapproval of US policy in the region is widely held, the Al-Qaeda line merely pushes it in a direction that sharpens the nature of the conflict. The debate is then about the desirability of particular actions – such as those that involve civilian casualties. Given this framing of the conflict, the correct course of action is for those who identify themselves as Muslims to give their support. This framing grows out of the analysis and strategy that underpins Al-Qaeda actions. As bin Laden put it in a 1999 interview, 'we seek to instigate the nation to get up and liberate its land, to fight for the sake of God, the Islamic law the highest law, and the word of God, the highest word of all.' In the interview he sought to polarize the situation: 'People were divided into two parts. The first part supported these strikes against US tyranny, while the second denounced them . . . The entire West, with the exception of a few countries, supports this unfair barbaric campaign . . . Mass demonstrations have spread . . . in the . . . Islamic world' (bin Laden, 1999).

In the period after 11 September 2001, the US and its allies were concerned precisely to counteract this attempt at polarization. Almost immediately the US emphasized that 'Islam is peace'. This theme was intended to protect American Muslims and to challenge Al-Qaeda's framing of the conflict (Bush, 2001d). This extract from a press conference given by the President's spokesman Ari Fleischer illustrates a concern both with international perceptions of the situation and with the need to counter the 'war on Islam' frame:

Questioner:
The President's visit to the Islamic center you mentioned has an important domestic purpose. Does it have an international purpose, as well? How concerned is the President that in defending ourselves we could ignite, not among the government of the region, but among the people of the region, a kind of religious conflict, a holy war?

Fleischer:
Well, I think it's fair to say that any actions the President takes domestically have international repercussions. The world is looking to us to see how we react to the fight against terrorism. The world will follow America's lead in many cases. And we will continue to work directly with many of those other nations.

But I remind you, also . . . that many of those nations have their own threats from within and they have to ask themselves if they fail to act against terrorism, will that further embolden the terrorists and send a signal that they can get away with more?

Questioner:
But is there a concern that this could degenerate into a conflict, not between terrorism and civilization, but between Islam and Christianity?

Fleischer:
This attack had nothing to do with Islam. This attack was a perversion of Islam.

(Fleischer, 2001b)

In the weeks that followed, the notion of a war on terrorism was taken up by political leaders and the media across the world. It is striking how much the leader of Al-Qaeda attempted to rebut the American framing. In the statements broadcast on Al-Jazeera, bin Laden demonstrated his familiarity with the comments of the Coalition leadership and the nature of the Western media response and sought to rebut them. 'The nature of this war is fundamentally religious. . . . It is a question of faith, not a war against terrorism, as Bush and Blair try to depict it' (bin Laden, 2001a). His communications sought to emphasize not just the basic injustice of Western policy but also the suffering caused by operations in Afghanistan (bin Laden, 2001b). Even from Afghanistan, bin Laden sought to make use of the new media environment to provide a counter-framing to that put forward by the US and to mobilize his own supporters.

Conclusion: the limits of spin

There are two conclusions to be drawn here, firstly about the importance of communications in international politics and secondly about how we study such issues. Changes in the political substance and communications context of international politics are making international strategies of political communications increasingly important. The US has devoted a great deal of effort in its attempts to shape perceptions of the conflict but this seems to have had little effect in the Middle East (Hazou, 2002). Yet this is indicative not of the unimportance of communications but of the difficulty in trying to craft and communicate a message in an increasingly complex and competitive transnational media environment. Given that media representations of the conflict are how policy makers as well as the public usually learn about events, this is an argument for paying more attention to communication rather than less. Although government communicators are trying to learn from the experience of domestic politics, the international media realm is vastly more complex.

Much of what is written about the media and international conflict is built around a concern with how the conflict is reported. Did the media accurately and objectively report events? Did the military use illegitimate means to restrict or shape the coverage? However, this presumes a separation between the event and its representation. This is reflected in the disciplinary division between communications studies and international relations. The analysis developed here suggests that this separation tends to hide the fundamental importance of communications in constituting the conflict. This is a two-fold development. Systems of communications place the actors in relation to each other but also actors respond to how the conflict is presented in the media. This is not to say that the traditional questions about military-media relations are unimportant but that they are insufficient to grasp the centrality of communications processes in the war on terrorism.

References

Advisory Commission on Public Diplomacy (1998) *Publics and Diplomats in the Global Communications Age*. Washington DC: ACPD.

Advisory Commission on Public Diplomacy (2000) *Consolidation of USIA Into the State Department: An Assessment After One Year*. Washington, DC: ACPD.

Advisory Commission on Public Diplomacy (2002) *Building America's Public Diplomacy*. Washington, DC: ACPD.

Allen, M. (2002) 'White House Angered at Plan for Pentagon Disinformation', *Washington Post*, 25 February.

Becker, E. and Dao, J. (2002) 'Bush Will Keep Wartime Office Promoting US', *New York Times*, 20 February.

bin Laden, O. (1999) 'Interview with Osama bin Laden'. Available at www.terrorism.com/terrorism/binladintranscript.shtml accessed 23 April 2002.

bin Laden, O. (2001a) 'bin Laden Rails Against Crusaders and UN', transcript of tape broadcast on Al-Jazeera, 3 November. Available at www.bbc.co.uk/hi/english/monitoring/media_reports accessed 15 March 2002.

bin Laden, O. (2001b) 'Transcript: bin Laden Video Excerpts'. Available at www.bbc.co.uk/hi/english/world/middle_east/newsid_1729000/1792882.stm accessed 25 April 2002.

Broadcasting Board of Governors (2002) 'New Middle East Radio Network to Go on Air', *International Broadcasting Board Press Release*, 21 March.

Broder, D. (2001) 'America's Muffled Voice', *Washington Post*, 4 November.

Brown, R. (2002a) 'Information Operations, Public Diplomacy and Spin: The US and the Politics of Perception Management', *Journal of Information Warfare*. 1 (3): 40–50.

Brown, R. (2002b) 'The Contagiousness of Conflict: E. E. Schattschneider as a Theorist of the Information Society', *Information, Communication and Society*. 5, 1, Summer.

Bush, G. Jr. (2001a) Statement by the President in his Address to the Nation, 11 September.

Bush, G. Jr. (2001b) Remarks by the President in photo opportunity with the National Security Team, 12 September.

Bush, G. Jr. (2001c) Radio Address of the President to the Nation, 15 September.

Bush, G. Jr. (2001d) 'Islam is Peace Says President: Remarks by the President at Islamic Center of Washington, DC', 17 September.

Centre for Strategic and International Studies (1998) *Reinventing Diplomacy in the Information Age*. Washington DC: CSIS.

Clandestine Radio (2001) 'Afghanistan Dossier'. Available at www.clandestineradio.com/dossier/afghanistan/index.html accessed 23 April 2002.

Cook, T. (1998) *Governing with the News: The News Media as a Political Institution*. Chicago: University of Chicago Press.

Dao, J. and Schmitt, E. (2001) 'Pentagon Readies Office to Sway Sentiment Abroad', *New York Times*, 19 February.

Defense Science Board (2000) *The Creation and Dissemination of All Forms of Information in Support of Psychological Operations in Time of Military Conflict*. Washington DC: Office of the Under Secretary of Defense for Acquisition, Technology and Logistics.

Deibert, R. (2000) 'International Plug 'n' Play: Citizen Activism, the Internet and Global Public Policy', *International Studies Perspectives.* 1 (3): 255–72.

DeYoung, K. (2001) 'US, Britain Step Up War for Public Opinion', *Washington Post*, 1 November.

Donovan, R. and Scherer, R. (1992) *Unsilent Revolution: Television News and American Public Life.* Cambridge: Cambridge University Press.

Eban, A. (1998) *Diplomacy for the Next Century.* New Haven, CT: Yale University Press.

Entman, R. (2000) 'Declarations of Independence: The Growth of Media Power after the Cold War,' in B. Nacos, R. Shapiro and P. Isernia (eds) *Decision-making in a Glass House: Mass Media, Public Opinion and American and European Foreign Policy in the 21st Century.* Lanham, MD: Rowman and Littlefield.

Fitzwater, M. (1995) *Call the Briefing!* New York: Times Books.

Fleischer, A. (2001a) Press Briefing, 12 September.

Fleischer, A. (2001b) Press Briefing, 17 September.

Florini, A. (ed.) (2000) *The Third Force: The Rise of Transnational Civil Society.* Washington DC: Carnegie Endowment for International Peace.

Gould, P. (1998) *The Unfinished Revolution: How the Modernizers Save the Labour Party.* London: Little, Brown.

Gowing, N. (2002) 'Don't Get in Our Way', *The Guardian*, G2, 8 April.

Hazou, M. (2002) 'Seale Sees Danger Signs in Poll Highlighting Muslim Anger at US', *Daily Star* (Lebanon), 28 February.

Hixson, W. (1997) *Parting the Curtain: Propaganda, Culture and the Cold War, 1945–1961.* Basingstoke: Macmillan.

Howard, M (2002) 'What's in a Name?', *Foreign Affairs.* 81 (1): 8–13.

Ingham, B. (1991) *Kill the Messenger.* London: Fontana.

Innis, H. (1951) *The Bias of Communication.* Toronto: University of Toronto Press.

International Organization (2000) 'Special Issue: Legalization and World Politics', *International Organization.* 54 (3).

Kaufman, G. and Svitak, A. (2001) 'War Prompts Reshuffling at DoD', *Federal Times*, 12 November 2001. Available at www.federaltimes.com accessed 13 February 2002.

Keck, M. and Sikkink, K. (1998) *Activists Beyond Borders: Advocacy Networks in International Politics.* Ithaca, NY: Cornell University Press.

Keith, K. (2002) Testimony of Ambassador Kenton Keith before House Appropriations Subcommittee on Commerce, Justice, State and Judiciary, 24 April.

Keohane, R. and Nye, J. (1977) *Power and Interdependence.* Boston, MA: Little, Brown.

Keohane, R. and Nye, J. (1998) 'Power and Interdependence in the Information Age', *Foreign Affairs.* 77 (5): 81–94.

Livingston, S. (2000) 'Transparency and the News Media', in B. Finel and K. Lord (eds) *Power and Conflict in the Age of Transparency.* New York: Palgrave.

Lord, C. (2000) 'The Past and Future of Public Diplomacy', *Orbis.* 42 (1): 49–72.

Maltese, J. (1994) *Spin Control: The White House Office of Communications and the Management of Presidential News*, 2nd edn. Chapel Hill, NC: University of North Carolina Press.

McLuhan, M. (1964) *Understanding Media.* Cambridge, MA: MIT Press.

Miller, D. (1994) *Don't Mention the War: Northern Ireland, Propaganda and the Media*. London: Pluto.

Muravchik, J. (2002) 'Heart, Minds and the War Against Terror', *Commentary*, May.

Murphy, C. (1994) *International Organization and Industrial Change: Global Governance since 1850*. Cambridge: Polity.

Nye, J. (1990) *Bound to Lead: The Changing Nature of American Power*. New York: Basic Books.

Nye, J. (2002) *The Paradox of American Power*. New York: Oxford University Press.

Nye, J. and Owens, W.A. (1996) 'America's Information Edge', *Foreign Affairs*. 72 (2): 20–36.

Price, R. (1998) 'Reversing the Gun Sights: Transnational Civil Society Targets Landmines', *International Organization*. 52 (3): 613–44.

Project on the Advocacy of US Interests Abroad (1998) *Equipped for the Future: Managing US Foreign Affairs in the 21st Century*. Washington DC: Henry L. Stimson Center.

Ricks, T. (2002) 'Rumsfeld Kills Pentagon Propaganda Unit', *Washington Post*, 27 February.

Rosenau, J. and Czempiel, E-O. (eds) (1992) *Governance without Government: Order and Change in World Politics*. Cambridge: Cambridge University Press.

Rumsfeld, D. (2001) 'Interview with Fox News Sunday', 16 September. Available at www.defenselink.mil/news/sep2001/ accessed 24 April 2002.

Safire, W. (2001) 'Equal Time for Hitler', *New York Times*, 20 September.

Scammell, M. (1995) *Designer Politics: How Elections are Won*. Basingstoke: Macmillan.

Schattschneider, E.E. (1960) *The Semisovereign People: A Realist's View of Democracy in America*. Austin, TX: Harcourt, Brace Jovanovich.

Shahdid, A. (2001) 'Fighting Terror; The Battle for Hearts and Minds', *Boston Globe*, 26 December.

Shaw, M. (2000) 'Media and Public Sphere without Borders? News Coverage and Power from Kurdistan to Kosovo' in B. Nacos, R. Shapiro and P. Isernia (eds) *Decisionmaking in a Glass House: Mass Media, Public Opinion and American and European Foreign Policy in the 21st Century*. Lanham, MD: Rowman and Littlefield.

Speakes, L. (1989) *Speaking Out: The Reagan Presidency from Inside the White House*. New York: Avon.

Summe, J. (2000) *Presentation to Multilateral Operations Symposium*, Joint Forces Staff College, November. Available at www.jfsc.ndu.edu/mso2000/j39.ppt accessed 20 December 2001.

7

'WE KNOW WHERE YOU ARE': PSYCHOLOGICAL OPERATIONS MEDIA DURING ENDURING FREEDOM

Philip M. Taylor

In the 16 minutes following the first strike on the World Trade Centre, New York's news media organizations scrambled their helicopters and were on hand to broadcast images of the attack on the second tower live to a global television audience. It was, many people said, like 'watching a movie'. The so-called 'war' against international terrorism thus began with a spectacular psychological operation by an asymmetric enemy against militarily the most powerful nation on earth.

The relationship between terrorism and publicity has always been a symbiotic one, but the power of *real-time* television images would appear to have eradicated the Thatcherite solution of attempting to 'starve' terrorism of the 'oxygen of publicity' by denying them a voice through the traditional free mass media. This has not prevented the administration of President George W. Bush from trying to do this, for example by requesting the American-based television networks not to air Osama bin Laden's video recordings for fear that they may contain coded messages to terrorist 'sleepers' in the United States. This request was not only bizarre because it would appear to reveal considerable ignorance about how television images are edited for nightly news bulletins, but it was also reflective of a failure to understand just how much the global informational environment had changed in the past few years.

Take for example the case of Al-Jazeera, the Qatar based satellite TV station to which bin Laden and the Taliban gave exclusive initial rights for his taped messages. After 11 September 2001, Al-Jazeera seemed to burst into the global informational environment as some kind of new rogue player – the 'Arab CNN' – in the war against terrorism. Or rather it was accused of providing a voice for the terrorists in the propaganda war against the West. In fact it was founded in 1996 and most of its staff were trained in the BBC, especially within the public-service broadcasting ethos of reporting objectively both sides of a case. This was a unique experiment within traditionally state-controlled Arab media systems that had been subjected to considerable censorship of both news and views. Al-Jazeera broke this mould by reporting within a democratic tradition, with dissenting and contrary voices visible and audible for the first time in the region. A measure of its uniqueness – and of its impact – was that nearly every Arab head of state had complained about its coverage. So when Western leaders began complaining about its 'propaganda output', they missed the point that Al-Jazeera was the first voice of Arab street public opinion ever seen in the Middle East. And when they asked Western networks to limit its usage in their own coverage, this was interpreted as merely revealing their 'hypocrisy' about Western democracy and the value placed upon freedom of speech, undermining still further any claims that this was not a 'crusade' against Islam. Rounds one and two of the 'propaganda war' went to the terrorists.

So did round three when the American led bombing of Afghanistan began on 7 October 2001. The Taliban, who understood the power of television so much that they had banned its reception in Afghanistan, also understood the 24/7 global news cycle developed and dominated by Anglo-American media organizations that Al-Jazeera had now infiltrated. Five hours ahead of London and ten ahead of Washington, Taliban spokesmen were able to set the daily news agenda with stories about 'collateral damage' or how they had shot down American helicopters. The time difference meant that London and Washington were on the defensive, responding to such claims. It was not until the creation of the Coalition Information Centres a month later in London, Washington and – most crucially – in Islamabad that this situation was reversed. But, by then, a lot of damage had been done to the coalition's cause. Serious doubts had been cast on the veracity of American claims about Al-Qaeda's responsibility for the 9/11 attacks, on the identity of the hijackers, even the so-called 'evidence' from the crash sites. Rumours were rife that 4,000 Jews failed to turn up for work on the day of the strikes, that footage of celebrating Palestinians aired on CNN had in fact been taken during the Gulf War, and that the strikes were a CIA-Mossad conspiracy to provide a pretext for war in Afghanistan motivated by the Bush family's oil interests (Taylor, 2001). This mixture of rumour, gossip and misinformation from Palestine to Pakistan was picked up in the Western media and, where it was not, on the internet. The global information environment had become so porous and so fast that the waging of any strategic information campaign could not merely be confined to the traditional mass media front.

Today, portable camcorders capable of high-quality digital resolution are everywhere, as are the people who buy them at affordable prices from high-street stores. Hence, when something happens that may not once have been captured for posterity on film, today still and moving images of a Concorde crash outside Paris are taken by a Japanese businessman on board another aircraft waiting for take off or by the wife of a Spanish truck driver filming her husband on a highway adjacent to the runway. A new generation of mobile phones is capable of transmitting images taken with in-built digital cameras, while the internet provides a global communications platform which anybody with the right equipment can access. New media, niche audiences and citizen journalists were emerging phenomena of the 1990s and extended the range of the information 'front'. In such a world, the terrorist knows that there is a very good chance that any 'propaganda of the deed' will command global attention. In a military sense, this would be regarded as a strategic information challenge.

Winning the information war

For the past ten years, amidst all the talk of a Revolution in Military Affairs (RMA), there has been much thought given to the idea of 'winning the information war'. This has in turn given rise to a new military doctrine known initially as Information Warfare (IW), now more commonly called Information Operations (IO). The latter is defined by the Pentagon as 'actions taken to affect adversary information and information systems while defending one's own information and information systems' (Joint Pub 3–13, 1996). This doctrine was at first concerned with protecting the communications and information systems on which military forces were becoming increasingly reliable as a result of the RMA, although it was always recognized that these systems were both vulnerable to what was termed 'an electronic Pearl Harbor' while at the same time providing opportunities for taking command and control of any battle front or 'combat space' of the future. In this respect, the Gulf War was termed 'the first information war' because it embraced this new thinking by taking out Iraqi air defense systems on the opening nights of the conflict, conducted precision strikes against enemy command and control facilities and even extended into shaping the global media perception about the progress of the war in the coalition's favour (Taylor, 1997).

The need to incorporate the mass media in emerging IO doctrine remains highly problematic, especially from the media's point of view. This is partly because IO embraces the idea of 'shaping the information space' by what is now being called 'Perception Management'. A euphemism for propaganda this may be, but the range of options available to democratic governments for waging war in the information age includes public diplomacy and international broadcasting, cultural exchanges and the exercise of 'soft power', deception and psychological operations. It is the presence of deception – a tried, tested and long accepted military necessity – which causes the problems. As the debacle of the newly created Office of Strategic Influence revealed in the spring of 2002, the media have a deep suspicion of military communications strategies. The idea of creating a propaganda machinery in Washington to win the global struggle for hearts and minds in the war against international terrorism was a gut reaction to the September 11 attacks and the subsequent agonising about 'why they hate us so much?'. Yet the media outrage at the Pentagon's explanation that deception would form part of this military struggle indicated a high degree of journalistic misunderstanding about military strategies, especially new ones such as IO.

Interestingly, there was no equivalent outcry at the announcement about another part of that machinery, namely the Office of Global Communications based in the White House. Perhaps this was because modern politicians – who survive or die on the altar of media and public opinion – are much more adept at 'spin' than their military counterparts. Perhaps it was because the media expect politicians to manipulate them as part of the democratic process in the information age. Or perhaps it was because military-media relations in Western democracies that have long abandoned conscription had deteriorated to such a point that mutual misunderstanding has become the norm.

Despite all the military lessons learned since the end of the Cold War about the importance of good media relations, many military officers continue to regard the media as at worst an enemy in their own right or at best a necessary evil that has to be 'managed'. To this end we have seen in the past decade the rise of Public Affairs (PA) as it is known in the US (Public Information in NATO and Media Operations in the UK) as a specialized branch of military communications. Referred to sceptically by some journalists as 'organ grinders', these PA officers are in the front line of any 'media war'. They have tried to keep their distance from IO because many of them maintain they are not in the business of influencing journalists, merely of providing them with as much information as possible within the confines of operational security. However, this is a slightly disingenuous argument because, as any journalist knows, the selection or omission of information helps to shape the views upon which opinions can be formed. The classic example in recent times was the provision to the media in the 1991 Gulf War of videotapes of precision guided missiles hitting their targets with uncanny accuracy, thus deflecting media attention away from the fact that 90 per cent of coalition bombing was with old-fashioned 'dumb' weapons.

If that was a successful 'media war', the record since then has been somewhat mixed. There was much talk in the 1990s of the 'CNN effect' by which military intervention in some countries (e.g. Somalia) but not others (e.g. Rwanda) was said to be driven by dramatic real-time television imagery (Robinson, 2002). In the conflict against international terrorism, the US military has at times proved itself ill-equipped to handle the media. One need only recall the surprise by the military at the hostile media reaction outside the United States when the Department of Defense (DoD) issued photographs of manacled Taliban and Al-Qaeda suspects detained at Camp X Ray at Guantanamo Bay. Equally, as the debacle of the Office of Strategic Influence revealed, the military failed to appreciate that the US media would lead the way in opposing the creation of a propaganda department which, it openly admitted, would use deception through the media if it would aid victory. In terms of strategic influence in the global propaganda war against international terrorism, one can only conclude that non-military organizations – such as the State Department, the Office of Global Communications in the White House and the Department of Homeland Defence (created in 2002) – are better placed to win 'hearts and minds'. At the tactical and operational levels of military deployment, however, the military can draw upon a wealth of experience and expertise in the area of Psychological Operations (or PSYOPS), as the experience of Afghanistan once again revealed.

Psychological Operations (PSYOPS)

The US defines PSYOPS as 'planned operations to convey selected information and indicators to foreign audiences to influence their emotions, motives, objective reasoning, and ultimately the behavior of foreign governments, organizations, groups and individuals' (Joint Pub 3–13, 1996). One should note that this definition explicitly states that PSYOPS are directed at exclusively external audiences. NATO has a slightly different definition, namely 'planned psychological activities in peace, crisis and war directed to enemy, friendly and neutral audiences in order to influence attitudes and behavior affecting the achievement of political and military objectives' (MC 402, 1998). To the best knowledge of this author, however, NATO has not yet conducted PSYOPS against a 'friendly' or 'neutral' audience (unless one includes material designed to communicate with the Kosovar Albanians in 1999). As such, military PSYOP tends to be deployed in support of a military mission of whatever kind (peacekeeping, war fighting, peace consolidation, 'humanitarian intervention'). Of course the sheer variety of these military missions has varied enormously in the 1990s and, accordingly, so have the PSYOPS. It is not just traditional psychological warfare techniques of dropping leaflets, broadcasting radio messages or the use of tactical loudspeaker teams to convince enemy soldiers to surrender, desert or defect.

The complexity of recent 'operations other than war', combined with the need to explain to local civilian populations and warring parties alike why international armed forces are intervening (rather than 'invading') has given rise to the need to conduct psychological operations other than traditional 'surrender or die' messages. This can involve a simple communication to the local residents of an area to stay off the streets while a convoy of humanitarian aid passes through their area (as in Somalia, 1992–3) or another message to local children not to point their toy guns at soldiers (as in Kosovo, 1999). After stability has been restored, PSYOPS teams have been heavily involved in campaigns to alert local populations as to the dangers of land mines, producing everything from join-the-dot colouring books containing different diagrams of land mines (an IFOR product for Bosnia 1995–6) to Superman comics with storylines alerting children to the dangers of wandering into minefields (another Bosnian product from 1997–8).

PSYOPS today, then, are no longer solely about dropping what the Americans in World War Two called 'bullshit bombs'. This role still exists – 29 million leaflets were dropped over Iraqi forces during Operation Desert Storm in 1991, while 103 million leaflets were dropped over Kosovo and Serbia during Operation Allied Force in 1999. But these were what might be termed somewhat old-fashioned inter-state conflicts in which 'combat propaganda' had been used, tried and tested since the British first pioneered the activity during World War One (Taylor, 1999). Having said that, the PSYOP campaign in Afghanistan during 2001–02 can be described in these classical terms. Conducted largely by the United States' 4th Psychological Operations Group (4POG), based at Fort Bragg and part of US Special Forces, the objective was to communicate certain messages within a complex theatre of military operations in which less than 10,000 coalition troops (mainly American and British special operations soldiers) were deployed to remove the Taliban and capture Al-Qaeda suspects.

This was not a campaign in which the media would feature prominently on the battlefront. Special Operations Forces have a policy of not allowing journalists to accompany them on combat missions. In Afghanistan, therefore, there were no media pools, as in the Gulf War. Journalists had to fend largely for themselves, and eight were killed trying to report what was going on. In a highly dangerous environment, reporters took considerable risks to provide erratic snapshots of the fighting, while the BBC's John Simpson even managed to broadcast live from the fighting front via his videophone (Simpson, 2002: 387ff). However, the media war was being fought largely outside Afghanistan, while the real war was fought largely within an information vacuum from the media point of view. It was that vacuum which PSYOPS tried to take command and control of.

The role of radio

The Taliban ruled partly through terror and partly through a rigorous control of Afghan media. Television was forbidden, but they did have radio stations, especially the *Voice of Sharia* (Islamic Law) in Kabul. This was bombed on 8 October 2001 and, although it was able to resume broadcasting briefly on 26 October, within hours it was taken off the air permanently by another air strike. Interestingly, there was no outcry from the world's media similar to that which took place when *Radio Television Serbia* (RTS) was bombed in 1999 during the Kosovo air campaign. But Afghanistan was a much poorer media environment than Serbia, and RTS was able to resume broadcasting within hours. There was a bigger fuss when Al-Jazeera's Kabul office was hit – accidentally, it was later claimed – by a cruise missile. Having taken out the Taliban's radio stations, the coalition had to provide an alternative voice. On 15 October 2001, a simple leaflet depicting a graphic of a radio tower with words in Pashto and Dari described 'Information Radio' broadcasting on certain frequencies from 5–10am and from 5–10pm.

This 'alternative voice' was to emanate from a flying broadcasting platform known as 'Commando Solo', a converted EC 130E aircraft operated by the 193rd Special Operations Wing of the Pennsylvanian National Guard which had been deployed on similar operations in the Gulf, Haiti and Kosovo. One of the heaviest – and therefore most vulnerable – aircraft in the American air force and capable of broadcasting radio and television messages on multi-frequencies, there was obviously no need for its television capability in Operation 'Enduring Freedom', and so its television transmitters were removed prior to deployment. This was significant because it enabled Commando Solo to fly around 5,000 feet higher than normal, thus extending its radio transmission range and proving it with a degree of added protection from ground-to-air missiles in the dangerous mountainous terrain over which it was being deployed.

Broadcasting was one thing; the ability of the local population to receive the programming was quite another. Although radio receivers were fairly common throughout Afghanistan, there was still felt to be a need for more, especially in areas without electricity. Accordingly, almost 40,000 AM/FM/SW receivers were distributed – complete with batteries – throughout the country by American forces or by USAID. The British, who had a much smaller PSYOP capability in the region, were also reported to have dropped wind-up radios requiring no batteries. As coalition forces gradually took more and more areas under their control, radio sets were distributed freely on the ground. But what kind of programming was being heard? An early example of Commando Solo's radio broadcast output is as follows:

> We have no wish to hurt you, the innocent people of Afghanistan. Stay away from military installations, government buildings, terrorist camps, roads factories or bridges. If you are near these places, then you must move away from them. Seek a safe place, and stay well away from anything that might be a target. We do not wish to harm you. With your help, this conflict can be over soon. And once again, Afghanistan will

belong to you and not to tyrants or outsiders. Then you will reclaim your place among the nations of the world, and return to the honoured place your country once held. Remember, we are here to help you to be free from this terrorism, despotism and the fear and pain they bring with them.

This theme was reflected in the second leaflet drop which depicted an American soldier shaking hands with an Afghan male citizen with the words: 'The Partnership of Nations is here to help you'. Commando Solo does not drop leaflets; that is done by other aircraft or by the M129 leaflet bomb which explodes in mid air and scatters the leaflets to the ground. Two Command Solos were deployed in Afghanistan and their broadcasts were supplemented by ground transmitters based in Bagram and Kandahar once those towns fell to coalition forces.

In total, over 6,500 hours of radio programming, including material produced by the *Voice of America* as well as that prepared by the Psychological Operations Task Force (POTF), was put out by ground-and air-based transmitters between October 2001 and the end of the combat phase of the psychological operation in March 2002. This consisted of 166 different radio programmes with over 500 scripts produced mainly in Pashto and Dari. A handful of these scripts were prepared in Arabic and targeted at the 'foreign terrorists' fighting for the Taliban. A great deal of the broadcast output was local music, which had been banned by the Taliban.

For a co-ordinated PSYOP campaign, all media deployed had to sing to the same tune. Because locals had never seen the television images of the strikes against New York and Washington, every effort had to be made in the initial stages to explain why foreign forces were once again fighting on Afghan soil. This was delicate in the light of the prior Soviet invasion, and indeed of the British occupation a century before that. PSYOP messages tried to turn the situation on its head by emphasizing that Al-Qaeda's Arab recruits were the foreign invaders, not US–UK forces, and that it was their terrorist attacks which prompted the arrival of US forces to seek justice. An early leaflet described how 'On September 11th, the United States was the target of terrorist attacks, leaving no choice but to seek justice for these horrible crimes'. Another leaflet was produced depicting Al-Qaeda terrorists targeted by the crosshairs of a sniper's rifle with the words: 'Drive out foreign terrorists'.

To further emphasize the theme that the Partnership of Nations was here to help the people of Afghanistan, not to subdue them, humanitarian aid became a key element of the campaign, including the PSYOP campaign. A leaflet produced at the end of Ramadan depicted a dish of dates with the message from the 'People of America': 'We wish that God will accept your prayers and fast. Have a blessed holiday'. The Taliban resented this campaign sufficiently for them to respond by claiming that the yellow parcels of humanitarian aid were either poisoned or that they were cluster bomb booby traps. It was true that cluster bombs were also yellow and this was of considerable sensitivity for humanitarian NGOs concerning the wider propaganda war beyond the borders of Afghanistan. Accordingly leaflets were dropped warning children not to pick up the brightly coloured food parcels, while the colour of their packaging was changed to blue. A later leaflet depicted food parcels clearly marked 'USA' being distributed to hungry Afghan children with the phrase: 'America has provided $170 million in aid to Afghanistan' with images of Taliban destruction of buildings on the reverse side.

The coalition was clearly attempting to divide Afghan civilians from the Taliban leadership with messages such as: 'Do you enjoy being ruled by the Taliban? Are you proud to live a life of fear? Are you happy to see the place your family has owned for generations a terrorist training site?' Leaflets were dropped over towns depicting a Taliban whipping a woman dressed in a *burqa* with the words: 'Is this the future you want for your women and children?' Other messages tried to convey a sense of solidarity between the ordinary people of the US and of Afghanistan. As one leaflet declared: 'No one should tell you how to live. The Partnership of Nations will help rescue the Afghan people from the Taliban criminals and foreign terrorists.'

Targeting the Taliban

The messages directed towards the Afghan civilian population were but one part of the PSYOP campaign. Another included classic military to military (or enemy propaganda) communications. Broadcasts targeting the Taliban forces included one which claimed:

> Attention Taliban! You are condemned. Did you know that? The instant the terrorists you support took over our planes, you sentenced yourselves to death . . . our helicopters will rain death down upon your camps before you detect them on your radar. Our bombs are so accurate we can drop them through your windows . . . you have only one choice, surrender now and we will give you a second chance. We will let you live.
>
> (Freidman, 2002)

Further leaflets depicting the dropping of the powerful 'Daisy Cutter' bomb (BLU-82) by parachute warned the Taliban soldiers in the mountains: 'We know where you are' and, on the reverse side, 'Stop fighting for the Taliban and live'. When, on 20 October, 200 American Rangers attacked a Taliban fortress at Kandahar in an attempt to grab Mullah Omar, they were accompanied by four PSYOPS officers. The raid sent a message that the coalition was now embarked on a manhunt for the Taliban leadership. The PSYOPS team left behind thousands of leaflets depicting a photograph of a New York fireman raising the American flag over the ruins of the World Trade Centre with the message: 'Freedom

Endures'. And when the raid on Tora Bora began, thousands of leaflets were dropped on the cave fortress depicting missiles raining down on the Taliban fighters in their caves: 'Al-Qaeda – do you think you are safe?' Impressive images of AC 130 gunships firing at the ground were depicted on some leaflets, while others contained photographs of attack helicopters to drive home American military superiority.

A prominent feature of the manhunt campaign revolved around a 25 million dollar reward for information leading to the capture of Mullah Omar and Osama bin Laden. The Taliban's spiritual leader had always forbidden photographs of himself, and so leaflets were dropped announcing the reward with Omar's portrait, and another even depicted his car's number plate taken from an aerial image. Other leaflets added additional senior Taliban commanders and, of course, bin Laden. One unusual leaflet depicted a clean-shaven (save for moustache) black and white photograph of bin Laden dressed in Western clothing in an attempt to undermine local myths about his Western connections. The caption reads: 'Usama bin Laden the murderer and coward has abandoned al-Qaeda. He has abandoned you and run away. Give yourself up and do not die needlessly. You mean nothing to him. Save your families the grief and pain of your death'. There was some discussion in the Western media about whether this photograph had been faked. If so, it would have broken one of the first rules of PSYOPS as practised in its 'white' form by Fort Bragg. This was that PSYOPS messages should never deliberately lie because, if found out, the credibility of future messages would be jeopardised. This does not mean that PSYOPS messages contained aspirational themes that went unfulfilled, as the targeting of Mullah Omar and bin Laden suggested. The objective was to sow seeds of doubt, to break the mystique of Taliban power and to demonise its leadership. For example, a leaflet was produced depicting bin Laden playing chess (also banned by the Taliban) with Taliban leaders as pawns on a chessboard. The message ran: 'Expel the foreign rulers and live in peace'. On the reverse side, bin Laden was depicted holding a chained dog with the head of Mullah Omar. The caption read: 'Who really runs the Taliban?' And, in a reversion to World War Two techniques, another leaflet was dropped containing morphed images of skulls over the faces of Taliban leaders with the words 'The Taliban reign of fear is about to end'.

It should be noted that these leaflets were released to the media by the Pentagon after they had been dropped. They were widely available on the World Wide Web, and thus put the PSYOPS campaign in Afghanistan under a public scrutiny never possible before in a near contemporaneous sense. During the Kosovo campaign, leaflets dropped on Belgrade and Novi Sad were picked up by citizens who displayed them to CNN camera crews, so there was no longer any point in trying to keep them secret. Indeed, even the broadcasts of Commando Solo were being monitored by radio hams outside the theatre of operations, translated back into English and placed on the web within days of their transmission. This is all a far cry from the situation that existed at the outbreak of World War Two when the RAF announced that its first air raid over Germany had been a leaflet-dropping mission. When the press asked to see the leaflets, the Air Ministry refused on the grounds that they were classified! Perhaps the Pentagon had understood how much the world had changed in the information age after all. It would have been futile to try and keep secret the 84 million leaflets, handbills and posters disseminated during the Afghan phase of Operation Enduring Freedom. Of these, just over 80 million were disseminated from the air, and almost two million by Tactical PSYOPS teams on the ground.

The point about all this is that there is really no such thing anymore as tactical information. A leaflet dropped in the remote mountains of Afghanistan will be picked up and scanned into a computer by somebody and, once on a website, can have a strategic impact. This made it even more important for the PSYOPS teams to be careful about what they said in their products. Although designed as a 'combat force multiplier', PSYOPS products invite closer public scrutiny and can reflect badly upon their producers if they deviate widely from 'the truth'. Moreover, because military forces are increasingly interacting with civilian audiences outside of combat operations, they need to produce messages which can resonate with those audiences. This became all too apparent in the immediate aftermath of the fall of Afghan towns and cities. Drawing on their experiences from Bosnia, Africa and South America, the PSYOPS teams launched themselves into mine awareness campaigns to minimize civilian casualties. Leaflets and posters were produced depicting different types of land mines with slogans such as: 'ATTENTION. Partnership of Nations forces are destroying unexploded ordinance and weapons to keep the citizens of this region safe. There is no reason to be alarmed. For your own safety, stay away! STAY AWAY'. And if this appears too alarmist, slightly 'softer' messages warned 'Danger! Unexploded ordanance [*sic*] can kill! Do not touch! Help us keep you safe.'

The final phase of the operation was the conduct of 'Consolidation PSYOP' designed to help reconstruct the physical and psychological health of the nation, as well as to build loyalties to the new government following the collapse of the Taliban. A tall order in a nation divided into factions for decades, consolidation products are only likely to succeed over time, probably at least for a generation. It remains to be seen how long this campaign will go on for, but in the early phase it consisted of educational programmes, including the reconstruction of Kabul University, the promotion of support for the new government, continued discrediting of Mullah Omar and other Taliban and Al-Qaeda leaders, mine awareness and an explanation of what the coalition had achieved and why it was still in the country. The Psychological Operations Task Force transformed into a Military Information Support Team

(MIST) and one of its early programmes was to construct a national radio network with transmitters throughout the country, from Mazar-e-Sharif in the north to Kandahar in the south. These were operated by local journalists, trained by Partnership of Nations forces where necessary, and capable of delivering themes with consolidation messages. *Radio Afghanistan* in Kabul was at the heart of this network and TV had already begun to reappear by the summer of 2002, with satellite dishes selling like hot cakes in the markets of the main towns.

The MIST began to notice that previous PSYOP products such as the reward leaflets and the mine awareness posters were being displayed widely in Afghan shop windows, in cars and on the side of trucks. Similarly, they were surprised to find local rug makers incorporating PSYOP product designs on prayer rugs being sold in bazaars. In Konduz to the north, a local coffee shop actually asked for taped PSYOP programming so that he could play it to his customers. These were all taken as measures of the effectiveness of the campaign. To keep up the momentum, the MIST produced leaflets with Afghans in black turbans shaking hands with men in white turbans, with the message: 'The time has come for all Afghans to make peace'. Another depicts three Afghans building a house together with the phrase 'brick by brick . . .' By this time, the shorter messages contained in leaflets were being supplemented by longer news-based articles in a bi-monthly newspaper, *ISAF News*, distributed free by the newly created International Security Force for Afghanistan.

It is still perhaps too early to assess fully the effectiveness of the PSYOP campaign. Certainly the anti-Taliban and especially the anti-Al-Qaeda messages resonated with many Afghans, although the fractious nature of Afghan politics meant this varied from area to area. When the Taliban forces suddenly left Kabul in December 2001, they were unable to rally much popular support in the areas they tried to regroup in. This was why they had to flee to their mountain cave complexes. On the other hand, bribery of local forces probably helped many more to get away completely. This use of anti-Taliban local fighting forces thus proved to be a mixed blessing. On the one hand, the use of Northern Alliance troops as a proxy force helped to underpin the theme that American and British forces were not the invaders but, on the other, a sense of Islamic brotherhood – backed up by local traditions involving money – meant that many of the targets of American 'justice' managed to escape. To date, the 25 million dollar reward for bin Laden and Mullah Omar has yet to be paid out. In this respect alone, the strategic PSYOP campaign against Al-Qaeda, reportedly with bases in 67 other countries, has yet to succeed.

In an asymmetric war against international terrorism, the battlefront is the global information environment. The military elements of the conflict, as in Afghanistan or possibly next in Iraq, may be the most visible from a traditional media point of view, but they are much less significant than the intelligence, financial, legal and psychological components of the struggle. Much of the 'war' will be fought in complete secrecy, far away from the prying gaze of the media. The most visible elements will relate to the next military phases in which troops are deployed and to the strategic psychological operation of convincing the Islamic world that this is not a 'clash of civilizations'. For the terrorists, however, it is very much a war against a way of life, and propaganda is a key weapon in their arsenal. Indeed, apart from further terrorist acts that constitute 'propaganda of the deed' – or the threat of them – it is their major weapon. As such the media, with their inevitable preoccupation with 'bad news', become a major battlefront on which the 'war' will be fought. But perhaps it will also be determined by the skill with which PSYOPS and Information Operations can be deployed not just in future combat theatres but throughout the wider strategic global information environment.

Note: on the PSYOPS output

Most of the leaflets described in this chapter can be found on the internet. Principal sites are www.psywarrior.com and www.leeds.ac.uk/ics/terrorism.htm The radio transcripts can be found at www.clandestineradio.com Many are also in the author's possession.

References

Friedman, H. (2002) *Psychological Operations in Afghanistan* available at http://psywar.psyborg.co.uk/afghanistan.shtml.

Joint Pub 3–13 (1996) *Joint Doctrine for Information Operations*, available at www.dtic.mil/doctrine/jel/new_pubs/jp3_13.pdf.

MC 402 (1998) NATO Psychological Operations Policy, NATO, Brussels. Available at http://www.nato.int/adac/fellow/96-98/combelle.pdf.

Robinson, Piers (2002) *The CNN Effect: The Myth of News Media, Foreign Policy and Intervention*. London: Routledge.

Simpson, John (2002) *News from No-Man's Land: Reporting the World*. London: Macmillan.

Taylor, Philip M. (1997) *War and the Media: Propaganda and Persuasion During the Gulf War*. Manchester: Manchester University Press.

Taylor, Philip M. (1999) *British Propaganda during the Twentieth Century: Selling Democracy*. Edinburgh: Edinburgh University Press.

Taylor, Philip M. (2001) Spin Laden: Propaganda and Urban Myths, in *The World Today*. London, Chatham House, 57 (12): 7–9.

Part 3

REPORTING CONFLICT IN THE ERA OF 24/7 NEWS

LIVE TV AND BLOODLESS DEATHS: WAR, INFOTAINMENT AND 24/7 NEWS

Daya Kishan Thussu

This chapter examines developments in international television news and their implications for the coverage of conflict situations at a time when the political, economic and technological contexts in which news organizations operate are becoming increasingly global. In the media-saturated world, with a constant flow of words, sounds and images, '24/7 News' (24-hour news, 7 days a week) has emerged as a television genre in its own right. Given the fiercely competitive commercial environment within which television news networks have to function, television has to be live and the most important 'live TV' is news, because of its contemporaneity and the ability to transmit it instantaneously to a global audience. This has been facilitated by a market-led broadcasting ecology and the availability of privatized satellite networks.

The demand for live 24/7 news, this chapter argues, can lead to sensationalization and trivialization of often complex stories and a temptation to highlight the entertainment value of news. Audience interest in news is highest at the time of conflict: news is largely about conflict, and conflict is always news, especially its rolling variety, as the global expansion of the Atlanta-based Cable News Network (CNN) demonstrates. CNN created a new paradigm of 24-hour news culture which has led to the 'CNNization' of television networks across the globe (Bennett, 2003; Volkmer, 1999). One result of these developments is that conflict reporting tends towards infotainment.

The chapter discusses the key features of war as infotainment: the obsession with high-tech reporting, using a video-game format to present combat operations, with complex graphics and satellite imagery, providing a largely virtual, even bloodless, coverage of war. Finally, it argues that this type of coverage is in the process of being globalized – given the power and influence of the Western, or more specifically, US model of television news. Such coverage has implications for foreign and security policy and portends ill for the proper understanding of distant wars both within Western societies and across the globe.

Television news and the 24/7 cycle

Television has become the most global of the media, taking advantage of its capacity to transcend linguistic and geographical barriers. Images carry greater influence in shaping opinion than words, especially in a world where, even in the twenty-first century, millions of people cannot read or write. Even in media-saturated countries such as the United States, television news is seen as 'authoritative' and therefore trustworthy (Iyengar and Kinder, 1987). In Britain, as a new report for the Independent Television Commission and the Broadcasting Standards Commission attests: 'television is now the supreme news medium, in the sense that it is used and respected by almost everyone. It is the only news medium presently capable of reaching across the whole of British society' (Hargreaves and Thomas, 2002: 5).

The growing commercialism of the airwaves, partly as a result of the privatization of global satellite networks and the technological convergence between media, computer and telecommunication industries, has fundamentally changed the international ecology of broadcasting. The shift from public-service to ratings-led television, dependent on corporate advertising and a heterogeneous global audience, has implications for news agendas and editorial priorities.

Developments in communications technologies, such as satellite and cable, and especially the availability of digital broadcasting, has made possible the global expansion of news and current affairs TV channels. The global television newsscape changed with CNN's ability to beam live, 24-hour news of the US bombing of the Iraqi capital during the 1991 Gulf War, making it the world's first 'real time' war (Bennett, 2003; Boyd-Barrett and Rantanen, 1998; Volkmer, 1999). There is little doubt that CNN, which now calls itself 'the world's news leader,' established the concept of a global round-the-clock TV news network, one which 'certainly changed the international news system – especially during times of international crisis and conflict' (Hachten, 1999: 151).

CNN claims to be the only network capable of covering international news instantly: with a network of 150 correspondents in 42 international bureaux and 23 satellites, it is able to beam its programmes across continents, reaching a billion people. In 2003, CNN was available in over 150 million homes in more than 212 countries and territories worldwide (CNN website). Though in peacetime all-news channels such as CNN have a small number of regular viewers, journalists and news organizations worldwide constantly monitor them for any breaking news stories. With increasing localization of content and availability of programming in other languages – including Spanish, German, Portuguese and Turkish – CNN has been able to expand its reach beyond English-fluent viewers.

The 24/7 news concept has been adopted by other news networks around the world – most notably by the BBC, whose BBC World, the 24-hour global news and information channel, was available, in 2003, in more than 241 million homes in 200 countries and territories worldwide. In operation as an international news network since 1995, BBC World claims to provide 'impartial and objective journalism of the highest standard,' drawing on the extensive news resources of the BBC – 58 international news bureaux and 250 correspondents worldwide. In the US, Fox News, part of Australian-born US citizen Rupert Murdoch's media empire, has a growing audience base. In Britain, apart from Murdoch's Sky News, available to subscribers across Europe on a digital platform, BBC's News 24 and Independent Television News (ITV News) are other major players. Other examples of 24/7 news networks include, in Asia, Star News (in English and Hindi), Zee News (in Hindi), news channels of state broadcasters in both India and China – *Doordarshan* and China Central Television (CCTV). In Latin America, the major news operation is Brazil's Globo News, part of TV Globo conglomerate. In the Arab world, the most significant new actor to emerge is the Qatar-based Al-Jazeera. South Africa's SABC Africa is the only 24-hour news channel dedicated to bringing 'Africans in touch with Africa.'

The global influence of these channels may vary greatly – some aim mainly at diasporic audiences, others are international in their coverage. Their proliferation may give a sense of a greater degree of democratization of global news flow, but the reality is that the dominant players in global information and entertainment industries are still Western. The globalization of media industries has strengthened the hold of Western, and within it US–UK conglomerates, on global media flows, despite small but significant trends towards a contra-flow in news and entertainment programming. The major players in most sectors of international media – news agencies, international newspapers and magazines, radio and television, music, book publishing, advertising and films – are mainly Western-based organizations (Boyd-Barrett, 1998; Thussu, 2000; Tunstall and Machin, 1999).

In the realm of television news, the globalization of a US-style, commercially driven news culture is affecting broadcasting in other parts of the world. Part of the reason for this is the structural dependence of the world's broadcasters on news footage supplied mainly by just two television news agencies – Reuters Television (part of Reuters news agency) and Associated Press Television News (APTN – the international television arm of Associated Press, 'the world's oldest and largest newsgathering organization'). With its 83 bureaux in 67 countries,

APTN is a crucial supplier of news footage to broadcasters across the globe. Reuters Television, with its 77 bureaux worldwide and a team of 2,500 journalists and photographers operating in more than 150 countries, is able to provide fast, reliable, high-quality video coverage in 'near real-time.' Reuters World News Service is used for coverage of international events by broadcasters worldwide. It also has regional feeds for Africa as well as a German and a Turkish news service.

The news footage that these agencies provide can be used in either ready-to-air format or re-edited or translated with a new voiceover to suit requirements of particular broadcasters. These agencies also supply entertainment news. APTN's *Roving Report* – the world's longest running international current affairs programme – comprises a mixture of stories including what might be termed infotainment reports and APTN Entertainment's daily news service provides entertainment news and features, including film, music and fashion, three times a day with a half-hour weekly review of show business. Reuters runs a Reuters Showbiz News Service. The entertainment stories are popular among broadcasters across the world as they act as useful fillers for 24/7 news networks. Apart from these, CNN and BBC World (the two key 24/7 news networks watched in newsrooms and diplomatic enclaves across the globe) have profoundly influenced global television journalism. This 'US/UK news duopoly,' can thus 'bestride the news agendas and news flows of the world' (Tunstall and Machin, 1999: 88).

The pressures of live reporting

Going 'live' to the sites of unfolding news is one of the defining characteristics of 24/7 news networks. According to a recent survey, a majority of audiences in the US 'prefer live reports from global trouble spots to other types of international news stories, including background reports and interviews with world leaders' (Pew Center, 2002). The pressure to be first with the news can create a tendency among news channels to sacrifice depth in favour of the widest and quickest reach of live news to an increasingly heterogeneous audience. There is a danger that such a news culture may be detrimental to the quality of news, as one commentator notes: 'By making the live and the exclusive into primary news values, accuracy and understanding will be lost' (MacGregor, 1997: 200).

Television journalists work under the tremendous pressure of 'deadlines every minute,' leaving them little time to investigate a story, research and reflect on it before it is transmitted. Their editors want to make the story as timely and dramatic as possible. In wartime reporting, when a great deal of disinformation/misinformation is in circulation, the journalist's task of sifting truth from half-truths, rumours or even downright lies, becomes much more complicated.

Even during the 1991 Gulf War, with all the problems – techno-logical and political – associated with 'live' reporting, CNN's Peter Arnett, one of the few Western journalists in Baghdad at the time of war, believed that because of its instantaneous coverage, CNN had become the world's 'most influential news organization' (Arnett, 1994: 359). Yet, this 'live' reporting was rarely live, as two seasoned observers of US television news later wrote:

> Television showed troops in preparation, convoys moving, artillery pieces firing on unseen targets, and fighter planes streaking down runways and dropping 'smart' bombs on factories and buildings. Much of this action, however, had occurred hours earlier. Apart from the opening scenes in Baghdad and the later flashes of Scuds and Patriots missiles rising in attack, little live action appeared on television during the hundred hours of the ground war.
>
> (Donovan and Scherer, 1992: 313)

Given the demands of a 24-hour news cycle, reporters may find it difficult to obtain sufficient material to fill the airtime. In the absence of any new information on an unfolding event and tight control in the name of security, journalists may sometimes use unattributed sources, indulge in idle speculation or produce slanted reports influenced by rumour. During the events of 9/11, television networks sometimes had to resort to speculation and supposition rather than accurate reporting. In such situations, reporters tend to use almost any new information, even remotely connected to the story, in order to be first with the news to beat rival networks. Often the elite media – such as CNN – may set the agenda while other networks more or less follow it. Such 'gang-reporting' is partly responsible for the generally similar editorial stance that television networks take on major international crisis situations.

One result of the proliferation of 24/7 news channels is a growing competition for audiences and, crucially, advertising revenue, at a time when interest in news is generally declining. In the US, according to a recent Pew Center survey, audiences for network television peak-time news bulletins have declined substantially, from 90 per cent of the television audience in the 1960s to 30 per cent in 2000, partly as a result of many, especially younger, viewers opting for on-line news sources (Pew Center, 2002). In Britain, the audience for current affairs pro-gramming fell by nearly 32 per cent between 1994–2001 – from 64.3 hours per year in 1994 to nearly 44 hours in 2001. 'Today,' laments a new report, 'only a small minority (16 per cent) regard themselves as regular current affairs viewers. Current affairs seems to have lost its place as regular, appointment to view television' (Hargreaves and Thomas, 2002: 6).

24/7 news or round-the-clock infotainment?

In a competitive media market, news-gathering, particularly foreign news, is an expensive operation requiring high levels of investment and, consequently, television executives are under constant pressure to deliver demographically desirable audiences for news and current affairs programming to contribute to profits or at least avoid losses. In the US, one major recent development has been the acquiring of key news networks by conglomerates whose primary interest is in the entertainment business: Viacom-Paramount owns CBS; ABC is part of the Disney empire; CNN is a key component of AOL-Time-Warner (the world's biggest media and entertainment conglomerate), and Fox Network is owned by News Corporation. This shift in ownership is reflected in the type of stories that often get prominence on television news – stories about celebrities from the world of entertainment, for example, thus strengthening corporate synergies (Bennett, 2003: chapter 3). Among the characteristics of this new form of television news are dramatic music, special effects, computer graphics, re-enactments, often presented by a glamorous anchor. The proliferation of all-news channels has also impacted upon European news networks, where there is a tendency to move away from a public-service news agenda – privileging information and education over the entertainment value of news – to a more market-led, 'tabloid' version of news, with its emphasis on consumer journalism, sports and entertainment. The harbinger of this type of news was the private network, Sky News, which 'offers a more dynamic package, complete with computer graphics, a one-person presenter (sometimes standing, sometime sitting), and interactive screen, complete with the occasional online vote' (Hargreaves and Thomas, 2002: 95).

In a consumer-oriented broadcasting environment, operating in a fiercely competitive and increasingly fragmented news market, contemporary television journalism is tending toward 'infotainment' – news where presentation becomes as important as the content of a report. Emerging during the late 1980s, the term 'infotainment' has become a buzzword – a neologism that refers to an explicit genre-mixture of 'information' and 'entertainment' in news and current affairs programming. For television news executives, infotainment appears to be the means to attract a younger generation of viewers, who have been influenced by a post-modern visual aesthetics – including fast-paced, eye-catching visuals, computer-animated logos and rhetorical headlines. Such 'McNuggets of news' seem to resonate with a generation growing up on computer games and MTV-style information (Kurtz, 1993). The increasing popularity of on-line news, with its multi-media and interactive approach, is also affecting the presentation of television news.

The growth of the new hybrid genre of 'reality TV' which blurs the boundaries between fact and fiction, using documentary narrative and soap-opera style characters, owes its success to 'tabloid sensationalism and similarly reflects the need to entertain and retain large audiences' (Roscoe and Hight, 2001: 39). Though these new genres of television, which combine, often skilfully, the factual approach of documentary with the entertainment values of television drama (Paget, 1998), may be making more audiences interested in television news, this seems to be happening at the expense of serious factual programming, which they often replace, with the danger of further eroding the level of public understanding of global affairs, prompting critics to declare that 'the international documentary is virtually dead' (3WE, 2002).

Evidence of such trends was also found in a major study conducted in 1997 by the Project for Excellence in Journalism, which examined the US mass media over a span of 20 years. The study noted: 'There has been a shift toward lifestyle, celebrity, entertainment and celebrity crime/ scandal in the news and away from government and foreign affairs'. Looking specifically at television networks, it reported: 'The greatest new shift in emphasis of network news was a marked rise in the number of stories about scandals, up from just one-half of one per cent in 1977 to 15 per cent in 1997. The next biggest shift in emphasis in network news is a rise in human interest and quality of life stories. On network TV, human interest and quality of life stories doubled from 8 per cent of the stories that appeared in 1977 to 16 per cent in 1997' (Project for Excellence in Journalism, 1998).

Some have cautioned against the 'infotainment scare' (Brants, 1998). Lifestyle programmes, reality TV, consumer-oriented news reports, docudrama and docusoaps may represent a greater diversity than traditional hard news, thus having a libratory potential and a more democratic character (Sparks and Tulloch (eds), 2000; Delli Carpini and Williams, 2001). However, the perceived dilution of news and information as a result of market-driven television journalism can have serious repercussions on the quality of public debate (Baker, 2002; Gitlin, 2002; Glasser (ed.), 1999). Given the growing power of media transnationals, there is a risk that the role of the media in contributing to an informed citizenry, essential for genuine democratic discourse, may be undermined (Bennett, 2003; Gitlin, 2002). If television news is trivialized and reduced to easily digestible sight-bites, it is likely to contribute to a structural erosion of the public sphere in a Habermasian sense, where the viewer, bombarded with visuals, may not be able to differentiate between public information and propaganda from a powerful military-industrial-entertainment complex.

War as infotainment

Apart from occasional positive news stories, good news simply does not make for compelling television, which thrives on violence, death and destruction – be that from natural causes (earthquake, floods, hurricanes) or human causes (wars, riots, murders). Television news requires visual impact and a dramatic story, and on this measure, wars and natural disasters score more highly than peacetime events. Wars and civil conflicts are, therefore, good news for 24/7 networks: audiences turn to news channels when there is a natural or man-made crisis. In fact it has been argued that the rolling news networks have to be conflict-driven or else they will cease to operate as successful businesses (Hachten, 1999).

Given the characteristics of television news – arresting visuals, dramatic pictures – wars and civil conflicts are particularly susceptible to infotainment. Writing in the wake of the 1982 Israeli invasion of Lebanon, one US commentator wondered how far television can record real tragedy or suffering. 'The uniformity of TV's view includes not just war's victims, but wars themselves. As the medium subverts all overpowering commitment, all keen belief and pain, so it equates jihad, class struggle, imperialist assault, blood feud, and border strife, never capturing whatever is peculiar to specific conflicts, and thereby reducing all wars to a vague abstraction known as War' (Miller, 1989 [1982]: 159). As the late French sociologist Pierre Bourdieu has noted, TV news sees the world 'as a series of apparently absurd stories that all end up looking the same, endless parades of poverty-stricken countries, sequences of events that, having appeared with no explanation, will disappear with no solution – Zaire today, Bosnia yesterday, the Congo tomorrow' (Bourdieu, 1998 [1996]: 7).

There are certain key features of the presentation of war on television that have emerged over the last decade of war reporting, which demonstrate the tendency to using entertainment formats: video/computer-game style images of surgical strikes by 'intelligent' weaponry; arresting graphics and satellite pictures, and 'chat-show' use of 'experts'. As a result of this homogenization of coverage of conflicts – bloodless and largely devoid of any real sense of death and destruction – the audience can be desensitized to the tragedy and horror of war.

TV news' obsession with high-tech war reporting has grown since the 1991 US attack against Iraq. CNN's coverage of the Gulf War, for the first time in history, brought military conflict into living rooms across the globe. In the hi-tech, virtual presentation of war, cockpit videos of 'precision bombings' of Iraqi targets were supplied to television networks by the Pentagon, thus presenting a major conflict, responsible for huge destruction of life and property 'as a painless Nintendo exercise, and the image of Americans as virtuous, clean warriors' (Said, 1993: 365). In this and subsequent US actions – in Somalia, Haiti, Bosnia, Kosovo and Afghanistan – the humanitarian dimension of the military intervention was constantly promoted by the US media, often in high moral tones. The responsible behaviour of Western forces in combat operations was underlined and the superiority of weaponry emphasized. When cockpit videos were first shown as part of news reports during the

Gulf War, the broadcasters always mentioned that they were procured through the US Defense Department. In those ten years, the process has been routinized to such an extent that this acknowledgement is not considered necessary anymore.

This kind of reporting was typical during the 2001 bombing of Afghanistan. Jamie McIntyre, CNN's military affairs correspondent, enthused about types of munitions and aircraft being used in the bombing (CNN World News, 7 October 2001). In what appeared like a post-modern version of tele-shopping, a price tag ($2.1 billion) appeared on the screen with each aircraft. McIntyre described the bombers, B1 and B52s as 'extremely accurate' and how they were successfully used in Iraq and Kosovo for carpet-bombing. An extraordinarily ironical aspect of the coverage was that he also reported, with similar enthusiasm, the humanitarian relief being dropped by C-17s. This was a new development – delivering bombs and food at the same time. It is interesting to speculate whether the reporting of the raids would have been any different had the Pentagon had its own 24/7 news network.

In addition to video clips providing visuals, news programmes are providing more and more complicated maps, graphics and studio models to illustrate the progress of war. Mimicking war-gaming, miniature tanks and aircraft re-create battlefields in the studio, where, more often than not, male correspondents and experts enthusiastically discuss tactics and strategies, reinforcing the feminist critique of war as 'toys for the boys'.

Another important source of visuals for reporting conflicts is satellite imagery. This is often used to illustrate the successes of aerial bombings, the pictures of sites of enemy defence installations, military barracks, etc. No one seems to question how these pictures are acquired (usually from military spy satellites) and the audience has to rely on 'expert' interpretations to 'see' what the often fuzzy and indeterminate images represent. Space has become the 'final frontier' in modern warfare, with the world's largest satellite fleet, Intelsat, effectively in the control of Lockheed Martin, one of the biggest defence companies in the world (Thussu, 2002). The Department of Defense considers space, information and intelligence major areas for further investment. Its annual report is unambiguous: 'A key objective of the Department's space surveillance and control mission is to ensure freedom of action in space for the United States and its allies and, when directed, deny such freedom of action to adversaries' (US Government, 2002). During the Afghanistan conflict, the US government purchased all the satellite imagery of the area from commercial providers – themselves mostly US-based corporations, not only for its own use but to prevent its use by others. It is worth reflecting on how Western governments and the media would react if the so-called 'rogue' nations had the capacity for space surveillance and then to broadcast on their television networks sensitive defence-related imagery taken from spy satellites over the US or Europe?

One outcome of such type of coverage is that the audience is not exposed to the real and ugly face of war. It is instructive to contrast the 24/7 news network's coverage of the efficiency of high-tech weapons with the death toll that these weapons caused (Herman, 2002). During the bombing raids on Afghanistan some of the worst wartime atrocities were inflicted upon the Afghans. More than 300 Afghans were massacred in *Qila-e-Jungi* in November 2001 in a CIA-managed operation, as revealed in later reports (Channel 4 TV, 2002). Up to 5,000 Afghan civilians were killed in bombing raids during 'Operation Enduring Freedom'; another 20,000 died as a result of indirect effects of the bombing (Steele, 2003: 23). The bloodless coverage, however, seemed to conform to the 'Pentagon's determination to control the flow of news from the front,' as Neil Hickey, the editor of the *Columbia Journalism Review*, noted. 'Images and descriptions of civilian bomb casualties – people already the victims of famine, poverty, drought, oppression, and brutality – would erode public support in the US and elsewhere in the world' (Hickey, 2002).

Apart from repetition by way of recaps and summaries, 24/7 news networks have to fill their schedules with 'talk' and 'speculation' (discussion, analysis, phone-ins etc.), which have much in common with the genre of the 'chat show'. Only certain categories of experts make it to 24/7 news screens. As Bourdieu wryly noted:

> . . . if television rewards a certain number of fast-thinkers who offer cultural 'fast food' – pre-digested and pre-thought culture – it is not only because those who speak regularly on television are virtually on call (that, too, is tied to the sense of urgency in television news production). The list of commentators varies little (for Russia, call Mr. or Mrs. X, for Germany it's Mr. Y). These 'authorities' spare journalists the trouble of looking for people who really have something to say . . .
>
> (Bourdieu, 1998: 29–30)

During the bombing of Afghanistan, most of the expert commentary came from hawkish voices – former or serving military men – or 'independent' experts, directly or indirectly connected with the military-industrial-informational complex. This was in ample evidence in the coverage on Fox News, for example, which tended to prefer live chat and an informal style of reporting. In addition, the presenters did not seem to worry too much if the boundaries between straight news and opinion were being crossed. An aggressive jingoism, often racist in its vocabulary, seemed to characterize Fox News' coverage from Afghanistan, as noted by two media observers: 'Just as the Gulf War marked an important milestone in the evolution of CNN, the war in Afghanistan appears to be a defining event for Fox News Channel. Fox may reshape the way wars are covered with its aggressive cheerleading for the US armed forces and their allies, and its hostile, even insulting portrayal of their opponents – who have been described by Fox personnel as "rats", "terror goons" and "psycho Arabs"' (Hart and Naureckas, 2002).

As an example, Hart and Naureckas recount how Geraldo Rivera, Fox News' main war correspondent, covered the events on 29 November 2001. Rivera: 'We've been in various conflicts, and we keep our chin up and keep focused on the fact that we want Osama bin Laden to end up either behind bars or six feet under or maybe just one foot under or maybe just as a pile of ash, you know. That's it.' To which Fox anchor Laurie Dhue replied: 'All right. Well said, Geraldo' (Hart and Naureckas, 2002).

The Fox approach of blurring the boundaries between news and editorial comment seems to have hit a chord with broadcasters elsewhere. Chris Shaw, Head of News and Current Affairs on Britain's Channel 5, is not worried by the lack of impartiality. Fox News, he says, 'is striking because it feels passionate. I'd be interested to see for regulatory reasons whether we could get away with that because they do take sides. Their anchors engage – they call it like they think it. For us, this would be unchartered territory, but if Channel 5 can't do it, I don't know who will' (quoted in Hargreaves and Thomas, 2002: 98).

Implications of war as infotainment

There are major implications of infotainment for public-opinion formation and its manipulation, not just within the West but indeed globally, given the extent to which US/UK news organizations can influence news agendas worldwide. US styles of presentation are becoming increasingly global, as news channels attempt to reach more viewers and keep their target audiences from switching channels. Such is the power of US-inspired television that even non-Western networks tend to follow the news agendas set by the West. This is particularly the case during times of conflict. Many regularly and routinely showed the cockpit videos of 'successful' precision bombings, procured through the Pentagon and broadcast satellite pictures of combat areas acquired through US spy satellites. They seemed to reproduce the war language and the imagery of the Pentagon: the coverage of the 'war on terrorism' in Afghanistan by Star News – India's best known 24-hour news channel – is a case in point. Given that Star News is part of Rupert Murdoch's global media empire, it used live coverage of the war from its sister 24/7 network Fox News, relaying, sometimes in their entirety, Pentagon briefings, as well as jingoistic studio discussions and US government press conferences.

Star News showed, on a daily basis, computer-generated maps and graphics, with a commentary from one of its top anchors, about the progress of the war, repeating, often verbatim, the US line. The channel also carried reports from its correspondent from the frontline, though he had limited access to the US sources. The tone and tenor of most of the reports broadcast during the conflict were much influenced by US networks. The footage of bombing raids and types of military aircraft provided by the US military, through news agencies or directly, was reproduced uncritically, as were the spy satellite pictures.

Since US-dominated television imagery is for consumption not only by US citizens but also by a global audience, this capacity to mould public opinion has a crucial international dimension. This dissemination helps to promote the US foreign policy agenda to a global audience through 24/7 networks: when US President George W. Bush addressed American citizens at the start of the US bombing of Afghanistan in October 2001, he was actually addressing the world, his message being broadcast live by CNN, BBC World, Star News, Fox News, Sky News, and Al-Jazeera, among others.

The ability for instantaneous media coverage of events across the globe has brought to the fore the role that the media, and especially television, play in the conduct of foreign policy. Variously described as 'the CNN effect,' or 'the CNN curve' – it is claimed that 24/7 news networks set the agenda at a time of an international crisis, though it has been argued that the visual media may be harnessed by powerful governments to advance their own political interests (Robinson, 2002). Governments seek cooperation, if not outright support, from the media to legitimize military action. Their increasingly sophisticated propaganda machinery ensures that the media generally support the government course of action during military operations and disseminate the official version of events.

Aware of the power of image diplomacy in the era of 24/7 news, the US government has successfully promoted a televised version of its foreign policy to international publics (Robinson, 2002; Seib, 1997). It can be argued that the world's view of US military interventions has, to a large extent, been influenced by the US-supplied images: 'Operation Just Cause' in 1989 in Panama; 'Operation Provide Comfort' in Northern Iraq, following the Gulf War in 1991; 'Operation Restore Hope' in Somalia in 1992; 'Operation Uphold Democracy' in Haiti in 1994; 'Operation Allied Force', NATO's bombing of Yugoslavia in 1999; and the 2001 'Operation Enduring Freedom,' the war on terrorism in Afghanistan. In these interventions, under the cloak of humanitarianism, Western governments, led by the US, have advanced their geo-strategic interests, whether it is in Kosovo (by changing the nature of NATO from a relic of the Cold War to a peace-enforcer whose remit now extends way beyond its traditional North Atlantic territory), or in Afghanistan (which has given the US government entry into the energy-rich Central Asian regions) (Chomsky, 1999; Rashid, 2001).

However, the dominant news discourse, especially on 24/7 television networks, does not seem to be interested in the analysis of geo-political issues and instead tends to provide justification of military interventions as necessary to protect human rights and promote democracy world-wide. In this version of post-Cold War military interventions, wars are just and have a high moral purpose. This kind of treatment helps create a 'feel-good factor' among Western publics – the West is literally being shown to do something to bring peace and prosperity to the world's hotspots.

Obsessed as 24/7 news appears to be with ratings and the resultant emphasis on infotainment, it seems to have failed to provide the economic or political context to help explain why there are conflicts in the world. What compounds this process is that, although most of the conflicts emanate from the developing world, the coverage on television of the global South has drastically changed in the past decade. Even in Britain, with its public service ethos of television, there has been a perceptible shift in the way television covers the developing world (DFID, 2002).

A report from the Third World and Environment Broadcasting Project, a consortium of UK-based non-governmental organizations, says that factual programmes in 'harder' categories such as 'history', 'politics', 'development, environment and human rights', and 'conflict and disaster' have fallen to their lowest levels since 1989, while 'softer', more accessible and entertainment-led formats now dominate. For example, 75 of ITV's 83 factual programmes on developing countries were in this infotainment category. These include travel and docu-soaps – which 'focus either on the experiences of British people abroad, or are presenter-or celebrity-led.' According to the report: 'Reality TV – putting British people into constructed environments located in developing countries, gets more television hours than the realities of life for the majority of the world's people' (3WE, 2002).

The situation is worse in the US, with a much longer history of commercial television, where 24/7 news has further reduced its already small window on the world (Pew Center, 2002; Utley, 1997). A recent survey showed 'powerful evidence that broad interest in international news is most inhibited by the public's lack of background information in this area. Overall, roughly two-thirds (65 per cent) of respondents said they sometimes lose interest in these stories because they lack the background information to keep up' (Pew Center, 2002).

Senior journalists are increasingly becoming alert to the deterioration of news reporting. In their book *The News About the News* Leonard Downie and Robert Kaiser (executive and associate editor, respectively, of *The Washington Post*) discuss the effects of the blurring of news and entertainment, drawing on interviews with such VIPs of US broadcast journalism – Dan Rather, Peter Jennings and Tom Brokaw. The demand for profits has, they argue, led to more sensational news coverage in order to boost ratings and a focus on entertainment and celebrities, reducing the amount of space or time given to international news (Downie and Kaiser, 2002).

As a result of such trends, television news rarely seems to cover the root causes of conflict in countries on the receiving end of neoliberal 'reforms' which have yet to deliver for a majority of the world's population (UNDP, 2002). The growing economic inequality in the world and its fallout is often dismissed in television reports as part of 'ethnic' conflicts. However, 'Third World threats', especially emanating from radicalized Islamic groups, have acquired deadly urgency in the wake of attacks on New York and Washington in September 2001 and its aftermath – the open-ended and global 'war on terrorism'.

Almost impervious to such dangers, increasingly vocal commentators speak with worrying regularity and confidence of the American empire (Ikenberry, 2002) or of 'the beginning of an American imperium' (Elliot, 2002: 85). As such formulations receive greater respectability both within academic and media discourses, it is likely that future conflicts will be progressively framed by television news within the context of an imperial discourse, being beamed around the world 24 hours a day, 7 days a week, with its virtual wars, live TV and bloodless deaths.

References

3WE (2002) *Losing Reality: Factual International Programming on UK Television, 2000–01*, Third World and Environment Broadcasting Project, London. Available at http://www.epolitix.com/forum/3WE.htm

Arnett, Peter (1994) *Live from the Battlefield*. London: Bloomsbury.

Baker, C. Edwin (2002) *Media, Markets, and Democracy*. Cambridge: Cambridge University Press.

Bennett, W. Lance (2003) *News: The Politics of Illusion*. 5th edn. New York: Addison Wesley Longman.

Bourdieu, Pierre (1998) *On Television and Journalism*. London: Pluto Press. Translated from the French by Priscilla Parkhurst Ferguson. Originally published in 1996 by *Liber – Raison de'agir*.

Boyd-Barrett, Oliver (1998) 'Media Imperialism Reformulated', in Daya K. Thussu (ed.) *Electronic Empires – Global Media and Local Resistance*. London: Arnold: 157–176.

Boyd-Barrett, Oliver and Rantanen, Terhi (eds) (1998) *The Globalization of News*. London: Sage.

Brants, Kees (1998) 'Who's Afraid of Infotainment?' *European Journal of Communication*. 13 (3): 315–335.

Channel 4 Television (2002) 'The House of War', *True Stories*. London: Channel 4 Television, 4 July.

Chomsky, Noam (1999) *The New Military Humanism: Lessons From Kosovo*. Monroe, ME: Common Courage Press.

CNN website (2003) http://www.cnn.com.

Delli Carpini, Michael and Williams, Bruce (2001) 'Let us Infotain You: Politics in the New Media Environment', in W. Lance Bennett and Robert M. Entman (eds) *Mediated Politics: Communication in the Future of Democracy*. Cambridge: Cambridge University Press: 160–181.

DFID (2002) *Making Sense of the World*. London: Department for International Development, October. Available at http://www.dfid.gov.uk/Pubs/files/makingsense.pdf

Donovan, Robert and Scherer, Ray (1992) *Unsilent Revolution – Television News and American Public Life, 1948–1991*. Woodrow Wilson International Center for Scholars and Cambridge University Press.

Downie, Leonard Jr. and Kaiser, Robert G. (2002) *The News About the News: American Journalism in Peril*. New York: Knopf.

Elliot, Michael (2002) 'The Trouble With Saving the World', *Time*, 30 December: 82–85.

Gitlin, Todd (2002) *Media Unlimited: How the Torrents of Images and Sounds Overwhelms Our Lives*. New York: Metropolitan Books.

Glasser, Theodore (ed.) (1999) *The Idea of Public Journalism*. New York: Guildford Press.

Hachten, William (1999) *The World News Prism – Changing Media of International Communication*. 5th edn. Ames: Iowa State University Press.

Hargreaves, Ian and Thomas, James (2002) *New News, Old News*. London: Independent Television Commission and Broadcasting Standards Commission.

Hart, Peter and Naureckas, Jim (2002) 'Fox at the Front – Will Geraldo Set the Tone for Future War Coverage?' *Extra!* January/February.

Herman, Edward (2002) 'Body Counts in Imperial Service: Yugoslavia, Afghanistan, and Elsewhere', *Z Magazine*. February. Available at http://www.zmag.org/

Hickey, Neil (2002) 'Access Denied – The Pentagon's War Reporting Rules are the Toughest Ever', *Columbia Journalism Review*. January/February. Available at http://www.cjr.org/year/02/1/index.asp

Ikenberry, John (2002) 'America's Imperial Ambition', *Foreign Affairs*. 81 (5).

Iyengar, Shanto and Kinder, Donald (1987) *News That Matters: Television and American Opinion*. Chicago: University of Chicago Press.

Kurtz, Howard (1993) *Media Circus: The Trouble with America's Newspapers*. New York: Random House.

MacGregor, Brent (1997) *Live, Direct and Biased? Making Television News in the Satellite Age*. London: Arnold.

Miller, Mark Crispin (1989) 'How TV Covers War', in his *Boxed In: The Culture of TV*. Evanston: Northwestern University Press, 151–172. Originally published in *The New Republic*, 29 November 1982.

Paget, Derek (1998) *No Other Way To Tell It – Dramadoc/docudrama on Television*. Manchester: Manchester University Press.

Pew Center (2002) 'Public's News Habits Little Changed by September 11 – Americans Lack Background to Follow International News,' June, Pew Research Center for the People and the Press. Available at http://people-press.org/reports

Project for Excellence in Journalism (1998) *Changing Definitions of News*, March 6. Available at http://www.journalism.org/resources/research/reports/

Rashid, Ahmad (2001) *Taliban: Islam, Oil and the New Great Game in Central Asia*. London: Yale University Press.

Robinson, Piers (2002) *The CNN Effect – The Myth of News, Foreign Policy and Intervention*. London: Routledge.

Roscoe, Jane and Hight, Craig (2001) *Faking It – Mock-documentary and the Subversion of Factuality*. Manchester: Manchester University Press.

Said, Edward (1993) *Culture and Imperialism*. London: Chatto and Windus.

Seib, Philip (1997) *Headline Diplomacy – How News Coverage Affects Foreign Policy*. Westport: Praeger.

Sparks, Colin and Tulloch, John (eds) (2000) *Tabloid Tales – Global Debates Over Media Standards*. Oxford: Rowman and Littlefield.

Steele, Jonathan (2003) 'Counting the Dead,' *The Guardian*, January 29, p. 23.

Thussu, Daya Kishan (2000) *International Communication – Continuity and Change*. London: Arnold.

Thussu, Daya Kishan (2002) 'Privatizing Intelsat: Implications for the Global South', in Marc Raboy (ed.) *Global Media Policy in the New Millennium*. Luton: University of Luton Press.

Tunstall, Jeremy and Machin, David (1999) *The Anglo-American Media Connection*. Oxford: Oxford University Press.

UNDP (2002) *Human Development Report 2002 – Deepening Democracy in a Fragmented World*. United Nations Development Programme. Oxford: Oxford University Press.

US Government (2002) Annual Report to the President and the Congress by Donald H. Rumsfeld, Secretary of Defence. Available at http://www.defenselink.mil/execsec/adr2002/index.htm

Utley, Garrick (1997) 'The Shrinking of Foreign News: From Broadcast to Narrowcast', *Foreign Affairs*. 76 (2): 2–10.

Volkmer, Ingrid (1999) *News in the Global Sphere – A Study of CNN and its Impact on Global Communications*. Luton: University of Luton Press.

THE ISRAELI-PALESTINIAN CONFLICT: TV NEWS AND PUBLIC UNDERSTANDING

Greg Philo, Alison Gilmour, Maureen Gilmour, Susanna Rust,
Etta Gaskell and Lucy West (Glasgow University Media Group)

If you do not understand the Middle East crisis it might be because you are watching it on TV news. This scores high on images of fighting, violence and drama but is low on explanation. A new study by the Glasgow University Media Group, financed by the Economic and Social Research Council, shows how this may influence public understanding. The Group initially interviewed 12 small audience groups (a total of 85 people) with a cross-section of ages and backgrounds. They were asked a series of questions about the conflict and what they had understood from TV news. The same questions were then put to 300 young people (aged between 17 and 22) who filled in a questionnaire. We asked these people what came to their mind when they heard the words 'Israeli/Palestinian conflict' and then what was the source of their answer. A small number of people had direct experience (two individuals) and listed accounts from relatives as what had come to their minds. But most (82 per cent) listed TV news as their source and to a lesser extent newspapers were also named. These replies showed that they had absorbed the 'main' message of the news, of conflict, violence and tragedy. We can see this in the following typical answers:

- Conflict, hatred, religion
- Palestinian kids being shot by tanks and artillery
- War, murder, religious hatred
- Shootings, war, suicide bombers, poverty
- War, suicide bombers, Jewish people
- War, repression, suffering
- Guns, fighting, explosions, bloodshed.

To pursue these issues further, we also interviewed journalists from the BBC, ITN, the press and other news agencies, who had actually reported on the conflict. We then established a further series of audience groups to which we invited these journalists. This made it possible for journalists, academics and members of the viewing public to discuss in detail the issues of representation and audience comprehension and belief which were being raised in the study.

The research showed that many people had little understanding of the reasons for the conflict and its origins. It was apparent that this lack of understanding (and indeed misunderstanding) was compounded by the news reports which they had watched. A key reason for this was that explanations were rarely given on the news and, when they were, journalists often spoke obliquely, almost in a form of shorthand. For the audience to understand the significance of what they were saying would require a level of understanding and background knowledge, that was simply not present in most people. For example, in a news bulletin, which featured the progress of peace talks, a journalist made a series of very brief comments on the issues that underpinned the conflict:

Journalist:
The basic raw disagreements remain – *the future, for example, of this city Jerusalem, the future of Jewish settlements and the returning refugees.* For all that, together with the anger and bitterness felt out in the West Bank, then I think it's clear this crisis is not about to abate.
(ITN 18.30, 16 October 2001, our italics)

There are several elements in this statement that require some background knowledge in order to be understood. 'Refugees' for example, are cited as a key issue. The journalist does not say which refugees but he means those who are Palestinians. The main audience sample of 300 young people were asked where the Palestinian refugees had come from and how they had become refugees: 80 per cent replied that they did not know. To understand the journalist's comments, the audience would need to have had the information that the refugees were displaced from their homes and land when Israel was established in 1948.

The Israeli historian Avi Shlaim has described how this came about. He shows in his very detailed history, *The Iron Wall*, how the military forces of what became Israel embarked on an offensive strategy which involved destroying Arab villages and the forced removal of civilians:

Palestinian society disintegrated under the impact of the Jewish military offensive that got underway in April [1948], and the exodus of the Palestinians was set in motion . . . by ordering the capture of Arab cities and the destruction of villages, it both permitted and justified the forcible expulsion of Arab civilians.
(Shlaim, 2000: 30)

The intention, as Shlaim comments, was to clear the interior of the future Israeli state of what were seen as potentially hostile 'Arab elements'. Shortly after, in May 1948, a major war broke out between

Israel and its Arab neighbours, which occasioned more people to flee. Many of the refugees moved to Gaza (which came under the control of Egypt) and to the West Bank of the Jordan river (under Jordanian control). In 1967 Israel fought a further war with its Arab neighbours and, in the process of this, occupied Gaza and the West Bank, thus bringing the Palestinian refugees under its military control. East Jerusalem, which has great religious and cultural significance for both Israelis and Palestinians, was also occupied (taken from Jordan). These military occupations were bitterly resisted by the Palestinians, not least because Israel built 'settlements' all across the militarily occupied territories. This was much more than simply building houses and farms. As Shlaim suggests, they were part of a policy of exerting strategic and military control, by for example 'surrounding the huge greater Jerusalem area with two concentric circles of settlements with access roads and military positions' (Shlaim, 2000: 582).

The settlements were also built so that they could exploit the crucial resource of water in the occupied territories. A report in *The Guardian* (2 November 1998) showed that the pattern of settlement construction since the 1970s was along the ridges and edges of aquifers and that 'this strategic consideration was part of the Jewish pattern in populating the area'. This was a central issue for Palestinians, since a third of their economy was agricultural and could not be sustained without water. The report also noted that 26 per cent of Palestinian houses had no water and that each Israeli was consuming over three times as much water as a Palestinian. Without such background knowledge, it is not possible to understand the significance in the above news report of the journalist's comments on 'Jerusalem', 'the future of the Jewish settlements' and the 'returning refugees'. Yet brief and cryptic as the comments were, they were still exceptional in that they existed at all in the news.

The Group analyzed TV news coverage of the major *intifada* (or uprising) by the Palestinians, which began in September 2000. We focused on the lunchtime, early evening and late night news on BBC1 and ITN, since these attract very large audiences. The bulletins from 28 September until 16 October 2000 (a total of 95 bulletins) were transcribed and the number of lines of text which were devoted to different themes were counted (e.g. how many described fighting/ violence, or peace negotiations or explanations of the conflict etc). In over 3,000 lines of text in total, only 17 explained the history of the conflict. The key issue of water was barely mentioned. There was a very brief reference on BBC2 when a journalist listed major issues for peace negotiations and commented that 'last but not least [there would need to be] an agreement on water rights' (BBC2 *Newsnight*, 3 October 2000). In our audience groups many people expressed surprise, because they had not heard about it before (only 2 people of the 85 interviewed knew of the issue).

It was apparent that many people did not understand that the Palestinians were subject to a military occupation and did not know who was 'occupying' the occupied territories. On TV news, journalists sometimes used the word 'occupied' but did not explain that the Israelis were involved in a military occupation. For example, a BBC bulletin referred to 'the settlers who have made their homes in occupied territory' (BBC1 18.00, 9 February 2001). The reference to settlers is interesting because it speaks of 'occupied territories', without making it clear that it is the Israelis settlers who are the 'occupiers'. It is perhaps not surprising then that many in the audience did not understand the nature of the 'occupation'. In the sample of 300 young people, 79 per cent did not know that it was the Israelis who were occupying the territories. Only 9 per cent knew that it was the Israelis and that the settlers were Israeli. There were actually more people (10 per cent) who believed that the Palestinians were occupying the territories and that the settlers were Palestinian.

So why does the news not give better explanations of the history and context of events? One reason is that the news, along with the rest of television, exists in a very commercial and competitive market and is concerned about audience ratings. In news presentation this translates to the view that pictures and action should dominate – news is to be essentially eye-catching and attention-grabbing. In this philosophy of news it is better to have great pictures taken in the middle of a riot with journalists ducking stones than to explain what the conflict is about. There is a second, perhaps more crucial reason why the TV newsrooms do not dwell on the history and origins of the Israeli/Palestinian conflict: to explain these or to refer to them as underlying the violence could be very controversial. Israel is closely allied to the United States and there are very strong pro-Israel lobbies in the US and to some extent in Britain. For a journalist to delve too deeply into controversial areas is simply to invite trouble (what Herman and Chomsky call 'flak', see Herman and Chomsky, 1988). It is much safer to stick with 'action' footage and simply recount the day's events. Israel has very powerful voices to speak for it and it combines this with a well-organized public relations apparatus which supplies 'favourable' stories and statements to the media and criticises those of which it disapproves.

The *Independent* newspaper reported in September 2001 that the Israeli embassy 'has mounted a huge drive to influence the British media' and that 'a senior Israeli official (has) publicly boasted that Israel has influenced the editorial policy of the BBC' (21 September 2001). The BBC denied these claims, but it is clear that a lack of discussion of the controversial aspects of the occupation would operate in favour of Israel. For example, Israel prefers to stress the attacks and bombings made upon it and the vicious anti-Semitism of some Islamic groups, rather than to have the legality of its own actions subject to public debate. The settlement policy is widely regarded as illegal in international law and this has certainly been the view of the British government. Newspapers such as *The Guardian* have routinely referred to the settlements as 'illegal' but this was not done on television news. The United Nations Human Rights Commission has also been severely critical, but there is little of such matters on TV news.

The occupation: social consequences for Israelis and Palestinians

From the Israeli perspective a major concern is security, and its continued presence in the West Bank and Gaza has been justified on these grounds. From the Palestinian perspective a central issue is that they are living under Israeli military control. The effects of the occupation on the everyday life of the Palestinians is substantially absent from media coverage. Phrases such as 'military occupation' or 'military rule' are not normally used. Yet the conditions which the military presence have imposed on the Palestinians are a major factor in the unrest. Human rights organisations have been very critical of the conduct of Israeli forces in the occupied territories. In December 1998, the *Observer* reported a survey, which had been published by B'Tselem, the Israeli human rights group, to mark the 50th anniversary of the Universal Declaration of Human Rights and B'Tselem observed: 'apart perhaps, from the article prohibiting slavery, the State of Israeli violates each and every one of the Declaration's provisions in its behaviour towards the Palestinians in the territories' (*Observer*, 13 December 1998).

B'Tselem found that the killing of Palestinians by Israeli settlers was rarely punished. It also reported that of the 1,000–1,500 Palestinian prisoners interrogated by the Israeli Shin Bet security services each year, 85 per cent were tortured. The use of torture by Israeli forces was outlawed by the Israeli High Court in 1999, but after the start of the *intifada* in October 2000, there were reports that it was again being widely used (*The Guardian*, 13 June 2002).

This was in the period before the *intifada* and, at this time, Palestinian security forces were working extensively with Israel to arrest and detain dissidents and militants who were opposed to the agreements which had been reached between the Israelis and Arafat's administration. The *Observer* reported that the 13 different Palestinian security forces had modelled themselves on Shin Bet and that three-quarters of their detainees had been tortured (13 December 1998). At the same time there were reports that thousands of Palestinians remained in Israeli jails, some from the time of the previous *intifada* in 1987 (*The Guardian*, 7 November 1998).

To live under such rule has had profound effects on the everyday lives of many Palestinians. From their perspective, the Israelis had used the peace to extend their military and economic dominance. It became more difficult for Palestinians to travel as more settlements and roads between them were built for the use of Israelis. These involved the bulldozing of large areas of Palestinian land and the development of extensive systems of checkpoints and military security. One of the journalists we interviewed for this study had been the head of a news agency in Jerusalem in the period before the 2000 *intifada*. He commented to us:

> My Palestinian neighbours could not go to the beach which you could practically see. They carry identity cards which tell everything about them. If an American viewer ever saw the extent to which the apartheid system is applied in the occupied territories – the pass laws make the South African system look benign . . .

> The Israelis say that [most] of the Palestinians are now under Palestinian Authority control. What they don't say is that they often can't even leave the town they are in.

He also commented that members of his Arab staff had been arrested and tortured by the Israelis. He made this criticism of TV news coverage of the conflict:

> They cover the day-to-day action but not the human inequities, the essential imbalances of the occupation, the day-to-day humiliations of the Palestinians.
>
> (Interview, 10 June 2002)

This is borne out by our analysis of news content. The consequences to the Palestinians of living under military occupation were very rarely explored. There were occasional comments in the news that obliquely raised the issue. The BBC, for example, mentioned in a report that the Palestinians were 'tearing down security cameras' referring to these as 'hated symbols of Israeli authority' (BBC1 main news, 6 October 2000). Another report describes undercover police grabbing a demonstrator noting that 'these officers, who never want to be identified, pretend to be Palestinians during a riot but when they spot a suspect they treat him with little mercy' (BBC1 early evening news, 13 October 2000). There are also occasional references to the occupation and occupied territories as, for example, when a BBC journalist says of young Palestinians that 'they don't trust the Americans and after all they say it's the occupation to blame' (BBC1 lunchtime news, 2 October 2000). It was clear from our audience studies that many people would not understand what such a reference meant. Because the Israeli presence is not described as a military occupation and the significance of this is not explained, it was not clear what the word 'occupation' actually meant. Some understood it to mean simply that people were *on* the land.

There were two other occasions when news events were reported, which could have been used to explain the nature of the occupation. On 13 October 2000 on BBC and ITV the Israelis were reported as stopping young Muslims from entering the old city to pray. And on 9 and 10 October, ITV news discussed how the Israelis had surrounded Palestinian areas to 'choke the life out of the revolt.' Both of these examples illustrate that the movement of Palestinians is subject to the wishes of the Israelis, but there was no commentary on how movement can be routinely controlled, nor any discussion of this as a feature of the military occupation. The clearest statement on this issue came in a brief statement from a Palestinian who said that people are 'penned like chickens, they can't move freely' (BBC 1 main news, 10 October 2000), but this comment was not taken up or developed by journalists.

There are two problems with coverage that does not explain the 'military' nature of the occupation and the consequences of this for the Palestinians. The first is that it is difficult for viewers to understand why the conflict is so intractable. It can appear simply as two communities who 'can't get on' and who are squabbling over the same areas of land. The second is that such coverage disadvantages the Palestinian perspective, as a key reason for their unrest and anger is left unexplained. Some observers have commented on their own surprise when viewing the conflict at first-hand. They noted how this revealed the limits of their previous understanding and of the accounts which were prevalent in the media. A businessman for example, wrote as follows in *The Guardian*:

> I have had business interests in the Middle East for many years, I often travel to Israel and the West Bank and I'm in contact with journalists, aid workers and UN officials there. I can state categorically that all those whom I have met, who have come to work on the West Bank with an open mind, or even, like me, with some prejudice in favour of Israel, leave with disgust and rage at Israeli brutality, racism and hypocrisy. Some are Jewish. It is experience on the spot that leads them to this perception.

He also commented how even a newspaper such as *The Guardian* 'seems never to address adequately the justice of the Palestinian position, or the frightening racism that seems to me to be at the core of Israeli arguments and actions' (Letter, *The Guardian*, 29 March 2001). Another correspondent discusses the role of the Israeli settlements in this system of control and also notes the absence of such analysis in media coverage:

> A few days ago the BBC showed an aerial film of a settlement. I was surprised by how unfamiliar it was to see one. I realised that few if any pictures are normally shown of settlements – their sheer scale, their facilities and their monopoly of the water supply. Nor is there any detailed map of their distribution . . . nothing prepared me for the shock of the prevalence and scale of the settlements when I visited the occupied

territories. It is as though every other hill-top in Devon and Cornwall was taken over by a Milton Keynes-like town and occupied . . . looking down triumphantly over the indigenous locals corralled in the valleys below.

(Letter, *The Guardian*, 26 May 2001)

The issue which this raises is that the settlements have a key military and strategic function in the occupation. The point of being situated on the top of hills is that this offers a commanding position. At the time of the signing of the Wye Accords (supposedly a land for security agreement), Ariel Sharon who was then the Israeli Foreign Minister urged settlers in the West Bank to 'grab the hill-tops' (*The Guardian*, 8 January 1999). Yet when the BBC went to visit a settlement at the beginning of the *intifada*, the journalist stressed that it was 'intensely vulnerable, high on a hill'. There were no comments on how it functions in the occupation:

> One regular target for Palestinian gunmen is the Jewish settlement of Passagot. It's intensely vulnerable, high on a hill, surrounded on all sides by Palestinian territory. Even a children's nursery had a bullet fired through the window. The settlers know they are in mortal danger. A dozen babies have been evacuated just a few minutes earlier to the settlement's bomb shelter. Settlers say Palestinians are trying to force them out.

The settlers were then interviewed but there were no questions on what the conflict is actually about:

Settler:
Well they want us out of here. They're shooting at us hoping that we'll pick up and leave.

Journalist:
Do you have any intention of leaving?

Settler:
No, no.

Journalist:
Some people would say you're crazy staying here with so many bullets flying.

Settler:
No, not crazy, we have our ideas and our ideals and we'll stick up for them and it's important to us.

(BBC1 main news, 5 October 2000)

The journalist then commented without explanation that 'This place looks more like a fortress than a settlement' – which seems to miss the key point that this is indeed what many settlements are. It is of course the case that some settlements are more exposed than others, and some are very small, but as Avi Shlaim notes, their overall impact is to exert strategic and military control, as well as to command land and water resources. It is this analysis which is missing from news reports which focus on vulnerability and the 'threat' to settlers, or even which present the Palestinians and Israelis as simply two warring communities. The key issue that remains unexplained is the structural division of society – one group is effectively controlling the lives of the other (with some resistance). This point of view is not put to the settlers and they are not asked if they think it is right that Palestinians have lost their land so that the settlements can be built.

In the following example from ITV the initial emphasis was again on Israel 'defending' and 'protecting' the 'small Jewish enclaves', while the Arabs were referred to as 'continuing their onslaught'. The reporter noted that the Palestinians regard the settlements as a 'symbol of the Israeli occupation'. But without an explanation of what this occupation is and what it signifies for the Palestinians there was no clear rationale for their action other than that they were 'driven by hatred' or that it was simply a 'cycle of violence'. The report began with a studio introduction which contrasted the peace talks with the ongoing violence:

Newscaster:
And even while those talks were on, the violence between Palestinians and Israeli security forces continued for the seventh day in a row. Among six Palestinians reported killed today was a boy of nine.

Line Journalist:
The cycle of violence is unbroken, the trouble spots are the same each day. The Israeli army has again been defending the small Jewish enclaves on the West Bank and the Gaza Strip – pockets in the midst of Palestinian towns and villages . . . here 400 people are protected by around a thousand soldiers. Some Israelis believe such little Alamos should be defended at all costs. The Arabs of course feel very differently and today *driven on by hatred* continued their onslaught and there's not much sign of conciliation here. These Palestinians regard the Jewish settlement here in Hebron as an affront, a symbol of the Israeli occupation that has not been brought to an end by the political process.

(ITV main news, 4 October 2000, our italics)

There are some qualifications which should be made to this analysis. Some reports did refer briefly to the *intifada* as a 'popular uprising', which does imply resistance though what it was to, and why, was less clear. There was also coverage in this sample period of attacks by settlers on Palestinians and sympathetic accounts of the deaths of Palestinian children. To this extent the consequences of the conflict for Palestinians were reported, but what remained unexplored was the nature of the military occupation and the distorted relationships which it produced between the occupiers and the subject population.

Israeli perspectives on security needs, terrorism and incitement

The official Israeli view on the settlements was that they are simply Jewish communities under threat from 'terrorists' and 'mobs', as in this report: 'Israeli soldiers are accused of using excessive force in response to the violence but insist they're only defending their communities from the stone-throwing mobs' (ITV lunchtime News, 4 October 2000).

While the Palestinians see themselves as resisting an illegal military presence, the Israeli perspective focuses on what they see as the vulnerability of their own nation. As Nomi Chazan, a member of the Israeli Knesset has commented, 'we are trapped in two narratives which both sides believe are incompatible: the Palestinian struggle for national liberation against Israeli occupation, [and] Israel's continued struggle to survive' (*Observer*, 18 August 2002). This sense that the Israelis have of being under threat is well expressed in the following report from the BBC. It is from the early days of the *intifada* and mentions the kidnapping of Israeli soldiers on the border with Lebanon as well as the conflict with the Palestinians:

> [The Israelis] say from their point of view that they feel as if they are under threat, as if they are under attack from all sides. They say, and they truly believe, that it was a concerted effort on the side of the Islamic militants in Lebanon to attack Israel when they took the three soldiers hostage yesterday, and there were also some stone-throwing incidents up here on the border from where I'm speaking. And the Israelis also feel as if they are under attack from the Palestinians, they blame all the violence on them.
> (BBC1 early evening news, 8 October 2000)

There were other references to Israeli fears, for example the comment that 'what is increasingly worrying the Israelis is the prospect of some kind of terrorist attack' (ITV early evening news, 13 October 2000). And on the BBC the same day: 'But what the Israeli security forces really fear now is a new wave of terrorist bombings by Palestinian extremists' (BBC1 main news, 13 October 2000). The similarity in the two comments suggests that they come from the same Israeli briefing. We found in this research that the word 'terrorist' was only used to describe Palestinian actions.

The Israelis were also described as feeling 'besieged' as in this report:

> And in the meantime Israeli troops are still on high alert. We visited this space in Gaza where snipers are on the look out for Palestinian gunmen who frequently open fire on them. The troops here showed us a network of breeze block tunnels they use to protect themselves. Many Israelis feel besieged at the moment by a Palestinian uprising they didn't expect.
> (BBC1 main news, 10 October 2000)

The above report was made without irony and there was no comment that the soldiers were actually imposing a military occupation upon the Palestinians. This raises a very significant point, that in the absence of such discussion, new developments in Israeli tactics can be presented as 'security' requirements (from the point of view of Israel) rather than as an extension of military control (which is how the Palestinians see it). Thus when Palestinians were prevented from entering the al-Aqsa mosque, the reason was reported as being because 'security forces' were 'afraid of a riot' (BBC1 main news, 13 October 2000). The Palestinians were shown as being angry at this treatment, but key elements of the reason for this anger were missing from the coverage. This absence also made it easier for the Israelis to present their account of the cause of the unrest. Rather than it being seen as a popular uprising against a military occupation, they suggested that the main cause was 'incitement' by Arab leaders and particularly by Yasser Arafat.

Without the discussion of wider origins and causes, we are left with accounts on the news of day-to-day events, in which it can appear that the 'normal' world is disrupted only when the Palestinians riot or bomb. This is of course the view of the Israeli Government and the news has tended to oscillate between this and the view that violence was per-petrated by both sides in a 'cycle' of 'tit for tat' killings. The Palestinians believe that they are resisting an illegal and violent occupation. From the perspective of the Israeli Government, the Palestinian militants are merely terrorists to whom they are 'responding.' There were many examples of the Israeli viewpoint being actively adopted by journalists and built into the structure of coverage which can be seen from reporting in the two years after the outbreak of the *intifada*. Palestinian bombings were frequently presented as 'starting' a sequence of events which involved an Israeli 'response', as in 'Dozens of Palestinians and Israelis have been killed in a relentless round of suicide bombings and Israeli counter-attacks' (BBC2 *Newsnight*, 22:30, 13 December 2001).

On Radio 4 it was reported that 'Five Palestinians have been killed when the Israeli army launched new attacks on the Gaza Strip in retaliation for recent acts of terrorism' (BBC Radio 4, 07:30, 6 March 2002). In another extraordinary exchange on BBC Radio 4, David Wiltshire MP was asked 'What can the Egyptians do to stop the suicide bombers – because that in the end is what is cranking up the violence at present?' He replies, 'Well that is one view, the Israeli view . . .' (BBC Radio 4, 17:00, 1 April 2002).

On Channel 4 News a journalist reported that 'the Israelis had carried out this demolition in retaliation for the murder of four soldiers' (Channel 4 News, 10 January 2002). The extent to which some jour-nalism simply assumes the Israeli perspective can be seen if the state-ments are 'reversed' and presented as Palestinian actions. The Group did not find any reports stating that 'The Palestinian attacks were in retalia-tion for the murder of those resisting the illegal Israeli occupation'. The incursions by Israeli forces into Palestinian towns in April 2002, occasioned heavy loss of life and much international criticism. On BBC Radio 4 News they were described using the phrase 'there is a determination to carry on until the job is done' (BBC Radio 4, 9 April 2002). Would Palestinian attacks be described in this fashion? A news journalism which seeks neutrality should not in fact endorse any point of view, but there were many departures from this principle.

The language of violence

The analysis of our main content sample found other differences in the manner in which Palestinians and Israelis were described in news reporting. Words such as 'murder', 'atrocity', 'lynching' and 'savage cold-blooded killing' were only used to describe Israeli deaths but not those of Palestinians. Terrible fates befell both Israelis and Palestinians but there was a clear difference in the language used to describe them. This was so even when the events being described had strong similarities. For example, on 10 October 2000 it was reported that Arab residents of Tel Aviv had been chased and stabbed. This was described on ITN as 'angry Jews looking for Arab victims' (ITN 18.30, 10 October 2000). There were also other attacks on Arabs in Nazareth. 13 Arabs were reported to have been killed and *The Independent* noted that Jewish mobs were chanting 'death to the Arabs' (11 October 2000).

In *The Guardian* (10 October 2000), these events were described as a pogrom. The reports on television news were extremely brief but two days later when two Israeli soldiers were killed by a crowd of Palestinians there was very extensive coverage and the words 'lynching' and 'lynch mob' were very widely used. This difference in the use of language is noteworthy. This is especially so since in this period, at the beginning of the *intifada*, over ten times as many Palestinians/Arabs had in fact been killed than Israelis. There was a disproportionate emphasis on Israeli deaths relative to those of Palestinians (both in terms of the amount of time devoted and the language used to describe them). This has apparently had an influence on viewers' perceptions. The news, on the occasions when it did give figures, stated that more Palestinians had died than Israelis, but in our sample of 300 young people from October 2002, 41 per cent believed that casualties were equal on both sides or that more Israelis had been killed than Palestinians. Our content analysis of television news of the first weeks of the *intifada* showed that Israelis spoke twice as often as Palestinians and there were many more headlines that expressed the Israeli view than that of the Palestinians.

The TV news did feature some criticism of Israel particularly for using 'excessive force', but it was clear from our work that such criticism was often muted. More severe criticisms emerged from within Israel itself when, for example Shimon Peres, the Israeli Foreign Minister, was reported in October 2001 as trying to 'rein in' the Israeli army. It was clearly stated that elements of the army were trying to 'wreck' a cease-fire:

> Aides of Mr. Peres have accused the army . . . of seeking to wreck the cease-fire he brokered last week with the Palestinian leader Yasser Arafat, by opening fire on stone throwing protesters. There are growing signs of disquiet with the army's operations in the West Bank and Gaza – including the use of live fire against unarmed protesters and 'surprise' checkpoints in the West Bank at which two Palestinian labourers were killed.
>
> (*The Guardian*, 2 October 2001)

In our research in October 2000, we found that some television news did report that Israeli soldiers were 'showing absolutely no restraint, firing live ammunition into crowds from metres' (ITN 18.00, 20 October 2000). But it was not suggested at this time that the actions of the army might be linked to a political agenda (i.e. to stop the peace process). In contrast the view put forward by the Israeli Government at the time that Arafat was encouraging violence for political ends – was widely reported and discussed on TV news. It is significant that the similarly critical view of the Israeli military emerged only briefly and when it came from an Israeli source. But this was rare and TV news did not develop this critical view as a theme in its reporting.

Public relations and production processes

The Israeli government was often able to present a coherent public relations perspective and to influence news agendas with their own way of seeing the conflict. In terms of the communications process this shows the clear links between information supply, production and news content. The veteran journalist Robert Fisk has commented on this and how the constant 'feeding' of stories and statements to the news machine led to imbalances in reporting:

> The journalist's narrative of events is built around the last thing someone has said and the last thing, given the constraints of time and the rolling news machine, that they have heard on the agency wire. So what you would find on television in the last few weeks is that every time an Israeli statement was made, it was pushed across at the Palestinians. So the Israelis would say, 'can Arafat control the violence?' And instead of the television reporter saying, 'well that's interesting, but can the Israelis control their own people?' The question was simply taken up as an Israeli question and became part of the news agenda. There seemed to be no real understanding that the job of the reporter is to analyze what's really happening, not simply to pick up on the rolling news machine, the last statement by one of the sides, and given the fact that the Israelis have a very smooth machine operating for the media, invariably what happened

is, it was Israel's voice that came across through the mouths of the reporters, rather than [having] people who were really making inquiries into both sides and what both people were doing.

(*The Message*, BBC Radio 4, 20 October 2000)

There were a number of other imbalances in the way in which the two sides were reported, for example, the Israelis spoke twice as much on television news as Palestinians. One very experienced journalist, a former BBC Middle East correspondent, described to us the production factors which influence television interviews. He made two important points. The first is that the Israelis have a very well-organized media and public relations operation. The second is that the Israelis limit what the Palestinians are able to do because of the impositions of their military occupation. As he commented:

The way you sound is terribly important for credibility. If you are in an absolutely sound studio setting, you have more credibility. If you are on a scratchy telephone line you are at a disadvantage. The reason the Palestinians suffer is their limited facilities – the Israelis have more money to spend and spend it on a sophisticated Western style of media communications and links. The second point is that the occupation limits Palestinians' freedom of access to the media. 99 per cent of the media is based in Jerusalem. If you have a Palestinian minister and you want him to come to a studio in Jerusalem then he can't or it will take him hours because of the restrictions [on the movement] of the Palestinians on the roads.

(Interview, 26 August 2002)

He also noted that the difficulties of movement applied to media teams trying to reach Palestinian areas and that this could affect coverage. This cannot be an acceptable situation for a publicly accountable broadcasting corporation which is committed to impartiality. Broadcasters cannot absolve themselves from the requirement for balance by accepting a status quo in which one side can ensure that it receives more favourable treatment by imposing restrictions on the other. The broadcasters really have to devote the necessary resources to make sure that both sides are properly represented. It should also be clearly indicated to viewers where the difficulties which Palestinians have in making their case result from the actions of the Israelis. For example, if a Palestinian is speaking down a scratchy telephone because of the limitations of movement imposed by military rule, then viewers should be told that this is so. To avoid doing this is to legitimize a structural imbalance.

The Israeli dominance in public relations combined with the sometimes muted approach to reporting criticism of Israeli actions led to a loss of impartiality in some areas of television news. The position is complicated for journalists by the closeness of Britain's relationship to the United States. In our sample we found very little criticism of US policy and this has probably become even more of a taboo area since the attacks on America of 11 September 2001. The BBC director general famously apologized for the content of a *Question Time* programme broadcast live, shortly after 11 September, in which such criticism had been made. In Middle Eastern politics, the US has sought to present itself as an 'honest broker' in the promotion of peace. But in practice it supplies around three billion dollars worth of aid each year to Israel, a large part of which is military hardware. This has led to considerable distrust on the part of the Palestinians towards the US. In our sample of news we found that this was sometimes reported, but the accounts normally stopped short of explaining why. As in this example:

Journalist (Visuals of fighting, stone-throwing)
A lethal game of cat and mouse in the narrow streets of Hebron. This is what the leaders (at peace talks) in Paris are up against. The idea that Washington might act as honest broker depressed these young Palestinians. It was a similar picture all over the West Bank again today but the level of violence was significantly lower. After six days of this people are getting tired, but in Gaza, Israel still wielded a big stick. Helicopters fired rockets killing at least one Palestinian.
(BBC1, 18.00, 4 October 2000)

There was no explanation of why the Palestinians do not trust the US. Other news also showed pictures of Palestinians burning an American flag but again did not say why or give the crucial information that the US was supplying the arms which were being used to attack the Palestinians. It was possible to find such information in news reports but it was very rare and was on the 'periphery' of TV news, i.e. late night on BBC2 or Channel 4, rather than on the mass audience programmes of BBC1 and ITN. This example is from Channel 4 news:

With two billion pounds of US money every year, much of it spent on arms, Israel has never been such a supreme regional power . . . Palestinians look up and see American-supplied Apache helicopters just as Hezbollah in Lebanon look south and see American supplied missiles, tanks and artillery.
(Channel 4 News, 19.00, 13 October 2000)

Without such information it is difficult to understand the actions or rationale of the people who are portrayed in television news stories. We asked our sample of young people why Palestinians might be critical of America and burn the US flag. In this group 66 per cent did not know, 24 per cent thought America 'supported' Israel and just ten per cent indicated that the US supplied money and arms.

The lack of explanation on the news about the origins of the conflict plus the differences in the manner in which both 'sides' had measurable effects on some public understanding. As one 18 year old in a focus group commented:

> You always think of the Palestinians as being really aggressive because of the stories you hear on the news. I always put the blame on them in my own head.
>
> (Interview, 25 May 2001)

It is hard to avoid the conclusion that the perspective of one side in the conflict occupies a privileged position in many news accounts. Viewers are not, however, uniform in their responses to this. Some for example, expressed support for the Palestinian 'side' and said that their judgement was informed not by the words that were spoken but by visual images which had shown the Palestinians as the 'underdog' – for example pictures of stone-throwers against tanks. Others cited 'alternative' sources which had led them to a greater sympathy for the Palestinian side – such as leaflets from campaigning groups, the internet and books, as well as press articles and some TV documentaries.

Overall the research suggests that the structure and content of much of TV news does not offer a balanced account of the range of perspectives on this conflict. This is in part a result of the success of the public relations initiatives undertaken by Israel, and the superior quality of their 'news machine'. Television is, however, required to achieve standards of balance and impartiality. Those who control it should think seriously about how to redress these imbalances and to offer a fair and impartial coverage. This is particularly important in an area where there are such clear and measurable effects on public understanding and belief.

References

Herman, Edward and Chomsky, Noam (1988) *Manufacturing Consent – the Political Economy of the Mass Media*. New York: Pantheon Books.
Shlaim, Avi (2000) *The Iron Wall: Israel and the Arab World*. London: Penguin.

MAPPING THE AL-JAZEERA PHENOMENON

Noureddine Miladi

Few could have imagined that a new and challenging way of understanding impartiality in communicating conflict would arise from an Arab television channel in a region where broadcasting has been stigmatized for decades by heavy censorship and complete state control. It was from the coverage of the 1991 Gulf War that CNN became the 'eyes and ears of the world'. In a similar fashion, Al-Jazeera, the pan-Arabic satellite television channel, ascended to the world stage after 11 September 2001, through the exclusive coverage of the war in Afghanistan. The unprecedented nature of this communication channel reached a climax when Al-Jazeera started regularly airing recorded videotapes of Osama bin Laden and press releases put out by Al-Qaeda. This ability to give airtime to the opposing viewpoint has made Al-Jazeera a distinct voice in Arab, and increasingly, international broadcasting.

This chapter briefly outlines the development of Arab broadcasting and examines the impact of the emergence of Arab satellite channels. Focusing on Al-Jazeera, the chapter analyses its programming output and how its editorial policies have affected broadcasting by other Arab television channels. It also looks at reception of the channel in the region and touches on the concerns and interests of Al-Jazeera's audiences through a survey the author conducted among members of the Arab communities in the UK. The chapter concludes by asking how the rise of Al-Jazeera may challenge the prevailing definitions of impartiality in news coverage, especially of the economically and geo-strategically important Middle East and central Asian regions.

Al-Jazeera, which in Arabic means 'the Peninsula', arose in 1996 from the ashes of the defunct London-based BBC Arabic television network, which was set up by the BBC in partnership with the Saudi government to establish a pan-Arab television service, with a view to dominating the Arab TV market. This market had steadily grown as a result of the proliferation of new commercial channels with the advent of satellite broadcasting in the early 1990s (Sakr, 2001). A conflicting vision of editorial policy culminated in the demise of the first-ever Western all-news channel for the Arab market. However, several key Arab journalists who worked for BBC Arabic were attracted to a new Arab-based news network, meeting their aspirations for an independent Arab voice on the world television scene, according to Hilal Ibrahim, News Room Chief Editor of Al-Jazeera (personal interview with the author, 7 July 2002).

Al-Jazeera, with a regular audience of 35 million and available to most of the world's 310 million Arabs, has redefined Arab broadcasting, making it a major regional network with ambitions to reach audiences outside its traditional constituency. The channel started by broadcasting daily news and current affairs as well as discussion and documentary programmes from Qatar, a tiny country in the Gulf region, only 60,000 square metres in size and with fewer than 700,000 inhabitants. The channel has become the most independent TV station in the region and essential viewing for millions both in the Middle East and among the Arab diaspora.

The success of Al-Jazeera can partly be attributed to the kinds of programmes it broadcasts, for example, giving airtime to critical voices from political parties, the academic community or human rights activists, and, in the process, provoking many Arab leaders. However, despite their initial and unsuccessful efforts to silence the channel, Arab governments have gradually come to terms with this plurality of opinion as a reality of twenty-first century, multi-channel broadcasting. The coverage of the tragic events of 11 September 2001 and their aftermath provided Al-Jazeera with a unique opportunity to make its presence felt outside the Arab world. Its capacity to provide live coverage from the theatre of war in Afghanistan and its determination to show pictures of death and destruction not seen on Western television networks angered the United States government, which tried in a number of ways to put heavy pressure on the channel to tone down its coverage.

The impact of satellite TV on Arab broadcasting

To make sense of the Al-Jazeera phenomenon, it is important to examine briefly the changing culture of broadcasting in the Arab world, brought about by the proliferation of satellite transmitters. Until the mid-1990s, Arab press in general, and broadcasting in particular, had been mono-polized by state-controlled media (Boyd, 1999; Rugh, 1979). The Arab countries launched their own satellite system, Arabsat, in 1985, with the aim of establishing a link between the state broadcasters. Three years later, Egypt became the first Arab country to have its own satellite system – Nilesat – marking a new era in satellite communication in the region. It was also the first Arab country to start satellite broadcasting, launching the Egyptian Satellite Channel in 1990. It was during the 1990s that all Arab countries managed to have their own state satellite channels, although their aims varied, from using these new channels for religious or political indoctrination, to fostering cultural ties and promoting tourism in their countries. These include Tunisia's Tunis-7, Libya's Al-Jamahiria, and the state controlled channels of Algeria, Syria, Iraq, Oman, Sudan, Saudi Arabia, Dubai, and Qatar. All these channels broadcast their programmes in Arabic, apart from two: Libya's Al-Jamahiria translates some of its main news programmes into French and Egypt's state-owned Nile TV International, established in 1994, broadcasts both in French and English.

The Arab satellite channels can be classified into two categories: state-owned and privately-owned. The state-owned channels were primarily targeted at citizens living outside their country – both long-term immigrants as well as those who go abroad for short periods of time to work or study – with the aim of maintaining a link between diasporic communities and their countries of origin (Yahyawi, 1997). However, such channels were characterized by tight editorial control of the content of programming, thereby rendering them little more than a tool for political propaganda, promoting the ideologies of the ruling parties. Complete editorial control was exercised over these channels by the Ministries of Information, whose officials were also involved in recruitment to the senior managerial and editorial positions (Kazan, 1993). However, it is necessary to point to the differences within the Arab media world – censorship in Egypt, Morocco and Jordan, for instance, is different and more lenient than in such authoritarian regimes as Tunisia, Algeria, Libya, Iraq and Syria. This kind of control was a reflection of the political realities in most of the Arab world, where for the past five decades non-democratic regimes have dominated the political landscape, rendering the possibilities of a free media very hard to achieve (Hafez, 2001).

The privatization of broadcasting, partly as a result of globalization and deregulation of telecommunications, has profoundly changed the face of Arab television. State-run media had to adapt to the pressure from private networks, which were seen to be more open in their approach to programming. With the emergence of private channels and the growing popularity of the internet, a new era seemed to have opened up. It has been argued that strict censorship laws in Arab countries contributed to what emerged in the 1980s as the 'migrating Arab press' thriving among the diaspora (Aish, 2001: 115). The 1990s witnessed the emergence of satellite channels, initially catering to the diaspora rather than focusing on audiences in the Arab world. For the privately-owned television networks, consumers not citizens are the key factor and therefore they tend to target general diasporic Arabs in addition to viewers in the Arab world, irrespective of nationality.

The first among these was the London-based Middle East Broadcasting Centre (MBC), which started broadcasting in 1991 and moved its operational headquarters to Dubai only in 2002. Owned by Saudi businessmen, MBC's programmes vary from soaps to entertainment to documentaries and news and current affairs. The other major players include: the Arab Radio and Television (ART), owned by Saudi businessman Salih Kamil, which started broadcasting on Arabsat from Italy in 1993; Orbit, owned by Al-Mawarid group from Saudi Arabia, which started its pay-TV service in 1994; and the Lebanese Broadcasting Corporation (LBC) and Future Television International (Lebanon), which are partly owned by the Lebanese Prime Minister, Rafiq al-Hariri.

The impact of deregulation in broadcasting was in evidence initially in Lebanon, where the audiovisual media law, passed by the parliament in 1994 and put into effect in 1996, broke the monopoly of the state on radio and television broadcasting, making it the first case of private TV channels broadcasting from inside an Arab country. This led to a proliferation of channels, ranging from LBC, Future TV, and Al-Manar TV, run by Hizbullah, broadcasting freely inside Lebanon and beyond, attracting viewers in the Arab diaspora. In the sphere of news and current affairs, the London-based Arab News Network (ANN), owned by Rifat al-Asad (brother of the former president of Syria), entered the market in 1997 as a rival to Al-Jazeera.

Al-Jazeera: revolutionizing Arab broadcasting?

The collapse of the short-lived partnership between the BBC Arabic television service and the government of Saudi Arabia gave the opportunity to Sheikh Hamad bin Khalifa, the new Emir of Qatar, to fill the gap in the broadcasting market by employing the technical infrastructure and the senior staff of the defunct service. Recognizing the need for a distinctive pan-Arabic news network broadcasting from Qatar rather than London, he allocated an initial amount of $150 million as a five-year loan from the Qatari ruling family to establish the channel, according to Nabil El-Kaisi, secretary to the Al-Jazeera's Board of Directors (personal interview with the author, 7 July 2002).

Attracted by competitive salaries and the promise that this would be the free-media zone of the Arab world, Arab journalists, editors, broadcasters and engineers were recruited from various Arab, as well as Western countries. About 500 employees now work for Al-Jazeera, from diverse political, cultural and religious backgrounds. From the very religious to the extremely secular, Muslims and Christians work side by side. Among the journalists/employees and correspondents there are nationalists, Islamists, Baathists (ideology of the ruling parties in Iraq and Syria), Marxists, feminists, liberalists, and apolitical people. All of them seem to agree on a common ground, which is freedom of expression, coexistence and the respect of the opposite opinion. From the outset, Al-Jazeera aimed at broadcasting 24 hours in classical Arabic, the language understood by a vast majority of the population in the Arab countries, as well as in the diaspora, regardless of their religion, culture and line of thinking.

Programming

Al-Jazeera has been perceived to have gained 'world fame' in the wake of the 11 September terrorist attacks in the US through its exclusive footage of video tapes of Osama bin Laden (BBC News, 15 November 2001). However, the channel was already popular in the Arab world and among diasporic Arab communities long before those events. Its programmes reflect the notion of public service broadcasting as pioneered by the BBC. The weekly talk shows and discussion programmes often tackle crucial, yet taboo subjects, like human rights, democracy and political corruption, women's freedom, banned political groups, polygamy, torture and rival interpretations of Islamic teachings.

Al-Jazeera appeals to Arab viewers with a variety of programmes, including home news, world news, sports, business analysis, documentaries, historical events, women's issues, religion, etc. Among the main programmes are: the talk show *Al-Ittijah Al-Mua'kis* (Opposite Direction), presented by Faisal Al-Qasim (Syrian) and modelled on CNN's *Crossfire*; a live discussion programme, *Akhtar Min Rai* (More than One Opinion), hosted by Sami Haddad (Lebanese); a one-on-one interview on topical issues called 'Without Limits', hosted by Ahmed Mansoor (Egyptian); *Al-Sharia' wal-Hayat* (Religion and Life), where the host Maher Abdullah invites notable Muslim scholars; an investigative series relying on 'tangible evidence and expert analysis' called *Top Secret*, produced and presented by Yusri Fouda (Egyptian); and *For Women Only*, a discussion programme geared primarily towards women and hosted by Muntaha Arumhi. The programme features academics, experts, and women activists from various venues and because of wide scope of topics, it attracts a large male audience, which is clear from the live phone-in participation.

On programmes like 'Opposite Direction', anchored by a Syrian presenter, Faisal Al-Qasim, 'Without Limits' conducted by Kuwaiti presenter, Ahmed Mansoor, and 'More than One Opinion' conducted by Sami Haddad, a Lebanese presenter with long experience in the BBC, Al-Jazeera opens the floor for free and often noisy debate on some of the most sensitive issues in Arab society – such as human rights, Arab-Israeli conflict, gender equality and democracy. Other Arab channels would not even consider screening such discussions, which might result in floods of telephone calls or criticism in the press or even encourage protests in the streets. The animated political discussions that were confined to private spaces in Arab countries have been brought into the open after decades of stagnation and state censorship, to be debated at a transnational level and the debates being conducted by anchors of different nationalities.

One can argue that this new public space could contribute to the construction of a 'public sphere' for Arab audiences (Habermas, 1989; Sparks and Dahlgren, 1995) and facilitate a pan-Arab debate on issues relevant to the region and help in reshaping a meaning for a global citizenship. Audiences have started to discuss issues not only relevant to their home countries but to other Arab or Muslim nations. Satellite networks like Al-Jazeera have provided a forum for Arab viewers and created a platform from which to express themselves. As Max Rodenbeck of the *New York Times* put it:

> Gone is the time when Arabs had to turn for the truth to the BBC, as in the Six Day War of 1967 . . . Some, like Al-Jazeera, rival and sometimes surpass Western models for the quality and timeliness of their reporting. It does not really require subtle manipulation to frame the ongoing tragedy as an epic struggle (in Jenin, Palestine) of the weak (Palestinians) against the strong (Israeli army). The imagery saturating Arab screens, of tanks crushing ambulances and helicopters rocketing refugee camps, is, alas, all too real.
>
> (Rodenbeck, 2002)

Another important aspect of the channel is its emphasis on live programming. In 2002, it had seven live programmes each week that allow phone-in and live participation by the audiences. This interactivity has helped increase its subscription base among the diasporic audience. There were more than 200,000 subscribers in the US and Canada in 2002, paying $22.99 per month to receive the channel on the Colorado-based Echostar's Dish Network (El-Nawawy and Iskandar, 2002: 65).

In the UK, where the channel is available on Sky Digital platform, several Arab cafés and *halal* shops have acquired the satellite service in order to cater for the needs of their customers. The popularity of the channel can be indicated by the claim by Abdullah Al-Hajj, Al-Jazeera's deputy manager, that, in many Arab countries, women have gone as far as to sell their jewellery to purchase a satellite dish, costing about $280, to watch its programmes (El-Nawawy and Iskandar, 2002).

A survey of the Arab community in the UK conducted by the author in 2001 found that among the ten Arabic language channels available in Britain, Al-Jazeera was the channel of choice for most people interviewed. The sample included 146 respondents (males and females from age 14 onward) and was constructed from the various venues where the Arab community is mainly found: like Arabic weekend schools, community centres, mosques, national clubs, student clubs and Arab shops and cafés in London's Edgware Road and Queensway. On a scale of 1 to 5, Al-Jazeera was rated highest by 47 per cent of those surveyed.

Aware of their channel's uniqueness, Al-Jazeera officials conducted a survey in the UK in July 2001 to prepare the ground for its long-term plan to become a pay channel. In total 426 interviewees were approached – 209 people from London, 119 from Sheffield and 98 from Manchester and Coventry. The sample consisted of Arab men only as they are the ones 'most likely to sign the cheques for subscription to Al-Jazeera' (Al-Jazeera Market Research, 22 July 2001). This research unveiled a high brand recognition score as 99 per cent of respondents had heard of Al-Jazeera, and 93 per cent of UK Arab viewers, from the sample interviewed, regularly watched the channel.

A common feature among the Arab community in the UK is their criticism of the lack of freedom of expression in their countries of origin, censorship of the media and absence of real democracy. A high percentage of them (about 55 per cent) are refugees who came to Britain in different waves of immigration. Issues of political and religious persecution reflect themselves on their everyday concerns, and therefore on their choice of television programmes. Also, a fundamental characteristic of this community – in spite of its complex cultural and ideological background – is its support for the Palestinian struggle for freedom and the right of return to the Palestinian refugees to their homeland. This is reflected in the audiences' preference for news and current affairs over entertainment programming (see Figure 10.1).

This explains the swift popularity of Al-Jazeera soon after its launch in 1996. Other channels broadcasting from outside the Arab countries, have not managed to attract such a wide viewing public, even though MBC, for example, had started broadcasting long before Al-Jazeera. Most private channels are entertainment-based and do not have a discourse that can be easily distinguished from that of the Arab state channels.

The availability of on-line communication has further widened Al-Jazeera's audience base. Its official website (www.aljazeera.net) has made considerable progress since its launch on 1 January 2001. During the year 2001, the activity of the site attracted 38 million hits, and more than 265 million pages viewed. The site provides daily international news analysis, special documentaries, portrayal of Arab and foreign press, in addition to transcripts of most of the discussion programmes, book reviews, and special reports. In January 2003, the site had over 80,000 members who can participate in TV programmes through the net and receive the daily newsletter through their e-mail service. After 11 September 2001, aljazeera.net became even more popular and the number of visits to the site substantially increased. During the month of October 2001, the number of web pages viewed soared from 600,000 per day before the 11 September to more than one million pages per day. By

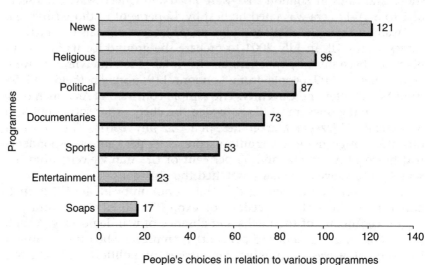

Figure 10.1 Viewers' preferences for programme types on Arab satellite TV in Britain

the beginning of January 2002, Al-Jazeera prided itself on having 70 million page views per month (Ben Thamir, 2002).

Al-Jazeera's reception in the Arab world

From the outset Al-Jazeera was perceived as a rival by Arab state channels, as well as by private ones, and it set the standard for quality broadcasting by which Arab audiences could compare the various channels. Viewers were suddenly able to judge the quality and balance of television coverage on a given topic through the ability to switch between tens of channels. The existence of Al-Jazeera has pushed the other Arab channels, particularly the private ones broadcasting from Europe, to improve their content and broadcast quality, and also to open up the scope of their operation to oppositional views. According to Mohammed Khawas, the editor of ANN: 'The channel excelled in every possible avenue; little room has been left to us for competition' (personal interview with the author, November 2001).

In order to attract their audiences back, MBC, for example, attempted to improve the quality of its news and current affairs programmes and to open up airtime to more diverse views, yet it was still restrained by the editorial policies of the Saudi princes who fund it. The growing popularity of Al-Jazeera has had a ripple effect on Arab broadcasting, as one Arab journalist, Noureddine Awididi working for the Quds Press remarked: 'Al-Jazeera has thrown a big stone in this stagnant sea' (personal interview with the author, 15 March 2002).

However, Al-Jazeera's policy of portraying 'the opinion and its opposite' has earned it criticism and even wrath across the Arab world (Sakr, 2001). The attack on the channel started long before the events of 11 September 2001. Kuwait's Information Minister flew to the Qatari capital Doha to complain in person after a programme on Al-Jazeera criticized his government for its stand on Iraq. Algeria's regime reportedly shut off electricity in parts of the country rather than allow Algerian television sets to pick up a debate on the country's bloody civil war. The Jordanian government closed down Al-Jazeera's news bureau in Amman after a talk show guest accused the late King Hussein of collaborating with Israel.

Tunisia's president called the Emir of Qatar to stop broadcasting a live programme discussing human rights abuse in Tunisia. The Moroccan Prime Minster, Abdurrahman El-Yousufi, accused Al-Jazeera of leading a campaign against the monarchy. He referred to discussion programmes which were tackling political corruption that included interviews with an exiled former army officer and a 1971 coup plotter against the late King Hussain. Morocco recalled its Ambassador in protest, although the Qatari Foreign Affairs Minister explained that 'Qatari media is free and we have no control over it'. He further argued that 'international television stations, newspapers and magazines are covering the Arab world much more than what we write about ourselves. Why be embarrassed when an Arab television station tackles our concerns?' (Reuters, 2000a).

Bahrain's Information Minister banned Al-Jazeera from reporting on the local elections that took place in May 2002. The government had been angered by Al-Jazeera's airing of footage of anti-American protests triggered by Israeli massacres in Jenin and the West Bank. The Information Minister, Al-Hamr, said that the station was biased towards Israel and against Bahrain. 'We will not deal with this channel', he reportedly remarked, 'because we object to its coverage of current affairs. It is a channel penetrated by Zionists' (BBC News, 10 May 2002). President Hosni Mubarak of Egypt frequently attacked Al-Jazeera as it aired programmes criticizing the Egyptian government and the violations of human rights and suppression of democracy in the country. More recently, Mubarak and the Egyptian media have openly blamed Al-Jazeera as a channel 'spreading friction, enmity and instability among Arab countries' (Al-Jazeera News, 30 April 2002).

Al-Jazeera is well known for conducting interviews with controversial figures that irk Arab governments. Earlier in October 2001 the Egyptian Information Minister again accused the channel of hostility towards Egypt, and towards the notion of Arab unity. After visiting the station,

Mubarak made the oft-quoted remark: 'All this noise from this match-box?'. His Information Minister remarked 'We have to know who is trying to break up the ranks. I may . . . stop all dealings with the Al-Jazeera channel concerning studios . . . satellite feeds or correspondents' (Reuters, 2000b). Some of the pressure has dissipated as Arab leaders develop a love-hate relationship with the news channel. Some, such as President Salih of Yemen, readily denounce it but cannot wait to appear on it. According to Nadim Shehadi of the Centre for Lebanese Studies at Oxford University, the rise of Al-Jazeera is a lesson in the perils of censorship. Shehadi argues that 'by trying to censor the BBC, the Saudis created an opportunity for the creation of something that was much worse for them. If you try to censor, you don't know what is going to come out' (quoted in Whitaker, 2001).

Response from the West

Al-Jazeera came to the notice of Western politicians, journalists and academics when, in 1998, it broadcast an interview with bin Laden in which he called upon Muslims to target 'American interests', but especially after the events of 11 September 2001, by regularly airing bin Laden's version of the 'war on terrorism'. It was praised by Arab as well as non-Arab observers as the first non-Western network to challenge the Western monopoly on global news reporting, and therefore, as a commentator noted in a Lebanese newspaper: 'Al-Jazeera provides a much more inclusive perspective, which gives you everything you get on CNN plus everything you don't' (Rath, 2002). The station's capacity of providing the 'other side of the story' while covering the war in Afghanistan provoked angry comments by top American diplomats, who demanded that Al-Jazeera should 'tone it down'. American politicians and journalists admitted that the channel had become the primary source of news for Arab viewers (Rodenbeck, 2002).

Faced with 'a battle for the hearts and minds' and the need to tell moderate Muslims that the US is not waging a war against Islam, in 2001 the US considered advertising on Al-Jazeera TV. Charlotte Beers, the State Department's chief of public diplomacy, said the State Department was investigating new ways to reach out to Arab audiences (Teinowtiz, 2001). The US government even planned to launch a TV station to rival Al-Jazeera. Initiative 9/11 put half a billion dollars into a channel that would compete in the region with Al-Jazeera, and that would be aimed specifically at younger Muslims who are seen as anti-American (Campbell, 2001).

Al-Jazeera's airing of bin Laden's tapes and its coverage of the war in Afghanistan made it pay a high price when the US military seemed to have deliberately bombed its Kabul office in November 2001. The channel's correspondent in Washington, Mohammad al-Alami, was detained as he was on his way to cover the Russian-American summit in Texas in the same month (BBC, 2001).

Fierce competition to reach out for Arab audiences through the net also led CNN officially to launch its Arabic website (CNNArabic.com) in January 2002, operated from Dubai by Arab journalists. The content of the site is complementary to CNN International. The Arabic service of the Voice of America (VOA) has also been suffering from a poor audience share in the Arab world. It has been estimated that only one to two per cent of Arabs listen to it since the 11 September events (Newton, 2002: 15). The US Congress, therefore, funded the renewal of Radio Free Afghanistan. Established in the mid-1980s, when Afghanistan was under Soviet domination, it was shut down when the Soviets withdrew, as the US mistakenly thought the service was no longer 'needed'. There is a growing concern that Arab satellite television channels headed by Al-Jazeera have weakened Arab audiences' interest in Western media services such as Radio Monte Carlo, the BBC and the VOA.

The events of 11 September 2001 and their aftermath posed new challenges to the mainstream Western and Arab state-run media. Al-Jazeera's coverage of the war in Afghanistan and the Israeli-Palestinian conflict turned out to be more than the American government could bear without fighting back. The battle to win over Arab and Muslim public opinion led to the launch of a new media strategy. If its plans to broadcast in English become a reality, Al-Jazeera could be seen to pose a challenge to traditional global media players. However, given the economics of satellite television there are several imponderables. Al-Jazeera became internationally known because it was covering a war where the Western cameras were not present, at least initially. How would it be received during peacetime, especially outside its Arab constituency? Will it be able to sustain itself on subscription and advertising alone? What happens if and when the state of Qatar stops subsidizing the channel? Given these uncertainties, it is safe to say that it will be a long time before it acquires the reach and influence of the Western television networks, in spite of the fact that in December 2002 it started broadcasts using English subtitles (MacAskill, 2002).

Nevertheless, if it could build on its initial success and continue to provide a fresh perspective on international issues, especially reporting the 'war on terrorism', Al-Jazeera may create a niche for itself in international broadcasting and thus enrich global media discourse. In a significant role reversal, it may even be able to influence Western public opinion. The question that remains to be answered is whether the world's only superpower would put up with a daring and different television satellite channel like Al-Jazeera, making its programmes accessible to a global public and helping to shape its opinions.

References

Aish, Mohammad (2001) 'Changing Face of Arab Communications', in Kai, Hafez (ed.) *Mass Media, Politics and Society in the Middle East*. New Jersey: Hampton Press.

Al-Jazeera News (2002) 'Mubarak Attacks Washington and the Arab satellite channels', 30 April. Available at http://www.aljazeera.net/news/arabic/2002/4/4-30-9. htm

BBC (2001) News bulletin at 11:18 GMT, 15 November.

BBC News (2002) 'Bahrain Bans Al-Jazeera TV', May 10. Available at http://news.bbc.co.uk/hi/english/world/middle_east/newsid_1980000/1980191.stm

Ben Thamir, Hamad (2002) 'Al-Jazeera achieves 265 million page views in its first year'. Available at www.aljazeera.net accessed on 6 February 2002.

Boyd, Douglas (1999) *Broadcasting in the Arab World*. Ames: Iowa State University Press.

Campbell, Duncan (2001) 'US plans TV station to rival Al-Jazeera', *The Guardian*, 23 November.

El-Nawawy, M. and Iskandar, A. (2002) *Al-Jazeera: How the Free Arab Network Scooped the World and Changed the Middle East*. Cambridge, MA: Westview.

Habermas, J. (1989) *The Structural Transformation of the Public Sphere*. Cambridge: Polity.

Hafez, Kai (2001) 'Mass Media in the Middle East: Patterns of Political and Societal Change', in Kai, Hafez (ed.) *Mass Media, Politics and Society in the Middle East*. New Jersey: Hampton Press.

Kazan, Fayad (1993) *Mass, Modernity, and Development: Arab States of the Gulf*. Westport, CT: Praeger.

MacAskill, Ewen (2002) 'Al-Jazeera broadcasts in English', *The Guardian*, 27 December, p. 17.

Newton, N. Minow (2002) 'Mass media can battle mass destruction', *USA Today*, 9 April, p. 15.

Rath, Tiare (2002) 'Media groups go multi-lingual to feed the post-Sept 11 hunger for Arab news', *The Daily Star* (Beirut), 7 February.

Reuters (2000a) 'Qatar defends free press in row with Morocco', 22 July. Available at http://www.arabia.com/news/article/english/0,11827,25537,00.html

Reuters (2000b) 'Egypt Deports Brother of Al-Jazeera TV Announcer', 27 October. Available at www.arabia.com accessed 30 October 2002.

Rodenbeck, Max (2002) Broadcasting the War. *The New York Times*, 17 April.

Rugh, William (1979) *The Arab Press: News Media and Political Process in the Arab World*. Syracuse, NY: Syracuse University Press.

Sakr, Naomi (2001) *Satellite Realms: Transnational Television, Globalization and the Middle East*. London: I.B. Tauris.

Sparks, Colin and Dahlgren, Peter (1995) *Communication and Citizenship*. London: Routledge.

Teinowitz, Ira (2001) 'US Considers advertising on Al-Jazeera TV', *Advertising Age*, 15 October. Available at http://www.adage.com/news.cms?newsId=33163 accessed on 25 October 2001.

Whitaker, Brian (2001) Battle Station. *The Guardian*, 9 October.

Yahyawi, Yaihya (1997) *The Arab World and the Challenges of Media & Communication Technologies* (in Arabic). Knitra, Morocco: Al-Bukeeli.

Part 4

REPRESENTATIONS OF CONFLICT – 9/11 AND BEYOND

11

WAR AND THE ENTERTAINMENT INDUSTRIES: NEW RESEARCH PRIORITIES IN AN ERA OF CYBER-PATRIOTISM

Jonathan Burston

'Militainment' and the end of the information/ entertainment binary

> Modeling and simulation technology has become increasingly important to both the entertainment industry and the U.S. Department of Defense (DOD). In the entertainment industry, such technology lies at the heart of video games, theme park attractions and entertainment centers, and special effects for film production. For DOD, modeling and simulation technology provides a low-cost means of conducting joint training exercises, evaluating new doctrine and tactics, and studying the effectiveness of new weapons systems . . . These common interests suggest that the entertainment industry and DOD may be able to more efficiently achieve their individual goals by working together to advance the technology base for modeling and simulation. Such cooperation could take many forms, including collaborative research and development projects, sharing research results, or coordinating ongoing research programs to avoid unnecessary duplication of effort.
>
> (NRC, 1996)

So begins a 1996 report sponsored by the US National Research Council (NRC) entitled *Modeling and Simulation: Linking Entertainment and Defense* (NRC, 1996). The report documents the findings of a conference convened in 1996 in Irvine, California by the NRC's Computer Science and Telecommunications Board, on behalf of the Department of Defense's Defense Modeling and Simulation Office (DMSO). DOD participants included individuals from the DMSO, the Defense Advanced Research Projects Agency (DARPA), the Navy and the Air Force.

Representing the entertainment industry were people from Disney, Paramount, the George Lucas special effects house Industrial Light and Magic (ILM), Pixar, and a host of other established and emerging players. Joining both groups were defense and computer industry executives and academic researchers in computer science and computer art and design. Their collective mission: to investigate the potential benefits of collaboration in creating 'the technical advances upon which future entertainment and defense systems will be built' (NRC, 1996).

Although there probably were a few in attendance in Irvine, one clearly does not have to be a rocket scientist to have noticed a growing compatibility between the entertainment industry and the military over the last decade or so. From the 'Join the Navy' feel of blockbuster military spectaculars like *Behind Enemy Lines* to the *SOCOM: U.S. Navy SEALs* video game, entertainment corporations and the military are cooperating with each other to highly profitable ends, and the crossover potential is apparent everywhere. Yet when reading official documents like the NRC's, one can still be taken aback by the persistent juxtaposition of these two ostensibly very different sectors: 'Both DOD and the entertainment industry would like to develop computer-generated characters that have adaptable behaviors and can learn from experience' (NRC, 1996). 'Oh', you think, 'like in that Spielberg movie with the blonde kid from *The Sixth Sense*. But for real'. Of course the DOD was already sponsoring research in the application of artificial intelligence (AI) technologies to the computer-generated characters (CGCs, or 'synthespians') inhabiting their own training simulations. But by the early 1990s it had become clear to the military that if they wanted to take it to the next level, it was time to get a little help from Hollywood.

Or better, Siliwood. For nowadays, if we wish to define 'the entertainment industry' accurately, we really ought to stop relying on Hollywood as its metonym. We need instead to recalibrate our understanding of both the form and the locus of heavy-hitting, media-transnational pop-cultural power. In North America, revenues from video and computer games have been matching or out-scoring conventional box office revenues for a few years now; one of the industry's largest producers, Electronic Arts, has twice as many in-house game developers as Disney has animators (Keighly, 2002). Silicon Valley certainly appears to be as 'natural' a home for video-gaming as Hollywood has long appeared to be for film and television production, though there is a fair bit of shuttle traffic and turf-swapping in either direction. In each instance, however, the speed of innovation (and the speed of digital technology itself) in fact continues to promote the steady dissemination of entertainment research, development and production across a far wider territory than the state of California. Indeed the chairman of Toronto-based, Academy Award-winning digi-house, Alias Wavefront, was one of the chief organizers of the DOD's Irvine conference. And recent American concerns about disappearing film, TV, animation and software gigs in Los Angeles and New York to so-called 'runaway' productions provide only one of many possible examples of the growing, if attenuated, globalization of what is usually still US-influenced entertainment production (Magder and Burston, 2001; Miller *et al.*, 2001).

Redefining the parameters of 'the entertainment industry' with such formal, geographical, political and technological rudiments in mind is, in fact, essential to forming an adequate understanding of the multiple forces working to represent war – in many different ways and for many different reasons – from inside the larger industrial formation that is transnational media capitalism. Yet most media scholarship investigating war and its representation has eschewed the examination of 'soft' entertainment product and production, choosing instead to focus on the 'harder' topic of news journalism. This hard/soft binary has of course been typical of media studies more broadly, where an empirical understanding of the politics of *information* programming is generally perceived to matter more than anything else because of its potentially salubrious effects on the health of the global public sphere. Though some important work within the media studies tradition does document the politics of producing popular culture (Hesmondhalgh, 2002; Negus, 1999; Toynbee, 2000), comprehending the politics of entertainment programming still generally seems to matter more as a buttress to the theoretical needs of media scholarship on news-gathering. Enquiries into the dynamics of entertainment capitalism are understood to be useful, in other words, only when they shed light on the octopean nature of media capitalism more broadly, or when they reveal emerging nuances in the realm of ideology. This is in part because entertainment, as a category of production, reception or analysis, has conventionally been understood as (somehow) more oriented toward the private or domestic sphere. But as work in cultural studies has long reminded us (e.g. Dyer, 1992), this particular hard/soft binary is as dangerous politically as it is untenable theoretically, sliding down the slippery slope from 'information/entertainment', through 'public/private', *all* the way down to the 'masculine/feminine' binary and the imprudent assumptions and blind alleys contained therein. For reasons that are now all too practical, however, recent events inside the entertainment sector reveal how entirely untenable the information/entertainment binary has become. The moment of 'militainment' is upon us, and we ignore its specificity at our peril.

Meet the neighbours: the military entertainment establishment

Irvine is not the only place military and entertainment types have been meeting and greeting over the last ten years or so. The US College of

Aerospace, Doctrine, Research and Education (CADRE) at Maxwell Air Force Base in Montgomery, Alabama has sponsored an annual conference called 'Connections' for the entertainment and defense simulation 'communities' during that same period, in order 'to increase the defense utility of all conflict simulations by facilitating their evolution toward greater comprehensiveness and accessibility' (CADRE, 2002). Then there are the Association for Computing Machinery (ACM)'s annual conferences, SIGGRAPH (Special Interest Group on Computer Graphics and Interactive Techniques) and SIGART (Special Interest Group on Artificial Intelligence) where, along with the North American Simulation and Gaming Association (NASAGA) annual event, all sorts of initiatives are brainstormed. The city of Orlando, Florida, constitutes its own perpetual industry confab. Orlando is headquarters for the DOD's Simulation Training and Instrumentation Command (STRICOM), whose mission is to create 'a distributed computerized warfare simulation system' and to support 'the twenty-first century warfighter's preparation for real world contingencies' (cited in Der Derian, 2000). It is also home, of course, to 'Team Disney' – the legendary cohort of R&D 'imagineers' at Disney World. Orlando is native soil in addition to a number of up-and-coming virtual reality outfits like Real3D, who cater to both the aerospace and the video game industries. It boasts regional offices for the likes of Silicon Graphics and defense giant Lockheed Martin too, more or less across the street from STRICOM. Finally, there are the nearby Universities of South Florida and Central Florida, the latter's Institute for Simulation and Training counting as only one of the academic enterprises adding sub-woofer power to the formidable node of the North American military entertainment establishment that STRICOM's own website likes to call 'Team Orlando' (www.stricom.army.mil).

But it was the DMSO-NRC event in Irvine in 1996 that spawned what is to date the most notable development inside this ominous new techno-industrial formation: the birth of STRICOM's California-based sister institution, the disingenuously-named Institute for Creative Technologies (ICT). The result of a $45 million grant from the US military and housed at the University of Southern California (USC), the ICT boasts an explicit and sobering mandate: 'to enlist the resources and talents of the entertainment and game development industries and to work collaboratively with computer scientists to advance the state of immersive training simulation' (ICT, n.d.). At the ICT, technologies of the digital spectacular are being developed simultaneously as entertainment technology and as cutting edge military technology. Housed in Marina del Rey offices planned by *Star Trek* production designer Herman Zimmerman, Hollywood management at the ICT includes former senior executives from NBC, Paramount and Disney. They work hand in hand with the military and with designers from the digital effects houses of Silicon Valley who are otherwise busy transforming movies, video games and amusement park rides.

Their activities are various. The ICT's Flat World project 'updates flats, a staple of Hollywood set design, into a system called Digital Walls' (Hart, 2001), transforming an empty room into a convincing 3D simulation of some far-away battle terrain (into which a trainee is 'immersed'). It is only one of the ICT's several state-of-the art virtual reality projects, all of them instantly evocative of *The Matrix*. In November 2002, for example, the ICT premiered its long-awaited Mission Rehearsal Exercise (MRE), a curved-screen simulation in front of which officers-in-training are presented with a number of different options for emergency action, each of which results in a different out-come, in a virtual Bosnian village. Trainees interact with digital actors, who themselves 'listen' and 'respond' with instantly variable 'emo-tions'. At another notable ICT event shortly after 11 September 2001, Hollywood creative talent – including *Die Hard* screenwriter Steven E. De Souza, television writer David Engelbach (*MacGyver*), and directors Joseph Zito (*Delta Force One, Invasion U.S.A.* and *Missing in Action*), Spike Jonze (*Being John Malkovich*) and David Fincher (*Fight Club, Seven*) – got together at the ICT to brainstorm narrative scenarios in the service of future US-sponsored counter-terrorism efforts (Gorman, 2001). Last, but certainly not least, Hollywood and Pentagon representatives at the ICT collaborate in the development of military training platforms that double as commercially available video games such as *C-Force*, and others in the pipeline (see www.ict.usc.edu).

The monstrous moral implications of all of this have already been well expostulated by James Der Derian. 'Virtuality,' he writes, 'collapses distance, between here and there, near and far, fact and fiction. It . . . disappears the local and the particular' (Der Derian, 2001: xviii). Thus the recent maturation of digital technologies of virtual representation constitute nothing less than 'the passage from material to immaterial forms of war'. On the battlefield, the enemy soldier has become nothing more than an avatar in a video game, 'an electronically signified "target of opportunity"' – one that we may eradicate with greater psychic ease than we can his carbon-based ancestor; one that is thus 'much easier to "disappear"' in both the symbolic and material register. 'In short,' Der Derian argues, 'we have the disappearance of war as we know it' (Der Derian, 2001: 120). New wars, instead, 'are fought in the same manner as they are represented, by military simulations and public dissimula-tions, by real-time surveillance and TV live-feeds' (Der Derian, 2001: xviii).

And indeed the military entertainment establishment appears to generate such public dissimulations in equal measure, aided in no small part by the increasing interconnectedness of players across its various sectors. Early on in the US offensive in Afghanistan, the Pentagon received a number of high-profile complaints from American journal-ists, subsequent to their being barred from American bases there, locked inside metal sheds so as to be prevented from covering stories and, of course, having their dispatches 'reorganized' on a more or less continual basis. Most notably, such events were taking place even as the ABC reality TV programme, *Profiles from the Front Lines*, and the MTV series *Military Diaries*, were granted wide-ranging access to Afghan sites otherwise deemed off limits (Barringer, 2002; Jensen, 2002). In April 2002, the CBS dramatic series *JAG* (Judge Advocate General), which is about legal life in the US military and is written by former military officers, aired an episode that imagines in the rosiest possible terms the first, dubiously constitutional US military tribunal to take place subsequent to September 11. The episode's scriptwriter 'learned details of the intensely debated rules on conducting the controversial tribunals two weeks before [Donald] Rumsfeld released them at a news conference on March 21' (Seelye, 2002). Pentagon officials do an equally fine job taking care of those Hollywood movie-makers happy to deliver appropriately 'patriotic' scripts in exchange for access to aircraft carriers.

That this sort of thing goes on is ultimately unsurprising: Hollywood cooperation with the US military is more or less as old as the movie business itself. It is the ubiquity, sophistication and complexity that has lately characterized this cooperation, however, that warrants our careful attention. Consider the recent instance of the NBC television movie, *Asteroid*, about an end-of-the-world scenario that is averted thanks to the deployment of an airborne laser owned by the US military. This piece of weaponry is actually in development, and a goodly chunk of its funding comes from General Electric (GE). GE is also the parent company of NBC. With properties like *Asteroid*, everybody inside the militainment nexus gets to do a deal and then go home happy. The film's producers agree to certain script recommendations from a Pentagon media liaison and, as reward, are granted full access to air force personnel, bases and aircraft for their shoot. At the same time, both the Pentagon and GE get the right kind of exposure for a new component of the still highly controversial 'Star Wars' weapons system (Down, 2001). It is the kind of PR coup the Pentagon's media office, widely regarded as the best in the entire US government, is pulling off with increasing frequency and aplomb.

A match made in PR heaven

But it is the ICT itself that constitutes the biggest PR coup that either the Pentagon or Hollywood (and here I do mean the Los Angeles-based movie business that makes up one part of the wider American entertainment industry) has seen in years. The ICT is a kind of gift from the PR gods, a match made in PR heaven for both parties, each of whom must contend with particularly persistent image problems on an ongoing basis. Table 11.1 suggests a number of commonly-held assumptions

Table 11.1 The Marriage of Hollywood and the military

Hollywood	The military
Glamour	Grit
Representation/Sensation	Action
Fake/Fictional	Real
Private/Domestic	Public
Sensitivity	Toughness
(World of emotion)	(World of calculation)
Feminine	**Masculine**
Gay friendly/Gay	Homophobic
Judeaophilic/Jewish	Near-exclusively Christian
Cosmopolitan	Patriotic/Jingoistic
Liberal/Leftwing	Conservative/Rightwing

about each group of actors. Each assumption contains both its truths and its falsehoods and the descriptors listed above are in no way meant to replace the real complexities embedded in each social formation. Yet deploying this schematic remains instructive if we wish to chart the potential for image management that the marriage of Hollywood and the military – at ICT and elsewhere – in fact represents for each party.

There are times when invested parties in Hollywood and the military each desire the general public to own *different* assumptions about their lifeworlds than the ones listed here (and for brevity's sake, we must tease out some of the table's broader implications by schematizing 'Hollywood' and 'the military' as individual actors rather than as complex groups of actors with contradictory and competing attributes and objectives). In the innermost register, represented in bold type in the table, Hollywood often appears preoccupied with its essentially feminine typification; the military can sometimes (though not regularly enough) appear uncomfortable with its masculine one. Consider first Hollywood's dilemma, from the top. Glamour is a Hollywood staple, and wartime anxiety, privation and loss often make its steady supply even more necessary. The same can be said, of course, for the gritty, patriotic genres of the Western and the war film. That Hollywood representations of gritty patriotism nonetheless fail to attribute to the movie industry the cachet of being 'a man's business', indispensable to any war effort, has a great deal to do with the next pair of assumptions. For if the realms of representation and sensation are Hollywood's to claim and the realm of action that of the warrior, then the worlds of commerce *and* of criticism still know whose claims to genuine social value they will ultimately endorse. Representation is only *representation*, after all. Nothing is really accomplished there – save, of course, those partially rehabilitated representations of real events, rather than fake or fictional ones, that are presented (adequately or otherwise) on the news.

Still the source of a powerful wariness, the world of representation and its suspect pleasures are best left to savour in times of quiet reflection, preferably in the private, domestic space of one's own home. Wiser to leave the public realm available for the real thing: mobilization, engagement, politics traditionally defined. Such calculated determination, naturally, requires a certain degree of toughness, of imperviousness to the allures of sentiment and emotional expression. Clearly, 'real men' don't work in Hollywood (and they don't write about it much either).

The military doesn't really have an image problem until we arrive at the table's centremost Feminine/Masculine dyad and proceed downward from there. Indeed one can easily imagine a Pentagon PR executive getting this far while doodling a similar list on the back of a napkin, then suddenly pushing back his or her chair in alarm. Surely a modern military, funded by a twenty-first century Congress and facing, consequently, twenty-first century recruitment challenges, cannot afford to convey the entire sweep of military experience as so exclusively masculine, thinks the executive. We know, of course, that progressive concerns such as these extend only so far: though women may now be firmly in the US military's recruitment sights, its resolve to retain institutionalized homophobia is also a matter of record. But the military's reputation as politically reactionary bodes badly nonetheless for recruitment strategies *vis à vis* its other target demographics. How does one successfully recruit Muslim-Americans to fight in a new 'cultural' war, for instance, from inside a corporate culture that is near-exclusively Christian? That often seems proud of the jingoism that attaches itself so easily to American patriotism? That appears to hold little esteem for any politics other than the conservative politics – now, perhaps, more than ever – of 'America: Love it or leave it'? All that is purported to be wholesome about life in the military is effectively jeopardized by these darker components of contemporary masculinism. What, thinks the executive again, is to be done?

Although the right normally loves to hate Hollywood for its effete, bleeding-heart liberal cosmopolitanism, it turns out the military actually needs some of these very qualities if it is to meet its new long-term goals. Under some crucially important circumstances and not a little paradoxically, the military now finds itself needing to appear *less* belligerent, *less* insensitive to issues of culture and identity as they play out in the wider world. That is to say, there are now times when the military needs to appear *less masculine* in conventional terms. Consider a paper co-written by a number of ICT staffers, presented in Montreal in 2001 at the creepily titled '5th International Conference on Autonomous Agents' (another name for computer-generated characters or synthespians, this one explicitly foregrounding artificial intelligence). The paper's authors scrutinized the story choices that were required in the above-mentioned immersive training environment, the Mission

Rehearsal Exercise (MRE). These were notably new story choices for the army: narrative scenarios emphasizing the emerging prominence of 'peacekeeping' and disaster relief in military life. 'Not only must [the military leaders of today and tomorrow] be experts in the Army's tactics, techniques and procedures,' the writers explained, 'but they must also be familiar with the local culture . . .'

> In the post-cold-war era, peacekeeping and other [similar] operations are increasingly common. A key aspect of such operations is that close interaction occurs between the military and the local population. Thus, it is necessary that soldiers understand the local culture and how people are likely to react.
>
> (Swartout *et al.*, 2002)

That the ICT actually proposes to meet the training challenge of cultural awareness by means of virtual technologies of immersion is a subject that cannot be addressed in this chapter, though it ought to become an urgent research priority for media studies.[1] Here, we need to remain focused on the changes to affective disposition that such training aims to achieve.

Indications abound across a wide spectrum of ICT documentation that 'feminizing' modulations in military discourse, from talk of war-making to that of peacekeeping, for example, continue to be highly desirable. Future Combat Systems LLC (FCS) is a joint venture between Sony Pictures, Imageworks Inc. and the Pandemic Group. FCS develops networked immersive training environments and is sponsored by the ICT, whose own role and purpose features prominently in an FCS pro-motional blurb along with descriptions of the role, purpose and future of virtual training technology itself:

> ICT foresees the expanded use of this advanced technology as a new system for immersive learning – the next step beyond the internet – with exciting applications to industry, entertainment and especially education. ICT aims to design these emotionally engaging immersive learning environments by tapping the nation's two greatest resources, technology and entertainment . . . Core technology to be developed by ICT includes: artificial intelligence which allows digital characters to react to situations like real people; incorporation of compelling, realistic story lines; systems which engage the senses of sight, sound, touch and smell; the next generation of computer hardware, from head-mounted displays to force-feedback devices; and computer networks through which hundreds of thousands of troops worldwide may participate together in live simulations.
>
> (FCS, 2002)

Harken, if you will, to all the words and phrases here that are nor-mally (if problematically) connected to the feminine sphere: learning, education, emotional engagement, compelling story lines, the sensa-tions of sound, touch and smell . . . Indeed the ICT's meta-meme, 'immersion' itself powerfully evokes qualities of tactility, embrace and maternal enclosure. One may now assume that the various training arms of the US military do not really train soldiers how to kill so much as they educate on matters of human narrative, emotion and culture, toward more effective peacekeeping inside the New World Order. 'My sense was, the Army wanted some fairy dust', ICT creative director James H. Korris revealed in the *New York Times*. 'They wanted to add some Hollywood creativity to their world . . . Just being able to come up with characters with a rooting interest, having a decent antagonist, all the things that are second nature for people here in L.A. – those were part of a tool set that represented a different point of view' (Hart, 2001).

Returning to our table, we discover how symbiotically Hollywood's dilemma continues to unfold alongside the military's. For if Hollywood's concerns about its feminized image as regards the politics of representation are sometimes partly submerged, the same cannot be said for its longstanding fears of being rejected by middle America as a haven for Jews and gay people ('they own the media', etc. see Carr, 2001 and Ehrenstien, 1998 respectively). Thanks to the ICT, however, Hollywood is no longer *about* Jews, homosexuals and the eccentric folks who love them 'entertaining' us with their fairy dust, their subversive flights of fancy. Now the word 'Hollywood' can evoke sentiments of patriotic responsibility rather than social decay. It can play a vital role in winning the war on terror. Hollywood, too, can help show the world who's boss.

Conclusion: researching the military entertainment establishment

A new and formidable technostructure (Galbraith, 1985) has been slowly but steadily emerging inside the North American polity for a couple of decades now. Adding multiple layers of practical and analytical significance to what was until lately reasonably termed the military-industrial complex, this new technostructure prominently features members of the entertainment industry working alongside academia, heavy industry, defense and other arms of government. It has been variously named: the Military Information Society (Levidow and Robins, 1989), the Military Entertainment Complex (Herz, 1997; Lenoir, 2000; Sterling, 1993), and, most recently, the Military-Industrial-Media-Entertainment Network (Der Darian, 2001). Although Der Derian's appellation is a bit of a mouthful, it possesses an admirable specificity, and this is now precisely what is required. Der Derian's book constitutes one of a very few attempts to chart empirically the key articulations of this highly complex, emerging macro-political formation,[2] and it is time for the rest of media studies to take up this task with greater energy and rigour.

In order to do so, however, we need to abandon media studies' previous commonplaces about the entertainment industry and start examining the real thing more closely. In the textual register, conceptualizing 'entertainment' merely as fluff or, conversely, as sinister ideological vehicle, appears increasingly incongruous to this North American eye and ear. Today, when nothing remains of mainstream US news media that is worth fighting for, Americans learn about how their government works more or less exclusively from *The West Wing*. Meanwhile, HBO has effectively replaced PBS as public broadcaster. In Canada, popular wisdom has it that more people turn to a CBC television comedy (*This Hour Has Twenty-two Minutes*) than to any other televisual source for political analysis of weekly events. And, as we have seen above, the easy dismissal of the entertainment industry is equally improbable in the realm of political economy, where entertainment revenues, not the great scientific enterprises of the former military industrial complex, are now driving twenty-first century high-tech innovation (Herz, 1997; Lenoir, 2000), and where conglomeration and other less formal instances of trans-sector cooperation work continually to consolidate the strength and durability of the military entertainment establishment.

This is not to say that the new military-entertainment entity – whatever one wishes to call it – enjoys a seamless and incontrovertible power. The ICT's above-mentioned, post 9/11 brainstorming session with Hollywood directors and screenwriters on future war narratives was the subject of considerable disapprobation among large portions of that town's liberal elite. Little, if any, public activity of a similar nature has taken place since (Teicholz, 2002). Though they may exist in fewer numbers in Silicon Valley and Orlando, liberal dissenters work inside the militainment machine everywhere. Media ethnographers need to talk to them, and soon. We need to uncover the regimes of control and spaces for agency that form their discourses, their work practices, their professional subjectivities, their sense of duty, and their sense of options. This is not as difficult an assignment as it may first appear. Despite the presence of some very large 'no-go' zones inside the military entertainment establishment, there remain numerous small, independent operations, sub-contracted digital animation companies, for instance, who are likely to be open to enquiry in ways that suburban Virginia has never been (and never will be). Indeed, the 'flexible', contracted nature of much work in Siliwood suggests that many people working behind terminals there have some connection, or know someone who has some connection, to software development somehow related to militainment. In any event and whatever the circumstances, fieldwork in the trenches of Siliwood is now absolutely essential if we are ever to make any sense of the many complicated sites of struggle on the new terrain of twenty-first century popular warfare culture. Given the stakes, rarely has an emerging research agenda mattered more.

Notes

1. Commendable in its attempts to theorize from the field (sometimes quite literally), James Der Derian's *Virtuous War* stands out as one of the very few recent attempts to delineate the social implications of such epistemic choices in a careful and systematic manner (Der Derian, 2001).
2. Also commendable in this regard is Kline, Dyer-Witherford and de Peuter (forthcoming, 2003). Most of the important work preceding these two volumes – and here one cannot fail to mention Virilio (1986, 1989) and Baudrillard (1995) in addition – is held too tightly by the reins of theory or is, conversely, less than entirely critical in its approach to the subject.

References

Barringer, Felicity (2002) 'Reality TV about G.I.'s on war duty', *New York Times*, February 21. Available at http://www.nytimes.com accessed April 2002.

Baudrillard, Jean (1995) *The Gulf War did not take place.* Bloomington: Indiana University Press.

CADRE (2002) 'Connections 2002: Educational Wargaming'. Available at www.cadre.maxwell.af.mil/wgweb/wgn/connections/default.htm accessed January 2003.

Carr, Steven Alan (2001) *Hollywood and anti-Semitism: A cultural history up to World War II.* Cambridge: Cambridge University Press.

Der Derian, James (2000) 'War games: The Pentagon wants what Hollywood's got', *The Nation.* 3 April: 41–44.

Der Derian, James (2001) *Virtuous War: Mapping the military-industrial-media entertainment network.* Boulder: Westview.

Down, John (2001) 'The song machine', 23 October. Available at www.open democracy.net/debates/article.jsp?id=1&debateId=67&articleId=369 accessed January 2003.

Dyer, Richard (1992) *Only entertainment.* London: Routledge.

Ehrenstein, David (1998) *Open secret: Gay Hollywood 1928–1998.* New York: William Morrow and Company.

FCS (Future Combat Systems LLC) (2002). Available at http://www.futurecombat. net Link available at ICT website: http://www.ict.usc.edu accessed December 2002.

Galbraith, John Kenneth (1985) *The New Industrial State.* 4th edn. Boston: Houghton Mifflin.

Gorman, Steve (2001) 'U.S. filmmakers mull terror scenarios for Army', *Variety Online,* October 9. Available at http://www.variety.com

Hart, Hugh (2001) 'Bringing Hollywood pizazz to military training', *New York Times.* Available at www.ict.usc.edu/press_archive/NYtimes11-15-01.html accessed December 2002.

Herz, J.C. (1997) *Joystick Nation: How Videogames Ate Our Quarters, Won Our Hearts, and Rewired Our Minds.* Toronto: Little, Brown.

Hesmondhalgh, David (2002) *The Cultural Industries.* London: Sage.

ICT (Institute for Creative Technologies) 'Welcome to ICT'. Available at http://www.ict.usc.edu/disp.php accessed January 2003.

Jensen, Elizabeth (2002) 'Reality TV eagerly marches off to war', *Los Angeles Times*, February 22.

Keighly, Geoff (2002) 'Could this be the next Disney? Electronic Arts makes one of every four videogames . . .', *Business 2.0/www.business2.com*. December. Available at http://www.business2.com/articles/mag/0,1640,45482,FF.html accessed December 2002.

Kline, Stephen, Dyer-Witheford, Nick and de Peuter, Greig (Forthcoming, 2003) *Digital Play: Technology, Markets, Culture*. Montreal: McGill-Queen's University Press.

Lenoir, Tim (2000) 'All but war is simulation: The military-entertainment complex'. Available at http://www.stanford.edu/dept/HPS/TimLenoir/ MilitaryEntertainmentComplex.htm accessed December, 2002.

Levidow, Les and Robins, Kevin (eds) (1989) *Cyborg Worlds: The Military Information Society*. London: Free Association Books.

Magder, Ted and Burston, Jonathan (2001) 'Whose Hollywood?: Changing relations and changing forms in the new North American entertainment economy', in D. Schiller and V. Mosco (eds) *Continental Order: Integrating North America for Cyber-Capitalism*. Lanham, MD: Rowman and Littlefield.

Miller, Toby, Govil, Nitin, McMurria, John and Maxwell, Richard (2001) *Global Hollywood*. London: British Film Institute.

Negus, Keith (1999) *Music Genres and Corporate Cultures*. New York: Routledge.

NRC (National Research Institute) (1996) *Modeling and Simulation: Linking Entertainment and Defense*. Committee on Modeling and Simulation: Opportunities for Collaboration Between the Defense and Entertainment Research Communities, Computer Science and Telecommunications Board, Commission on Physical Sciences, Mathematics, and Applications. Available at http:// bob.nap.edu/html/modeling accessed December 2002.

Seelye, Katharine Q. (2002) 'Pentagon plays role in fictional terror drama', *New York Times*. March 31: 12.

Sterling, Bruce (1993) 'War is virtual Hell', *Wired Magazine*, Vol. 1, No. 1. January. Available at http://www.wired.com/wired/archive/1.01/virthell.html accessed December 2002.

Swartout, W., Hill, R., Gratch, J. *et al.* (2002) 'Toward the Holodeck: Integrating Graphics, Sound, Character and Story', proceedings of 5th International Conference on Autonomous Agents, Montreal, Canada, June 2001. Link available at http://www.ict.usc.edu/disp.php?bd=pub_ai accessed December 2002.

Teicholz, Nina (2002) 'Privatizing propaganda', *The Washington Monthly Online*. December. Available at http://www.washingtonmonthly.com accessed December 2002.

Toynbee, Jason (2000) *Making Popular Music: Musicians, Creativity and Institutions*. London: Arnold.

Virilio, Paul (1986) *Speed and Politics*. New York: Semiotext(e)

Virilio, Paul (1989) *War and Cinema: The Logistics of Perception*. London: Verso.

12

THE NEW MEDIA ENVIRONMENT, INTERNET CHATROOMS, AND PUBLIC DISCOURSE AFTER 9/11

Bruce A. Williams

After two decades of declining news audiences, increased newspaper readership and skyrocketing ratings for network and cable news in the wake of 11 September 2001 was a relief to many. Professional journalists especially saw it as reassuring evidence that, when it really mattered, Americans still turned to them. While the nightly news broadcasts drew increased audiences, the big winners, with the most dramatic and long-term increase were the cable news networks. 'In the aftermath of the September 11 attacks, the Pew Research Center found, nine of ten Americans were getting their news primarily from television – but 45 per cent turned to cable, 30 per cent to the broadcast networks' (Kurtz, 2002). As significantly, ratings increased dramatically among the young, who had been abandoning 'serious' news for decades. In the wake of 9/11, 45 per cent of 18–34 year olds watched CNN, as opposed to 16 per cent in August. The figures went from 20 to 30 per cent on MSNBC and from 12 to 28.9 per cent at Fox News (Walker, 2001). The increased audience was not limited to television. Newspaper circulation increased, as did the circulation of newsweeklies like *Time* and *Newsweek* (up by almost 80 per cent in the weeks after the attacks) and of *The Atlantic Monthly* (Engel, 2002).

However, a closer look at the patterns of media consumption during this crisis suggests that journalists are 'whistling past the graveyard' if they conclude that Americans rely on them as they have in the past. According to an ABC News poll, almost half of all Americans now get news over the internet and over a third of them increased their reliance on online sources after September 11. Moreover, when seeking out information online, people were not limiting their search to traditional sources. For example, the website of Matt Drudge, the notorious political gossip, was the 20th most popular destination on the internet for the week following the terrorist attacks, the first time it had ever rated that highly. This made it more popular than the online *New York Times, Washington Post* or *USA Today*.

In this chapter, I argue that, given the performance of American journalists and the mainstream media after 9/11, heavy use of the internet and other new sources of information available in a changing media environment was a positive development. During coverage of this crisis, as is typical for most 'media events', the range of political discourse dramatically narrowed in mainstream journalism (Dayan and Katz, 1994). At the same time, the range of political debate was opening up on the internet, especially in the chatrooms upon which this chapter will focus.

One does not have to look very hard at the coverage of the terrorist attacks to find strong evidence that journalists quickly abandoned all pretense of objectivity and became the uncritical mouthpiece of the US state. For example, Dan Rather, host of the *CBS Evening News*, told the nation in his 17 September 2001 appearance on the *David Letterman Show* that: 'George Bush is the president, he makes the decisions and, you know, as just one American, he wants me to line up, just tell me where' (quoted in Engel, 2002). He was not the only journalist to 'line up' for the administration. Tim Russert on NBC, Fox news network correspondents, and many local broadcasters donned American flag pins (Hertsgaard, 2002). Those who refused to adopt this practice were vulnerable to retaliation. In Missouri, Republican state legislators threatened to withhold funding from the University of Missouri School of Journalism after the news director of the campus TV station banned the wearing of flag pins and ribbons on camera (Brazaitis, 2001).

The collapse of any sort of critical distance went beyond donning lapel pins or broadcasting American flag logos in the corner of screens. An Excellence in Journalism study funded by the Pew Charitable Trust concluded that post-9/11 coverage in American newspapers and television heavily favoured US positions. About half of the stories contained only viewpoints in line with the Bush administration policy. Television news stories, especially, only rarely included any criticism of the administration (Jurkowitz, 2002). On Fox (the highest-rated cable network), Brit Hume dismissed civilian deaths in Afghanistan as unworthy of news coverage (Hertsgaard, 2002: 13). CNN President Walter Isaacson required reporters to mention civilian casualties in Afghanistan only if they also recalled Americans killed in the September 11 attacks. Tellingly, this applied only to domestic, not international, CNN broadcasts (Hertsgaard, 2002: 14). Nor was the suspension of the normal values of professional journalism limited to the electronic media, as newspaper columnists in Texas and Oregon were fired for publishing criticisms of the President's handling of the attacks (Carter and Barringer, 2001).

A little further afield, when Bill Maher, the host of the ABC talk show *Politically Incorrect*, suggested that whatever else they were, the suicide attacks were not cowardly, as opposed to those who launched cruise missiles from hundreds of miles away, he was roundly criticized by presidential spokesperson Ari Fleischer. While admitting he had not seen a transcript of the broadcast, Fleischer nevertheless commented that 'it's a terrible thing to say; and it's unfortunate [and that] the reminder is to all Americans that they need to watch what they say, watch what they do, and that this is not a time for remarks like that. It never is'. Sponsors abandoned the show and ABC eventually canceled it (quoted in *Washington Post*, 2001: C7).

It should not be surprising to media scholars that discourse on mainstream media narrows during media events like the terrorist attacks of September 11. For a variety of reasons, in times of national crisis journalists are more likely to act as the voice of the state than as professionals searching out competing perspectives on the day's events. Daniel Hallin illustrates one dimension of this process in his study of media coverage of the Vietnam War (Hallin, 1986). Journalists believe that a story is defined by what credible sources are willing to say and that credible sources are primarily political elites. So, while reporters also believe that objectivity and fairness means telling both sides of a story, if elite opinion is uniform, then professional journalism is likely to reflect a quite limited range of political views. In the immediate aftermath of an event like the terrorist attacks, elites are likely to be most cautious about any criticisms of the government and, as a result, mainstream journalism is limited to this uniform perspective, excluding criticism and simply reflecting the perspective of the state. Moreover, these limitations of mainstream journalism are reinforced by the sensitivity to ratings and public opinion of news divisions and the media corporations that own them. As a result, in times of national crisis, when there are strong 'rally round the flag effects', journalistic coverage is likely to be very cautious about offending a patriotically aroused audience by criticizing the views of government officials.

Murray Edelman argues that the function of the media, especially mainstream journalism, during such 'political spectacles' is not to inform a democratic citizenry and enable them to form educated opinions about events, but rather to mobilize the public in support of already determined government policies. He draws the depressing conclusion that the only real option for citizens is not to pay attention (Edelman, 1985).

While the line of arguments advanced by media scholars may accurately describe the role of professional journalism, it is significant that the broader environment within which mainstream media operate has changed fundamentally in the last few decades. These changes, resulting in what I will call the new media environment, have destabilized the provision of political information (Williams and Delli Carpini,

2000, 2002). In particular, through proliferation of the sources from which political information can be gleaned and analyzed, this new environment has undercut the power of mainstream journalists to set the public agenda and act as gatekeepers. The most obvious change is the internet, which provides myriad sources of information, from actual newspaper articles from around the world to much more dubious and difficult to judge sources of information. The proliferation of cable stations, talk radio shows and so forth, all provide further new conduits of political information.

> Instead of a monolithic US government point of view, the audience today is receiving a global perspective, seeing news from the BBC and from Al-Jazeera, the Arab television station that first carried the bin Laden and Al-Qaeda tapes. The diversity of sources exists whether the American networks want to admit it or not . . . The audience is now in the position of juggling multiple viewpoints, like the reader of a novel with several unreliable narrators. . . Active viewers can flip around and get entire broadcasts from Britain or Canada, American allies who report with a vastly wider perspective and greater range.
>
> (James, 2001: 88)

Against this backdrop of a changing media environment, this chapter provides an analysis of discussions that occurred in a variety of internet chatrooms (chosen for their ideological diversity) on 11 September 2001 and the days immediately following the attacks. Despite Fleischer's injunction, chatrooms provided a place for Americans to say what they wanted, when the government was warning them to watch what they say.

This data was collected as part of a larger project examining the implications of the new media environment for American democracy. As part of this broader project, I have been collecting chatroom discussions on eleven sites. All discussion threads relevant to the 9/11 attacks on these sites were downloaded and analyzed. On the far right are the neo-Nazi Stormfront and Crosstar. On the more moderate right are Conservative Politics and the Conservative Political Action Conference's Free Republic Forum. On the far left are the anarchist AlterNet, Anarchist Anti-defamation League and Guerrilla News Network. On the more moderate left are MC Forums, hosted by Media Channel and Salon.com. Reflecting unique perspectives, difficult to classify politically are the Forum of the Black Entertainment Television Network and the chatrooms of the *Jerusalem Post*.

Internet chatrooms and media events

Preliminary analysis of the chatroom discussions reveal at least five ways in which they provided a space for the development of a much broader and more critical perspective than was available in mainstream coverage of the terrorist attacks: interactivity; availability and use of diverse sources of information; critical and collective examination of mainstream media texts; insularity of conversation, and civility. It is important to emphasize at the outset of this analysis that these characteristics are not the normal state of affairs on these chatrooms. Instead, as the mainstream media returned to more routine practices as the attacks receded in time, so too did the chatrooms. In short, alternative new media, like chatrooms, have a subtle and changing relationship to the patterns, practices, and diversity of mainstream journalism. If we are to fully understand the pitfalls and possibilities of public discourse and democratic politics in this new media environment, we must develop a fuller understanding of this relationship.

Interactivity

The chatrooms took advantage of the interactivity of the internet, through both synchronous and asynchronous discussions among individuals separated by vast distances, but united by common political, cultural, or social concerns. This meant that from the first moments of the attacks, while television broadcast images of the World Trade Center collapsing, many citizens tuned simultaneously to chatrooms in an attempt collectively to make sense of what they were seeing on the mainstream media. The possibilities opened up by interactivity resulted in fascinating, diverse, and quite sophisticated critical conversations among participants as they struggled, almost in real time, to interpret events being reported in the mainstream media. For example, on Salon.com, one participant identified Osama bin Laden as the primary suspect almost immediately (9:31 AM Eastern Time, 11 September 2001), long before the mainstream media broadcast this speculation.

Participants did not abandon their political ideologies. For example, on the extreme right-wing sites Stormfront and Crosstar, racist and anti-Semitic attitudes were still in evidence. On the former site, there was immediate speculation that the attacks were engineered by the Israeli Mossad because Arabs were not sophisticated enough to pull off such attacks on their own. One participant noted that 'It's all running on a ZOG script.' For the uninitiated, ZOG stands for 'Zionist Occupation Government', the 'true' rulers of the United States. But participants clearly wrestled with where such values left them with respect to the terrorist attacks. Another Stormfront poster cautioned about leaping to conclusions about who was to blame: 'Propaganda is going to get really thick and deep and we should reserve judgment'. The result was a pattern of much more diverse opinions, and even civil debate than was the usual case on these sites, or, as we have seen was the case in mainstream coverage of the attacks.

Availability and use of diverse sources of information

Chat rooms and their host sites, took advantage of the ease with which diverse sources of information were easily accessible over the internet. So, for instance, if one used the search engine of Yahoo and entered the term 'Afghanistan' (this was one of the five most popular search terms in the week following 9/11), the result was a list of links to news articles, some from the US press, but many from abroad. One of the articles, for example, came from a Pakistani English language newspaper and provided a detailed historical analysis of the Northern Alliance. This story was remarkable both because it provided much more information on this crucial alliance than appeared anywhere in the American press and because it could be so easily accessed. Interestingly enough, despite being printed in a military dictatorship, the article was far more critical of US and Pakistani policy than anything in the linked articles published in the US press.

The degree to which this availability of diverse sources of information challenges the hegemony of mainstream journalism is captured by Carrin James of *The New York Times*:

> American reporters and anchors are clearly uncomfortable with this influx of foreign information, whether it's friendly or not. On MSNBC, Brian Williams was almost apologetic about showing the bin Laden tape so often, saying with a tone of resignation that we do have a free press and, anyway, the tape would have gotten out somehow. (In the pre-cable, pre-internet era, it probably would not have.)
>
> (James, 2001: B8)

The chatrooms themselves took advantage of this characteristic of the new media environment with many cross-postings of articles from quite diverse sources. These diverse sources were almost always examined from the perspective of the chatroom's ideological position and used to buttress arguments being made by participants. Some sources were obviously dubious, but used nevertheless. So, for example, there was much reference on Stormfront to a story, originally published in the Arabic press, that Jews had been warned to not show up at their World Trade Center offices on the day of the attacks. This was used as evidence to buttress the arguments, noted above, that the Mossad was behind the attacks. Yet, as we shall see, this site also saw the posting of an article from 1911 by the Jewish writer and anarchist Emma Goldman.

On the moderate left-wing Media Channel chatroom, in response to television's repeated showing of a video of cheering Palestinians, there were links to a *Guardian* (London) story on how the US fails to understand anti-American sentiment abroad as well as links to articles in Singapore newspapers warning against blaming all Muslims for the attack. Another participant posted the text of a 1983 Presidential proclamation praising Afghan freedom fighters, many of whom went on to establish the Taliban state.

Critical and collective interrogation of mainstream media

Interactivity and the ease with which diverse sources of information can be accessed led to a third characteristic of these conversations: the critical examination of mainstream media coverage and, more broadly, government responses to the attacks. Across the ideological spectrum, conversations routinely interrogated the connection between US foreign policy and attacks. This sort of critical examination of the images provided by the mainstream coverage was not limited to moderate sites.

On Stormfront, in response to repeated showing of the images of cheering Palestinians just mentioned, one poster asked: 'What is the difference between Arabs dancing in the streets and us celebrating the bombing of Yugoslavia?'. On 13 September, a thread entitled 'Patriotic Idiots' started and one poster asked, 'What about US bombing of Serbia or pharmaceutical factory in Afghanistan [*sic*]'. At the other end of the ideological spectrum, on the Anarchist Anti-defamation League, one participant asked: 'Have you seen the Palestinians and the Egyptians celebrating these attacks? The sad thing is, most Muslims are actually glad this happened'. Another poster immediately replied:

> That is absolute crap. You saw the unreflecting, instant reaction of about 20 Palestinians over and over, who have had their lives torn apart by American hardware. Their reaction was of course totally wrong. You are allowing the media to draw you in to their war drum beating. Obscenity was seen on a much larger scale in 1991 when thousands of Americans cheered in pubs the deaths of 200,000 Iraqis. You know now what the destruction of 2 buildings is like. Imagine whole cities destroyed, if that is possible without experiencing it. WE DON'T WANT MORE WAR. Stay Sane. Keep Cool. God bless.

Indeed, on chatrooms across the ideological spectrum, there was vigorous debate about the connection between US support for Israel and the 9/11 attacks. This sort of analysis was common in the foreign press. For instance, on 14 September, the London-based *Independent* ran a commentary calling for a reconsideration of US-led anti-Iraq sanctions and unreflexive support for Israel. Yet in the mainstream US press, any examination of the connection between US foreign policy and the attack was virtually absent and, if voiced, labeled as treasonous, as Susan Sontag found out after publishing a critical piece in the *New Yorker*. Only in chatrooms, often in the most politically extreme, were such arguments seriously debated in America. So, again on Stormfront, one participant posted a quote from Osama bin Laden claiming that attacks were in retaliation for US support of Israel.

On the far left Guerrilla News Network a participant wrote:

> What really lies at the heart of this issue is the painting of all Arabs as terrorists or nameless/faceless religious heretics who don't really DESERVE their own country, their own freedoms, their own rights. Given this attitude of the American people, who, on average, don't give a F**K about Arab rights, the political machine is free to outright (i.e. outrageous) support of Israel regardless of the atrocities they commit. Granted the problems in the M/E are not easily resolved, but the Israelis and Bush are moving towards policies of intolerance, which is only inflaming the Palestinian refugees who have no hope other than that provided by (a) the solidarity of the international community towards their plight or, failing that (b) the armed resistance against their oppressors. Its NOT an attack on freedom (duh), its a wake up call to the Americans. The export of terrorism WILL boomerang back. Remember that there are some 6M Palestinians in camps who have never known any of the freedoms that America espouses. The suicide bombers come from these camps, second and third generation welfare recipients with no hope for a normal life.

Insularity of conversations

A fourth feature follows from the way chatrooms create the opportunity for relatively insular conversation amongst only like-minded individuals who may be separated by time and space. While the mainstream media reiterated themes of national unity, the chatrooms allowed different groups of Americans to debate what the impact of the attacks was for them specifically. This allowed the critical interrogation of the role of the state (and the use of the media to mobilize support for administration policies).

At a time when many boards were seeing a dramatic increase in traffic, many by new participants, there were often debates over how (or whether) to maintain group boundaries and ideological purity. On Stormfront there was concern over both the need to guard against 'blind haters' as well as a concern about 'liberals' coming on the board to foment discord. On Crosstar, a board that had much less traffic than Stormfront, there was an initial flurry of discussion about keeping 'dissident voices' (i.e. liberal) off the board. One poster objected to allowing a particularly argumentative participant (Crimson) to contribute messages to this moderated discussion:

> There are plenty of chat rooms where 'Crimson' (appropriately named) can spout his ideology, but this is not one of them. Neither is Crosstar receptive to those trying to 'disguise' themselves as 'one of us,' to try to smear or distort us. Crosstar is for Nationalists, those seeking information about Nationalism and Nationalists dissecting points and sharing information among themselves.

This boundary maintenance was defended by another poster who argued, ominously, that: 'Crosstar Forum is moderated to be free of "noise" by would-be detractors, as well. Nationalists have fought hard for their internet "place in the sun" and they are not about to waste time arguing with their foes on their own turf. And it will be the same when we say of all of America: "This land is our land."'

While disturbing when defended in this manner, in many ways insular conversations that are not easily accessible to the wider public play a positive role by allowing marginalized groups to clarify their distinct values in opposition to those of the society-at-large within the safety of a sympathetic and homogeneous group. This is especially important during media events, when the perspective of mainstream coverage is particularly hegemonic. So, for example, on a chatroom hosted by the BET Network, there was a thoughtful discussion of how African-Americans were responding to 9/11. The conversation centered on whether it was possible to reconcile black beliefs about racist police and fire departments with the heroic images of these institutions in the wake of the terrorist attacks. A particularly interesting thread was prompted by the appearance on the television show *Saturday Night Live* of surviving firefighters – all of whom were white. Posters wrestled with how the undeniable heroism of these individuals contrasted with their participation in the Fire Department's discrimination against blacks.

Interesting debates also took place on left-and right-wing sites about the degree to which the current crisis did, or did not, justify forgetting past criticisms of liberals or conservatives, as the case may be. On the anarchist AlterNet, there was much admiration of the actions of Mayor Rudolph Giuliani and defense of President Bush's failure to return quickly to the White House. What makes these perspectives distinct from their expression in the mainstream media is the degree to which they are always challenged in these political sites. So, an atack on the defenders of these two politicians usually vilified on this board started: 'So tell me, all you wimps . . .'

On Salon.com a participant wrote: 'I absolutely cannot stand George W. Bush, but this is just one of those times to rally behind the President, as well as Cheney, Powell, and Rumsfeld. Sometimes extraordinary events spur ordinary men to greatness. I hope this is one of those times'. On this same board, after attacks on defenders of Bush, a participant wrote (placing the remarks of another poster in italics):

I would like to say a few things . . .

A lot of you have said some incredibly stupid things, and it reveals a stupidity that runs pretty deep. *'This would have never happened if Clinton were in office!'* Bullshit. Who was in office the last time the WTC was bombed? *'Where's Bush now? We need leadership! His response is ineffective!'* What the hell do you expect him to do? He's the President, he's in a secure location, and he's formulating a response. That's what Presidents do. *'In his first address, he acted like it was over, and it wasn't'* How was he supposed to know? If he would have waited, you would have screamed and whined because he didn't come out and say something to you. *'Bush should resign for this. His job is to protect the people, and he didn't do that!'* Good grief . . . that doesn't even warrant a response.

Let's drop the partisan crap, for one brief moment, and look at what we're saying. Thousands of innocent people have died, and some of you would like to think that GWB did this? ON PURPOSE?!! Or that he's HAPPY ABOUT IT? Good God, people, listen to yourselves. Whether or not you like his politics, he is human, like the rest of us. This is a tragedy for America, and the world. This administration may not be perfect, and you may disagree with them on policy, but I guarantee they are grieving just as much as you are. With the thousands of people dead, do you think they don't have friends and family affected by this?

Think before you post, please.

Perhaps the most interesting debate I found occurred on Stormfront. Some posters immediately called for closing the borders and excluding all immigrants (here, they reflected the sentiments voiced by many political leaders on television). However, many disagreed, expressing concern about the closing down of civil liberties and the implications for domestic right-wing groups who might be blamed for the attacks. On the 'Patriotic Idiots' thread, noted above, debates developed over how white racists should respond to the attacks. One poster asked: 'Why be sad over attack on NYC/WTC which are hubs of anti-white, anti-human activity?' But another responded: 'My grandfather enlisted the day after Pearl Harbor . . . All politics/ideology aside, our COUNTRY WAS ATTACKED YESTERDAY.'

One poster launched a diatribe against ZOG arguing that Jews do not fight for their country, they only manipulate others to do so. She went on to argue that it was the manipulation of patriotism and nationalism by the media, in the service of the state (both, in her view controlled by Jews), resulting in a tendency to drop any specific grievances that groups might have against the government, that was the great danger during times of crisis (compare this argument, minus the Jewish conspiracy, of course, with Edelman's arguments, discussed above). Somewhat amazingly, she posted an article from 1911 by the Jewish writer Emma Goldman criticizing the uses of patriotism for just these purposes. However, this argument was attacked by a participant who pointed out that Jews have actually served and died in the armed forces well out of proportion to their small number in the population.

On 14 September a Stormfront participant quoted John Locke's warning about the dangers of giving up power to the legislature in support of a thoughtful critique of the power of government to act unaccountably in times of crisis. Finally, there was a poster who argued that American Aryans have far more in common with Jews than with Arabs and called for something he called 'a non-racist white nationalism.'

Civility

The final characteristic of the chatroom discussions was the general tenor of tolerance to those with whom one might disagree. In the immediate wake of 9/11, even the most extreme sites adopted, or tried to adopt, a tolerance to divergent views which was decidedly uncharacteristic of their rhetorical styles in ordinary times. Such civility is essential for political debate and here it greatly expanded the range of views expressed, even on the most ideologically extreme sites (like Stormfront).

On the moderate Conservative Political Action Conference, one poster, adopting the usual tone of the board, blamed Clinton and liberals:

> They've put down our President over the past 8 months plus – That contributed to showing our Country as being WEAK enough to prompt outsiders to Attack Us? Bad enough that so many backed and defended Clinton cutting our defense so much during his years. So NOW can we at least rally and all come together?

However, the response was quite atypical for this board:

> It's really impolitic to use this occasion as a means to launch into partisan political arguments. One could just as easily criticize the Bush decision to spend money on his missile defense system. I've been arguing to people on this forum for months now that the real threat now to our national security is HERE, in THIS country, from people like those who did what happened on Tuesday. This event bears out what I was arguing. Clinton's policies probably deserve some criticism, but so do Bush's. What's important is that we can now move in a definite direction. I think we all can come together now and agree. The battle has been joined by everyone.

Similarly, on the moderate left-wing Salon.com, after a poster argued that President Bush was cowardly for not returning immediately to the White House after the attacks, another participant responded:

> I hate Bush as much as anyone here but these comments about him protecting his ass as though he were cowering under a school desk somewhere instead of broadcasting from the oval office where he belongs are every bit as asinine as the idiots who are inciting violence against the 'towel heads in 7-11'. Grow up, people. This is likely an act of war, not a photo op for the shrub.

To which another poster added: 'He's not the President we want, but he has to do the job. Let's let him do that'.

At a more extreme position on the ideological spectrum, the anarchist AlterNet hosted an interesting debate over the meaning of displaying the American flag and whether or not participants were going to attend anti-war rallies. Many argued that, while they usually supported such demonstrations, they could not attend right now, given the magnitude of the attack on the United States. The divergent viewpoints and civility with which these positions were treated was strikingly different from the more normal ideological uniformity, enforced by vicious flaming.

I don't want to claim, however, that this tone of tolerance was universal, either within or across sites. So, on the Anarchist Anti-defamation League Site, when a participant from the UK said: 'It's about time someone showed those yanks a lesson, if I knew who was behind it I would shake them firmly by the hand'. The responses were first: 'What are you talking about, Limey?' And then: 'Turn on the TV! REMEMBER THE TOWERS! KILL SAND NIGGERS!' Or on Stormfront, to the argument mentioned above that Jews had actually served in the armed forces out of proportion to their numbers, came this response (by the same person who posted the article by Emma Goldman): 'You little Jew commie socialist lover . . .' To which the target of this attack replied simply: 'This conversation is over'.

Additionally, this spirit of tolerance, even when it did emerge, was quite short-lived on most sites. Yet, it is important to also remember the intolerance to alternative viewpoints in the mainstream media as witnessed by the reaction to Susan Sontag and Bill Maher.

Conclusions

What conclusions can we draw from this snapshot of chatroom discussions in the wake of the 9/11 attacks? First, the new media environment makes the dynamics of media events quite different than was the case when the mainstream controlled virtually all the gates through which political information flowed to the public. If one limited oneself to simply watching mainstream print and electronic journalism, the conclusion might be that coverage was pretty much par for the course during media events. However, the most significant influence of the new media environment is precisely that we are no longer limited to the mainstream media. Now, those new axes of political information open up, as they gain larger audiences and draw participants from a wider variety of backgrounds, at precisely the time that the viewpoints examined in mainstream coverage are closing down. These alternative venues also can draw upon a wider variety of information than formerly available.

Secondly, chatrooms, in particular, allow the collective interrogation of mainstream media. While it was always possible to criticize the media by 'talking back' to the television, as many of us do, this is usually a solitary and often alienating activity with little potential for collective action. Chatrooms, in contrast, allow groups of like-minded individuals to develop a collective and social perspective on events of the day. The chatroom provides an opportunity for a form of collective and critical resistance to hegemonic messages not easily available before. It is the ability to hold asynchronous and synchronous conversations, combined with the wide availability of diverse sources of information, that gives chatrooms and other similar new media venues their potential for new forms of political action. In this way, for better or worse, they provide a way to resist mainstream messages, providing an alternative to Edelman's dismal conclusion that the only way to resist is to ignore those messages.

Third, despite their political potential, it is important not to over-estimate the significance of these chatrooms. Against the massive audiences for the mainstream media, the numbers of individuals turning to chatrooms is, indeed, miniscule. Moreover, while some of the chatrooms I monitored saw dramatically increased postings, others virtually shut down during the crisis (in my sample, the Conservative Politics chatrooms, for example), suggesting that their members were turning to other sources of information, most likely the mainstream media.

Finally, despite their often ominous and offensive discourse, it is important to emphasize the value of chatrooms and other new media venues especially during times of crisis. In many ways, the routine coverage of the major media outlets (and here I include most mainstream internet outlets) is more troubling than the most hateful rhetoric on neo-Nazi sites. This is so because no non-believer (nor most believers) accepts that such sites are providing the balanced truth, but this is not true of mainstream media, especially during times of crisis. Indeed, during crisis, the diversity of discourse opened up on even the most extreme web sites, precisely as diversity closed down in the mainstream. It is the dynamics of this relationship between mainstream, more traditional sources of political information, and the sources offered by new media, that require more study by media analysts. As well, this relationship warrants study by those concerned with the pitfalls and possibilities for enriching democratic politics posed by the new media environment. This new environment opens up the possibilities for critical discourse which, as always, demands far more of individual citizens than do more elite-driven approaches to politics.

References

Brazaitis, T. (2001) 'Lamenting the Loss of Free Speech', *Cleveland Plain Dealer*, 30 September, p. H3.

Carter, B. and Barringer, F. (2001) 'A Nation Challenged: Speech and Expression – In Patriotic Times, Dissent is Muted', *New York Times*, 28 September, A1.

Dayan, D. and Katz, E. (1994) *Media Events*. Cambridge, MA: Harvard University Press.

Edelman, M. (1985) *Constructing the Political Spectacle*. Chicago: University of Chicago Press.

Engel, M. (2002) 'Has Anything Changed?' *The Guardian*, Media Section, 2 September, p. 3.

Hallin, D. (1986) *The Uncensored War: The Media and Vietnam*. Oxford: Oxford University Press.

Hertsgaard, M. (2002) *In the Eagle's Shadow*. London: Bloomsbury.

James, C. (2001) 'A Public Flooded with Images From Friend and Foe Alike', *New York Times*, 10 October, p. B8.

Jurkowitz, M. (2002) 'Fighting Terror/the Home Front the Media; Pro-Us Tendency is Seen in Survey', *The Boston Globe*, 28 January, p. A9.

Kurtz, H. (2002) 'Troubled Times for Network Evening News', *Washington Post*, 10 March, p. A1.

Walker, J. (2001) 'Younger Audiences', *Media News*. 34 (44) 7 November, p. 4.

Washington Post (2001) 'WJLA Pulls 'PI' a Second Time', 28 September, p. C7.

Williams, B.A. and Delli Carpini, M.X. (2000) 'Let Us Entertain You: The Politics of Popular Media', in *Mediated Politics: The Future of Political Communication*, edited by Lance Bennett and Robert Entman. Cambridge: Cambridge University Press.

Williams, B.A. and Delli Carpini, M.X. (2002) 'Political Relevance in the New Media Environment', *The Chronicle of Higher Education*, 19 April.

13

THE MEDIA, THE 'WAR ON TERRORISM' AND THE CIRCULATION OF NON-KNOWLEDGE

Cynthia Weber

What has the media been telling us about the 'war on terrorism'? This is a question that currently engages many scholars, commentators, and viewers of the media. When not asking what the media is telling us, we ask instead what the media is not telling us. This essay is concerned with a particular combination of these two questions. Its focus is on what the media is not telling us when the media is telling us about the war on terrorism. My argument is simply this: that it is at least as important to examine what I call the media's circulation of non-knowledge as it is to examine the media's circulation of knowledge. The circulation of non-knowledge is the incessant, conscious exchange of some narratives, images, and ideas so that others remain unconscious, even when we are reading stories that engage them or are viewing images that portray them. The media – be it news media, entertainment media, or programs and networks in which news and entertainment overlap – circulate non-knowledge not by ignoring news stories but by representing them in such a way that their exclusive focus on one aspect of the story makes it possible to neglect other, potentially more important aspects of the same story.

A prime example of a network that circulates non-knowledge is CNN, especially its 24-hour Headline News channel. What makes CNN so interesting is not only its fusion of news and entertainment but also the declaration its acronym makes. CNN does not only stand for the Cable News Network. Employing phonetic license, the acronym CNN announces that this network stands for the Circulation of Non-kNowledge.[1] In the remainder of this essay, I tell a story that illustrates how non-knowledge circulates in American media representations of 'the war on terrorism', with CNN as well as Hollywood cinema being primary sites of such representations. What interests me about these media representations is not only what they do and do not tell

Americans about 'the war on terrorism', but also – and arguably more importantly – what they do and do not tell Americans about themselves.[2]

American media representations of the 'War on Terrorism'

My story begins in Pearl Harbor – the site of 'the first great sneak attack on America' (Harden, 2001) by the Japanese during World War Two – and moves to Palm Harbor – the site of the latest 'sneak attack' on America. Palm Harbor was the home of 15-year-old white American male Charles Bishop. Less than four months after hijacked commercial airliners crashed into and caused the collapse of the World Trade Center Twin Towers, Bishop stole a single-engine Cessna and flew it into the 42-story Bank of America tower in downtown Tampa. In a suicide note found at the scene, Bishop expressed sympathy for Osama bin Laden and the September 11 hijackers.

All sorts of knowledge and non-knowledge about 'the war on terrorism' and America's self-image circulate in the Pearl Harbor/Palm Harbor story. These forms of knowledge circulate not only through the Cable News Network but also through other networks of non-knowledge, like Hollywood cinema. While Hollywood films like *Black Hawk Down* (Sony Pictures, 2001) and *Behind Enemy Lines* (Fox, 2001) have dominated discussions of America's representations of war in the wake of September 11, I find the American re-release of the film *Pearl Harbor* (Touchstone Pictures, 2001) just after September 11 to be more telling.

The film *Pearl Harbor* is of interest because the idea of Pearl Harbor functions in an American imaginary as the moment when, in America's own narration of its history, America's legacy of sustained heroic global engagement began. While this is the sort of knowledge Americans absorb simply by living in America, this knowledge was made explicit by President George W. Bush on 7 December 2001, the 60th anniversary of the Japanese attack. President Bush said, 'What happened at Pearl Harbor was the start of a long and terrible war for America. Yet, out of that surprise attack grew a steadfast resolve that made America free-dom's defender. And that mission – our great calling – continues to this hour, as the brave men and women of our military fight the forces of terror in Afghanistan and around the world' (Bush, 2001a).

Given the dramatic re-circulation of ideas, images, and emotions about Pearl Harbor, it is not surprising that Pearl Harbor itself became a material site of return for relatives and colleagues of the firefighters, police officers, and rescue workers killed or injured on September 11. They visited Hawaii at the invitation of the state's governor over Pearl

Harbor remembrance week. Since September 11, World War Two veterans of Pearl Harbor have been experiencing renewed popularity. As they returned to Pearl Harbor on the 60th anniversary of the attack, 'they have been applauded in airport departure lounges, beatified by pilots in midflight monologues and pestered for autographs in Honolulu hotel lobbies' (Harden, 2001). Americans seem to be thanking Pearl Harbor vets post-September 11 not only for their past protection of the nation's land and lives but also for their present protection of the nation's image.

As circulated in cinemas, editorials, and official policy statements, America's narrative about Pearl Harbor unleashed some powerful ideas about 'the war on terrorism' and about America itself. In addition to heroizing the global mission of America as the benevolent leader of the 'free world', loved and admired within and beyond its shores, Pearl Harbor morally justified US 'war on terrorism' by aligning this war (if it is a war) with a time before America questioned its moral purity, i.e. before America dropped the nuclear bomb on Hiroshima (Engelhardt, 1995). By twinning Pearl Harbor with September 11, America reclaims its legacy to moral purity which it enacts in its war against terror. As one American commentator speaking about the United States' war on terrorism in early November 2001 put it, 'Certainly in the States right now I don't think you have any sense of moral ambiguity about the rightness of this particular cause that America's engaged in. September 11 has an almost December 7 kind of clarifying impact on Americans. So I don't think that the war on terrorism is going to be fraught with ambivalence and ambiguity, at least in the American imagination' (Doherty, 2001). Whereas Tom Engelhardt argues that America's own sense of moral purity ended when it dropped the nuclear bomb on Hiroshima, President Bush reinvested America with moral purity in its response to September 11 by reciting a World War Two narrative that claimed 'the terrorists are the heirs of fascism' and temporally linked that claim to Pearl Harbor, before the United States dropped the bomb (Bush, 2001a; Engelhardt, 1995: 10).

Pearl Harbor also taps into America's pre-Vietnam belief that its history is the history of progress. In this view, American victory in any war – including America's 'war on terrorism' – is inevitable. As Engelhardt explains, 'Triumphalism was in the American grain . . . . After all, hadn't American history [as Americans told it to themselves] been a processional of progress from the moment European explorers and settlers first set foot on the continent?' (Engelhardt, 1995: 10–11). Engelhardt argues that the United States' belief in its inevitable triumph was finally frustrated in Vietnam. But President Bush's appeal to Pearl Harbor in the wake of September 11 reactivated what Engelhardt calls its 'triumphal certainty of World War II' (Engelhardt, 1995: 13), something the American mood longed for in the aftermath of its most recent tragedies. This is why President Bush could tell the nation: 'We are fighting to protect ourselves and our children from violence and fear. We're fighting for the security of our people and the success of liberty. We're fighting against men without conscience, but full of ambition – to remake the world in their own brutal images. For all these reasons we're fighting to win – and win we will' (Bush, 2001a).

Finally, Pearl Harbor marks America's enemy as a racial and religious other who is primarily located outside of America and who, when located within America, can be neutralized through internment as Japanese-Americans were after the bombing of Pearl Harbor. In this American narrative, Shinto and Buddhist Japanese are replaced by Muslim Arabs. While the internment of Muslim Americans as portrayed in the film *The Siege* (Twentieth Century Fox, 1998) did not materialize in post-9/11 America, and while President Bush argued that 'Islam means peace' and America was not at war with Islam, racial and religious profiling across America has been employed in an attempt to secure United States' territory (Bush, 2001b). In this narrative, Arabs and Muslims become anticipated terrorist threats to American 'homeland security', while non-Arabs and non-Muslims are marked as unantici-pated threats to America. Furthermore, even when non-Arabs or non-Muslims act violently against the American homeland, they are rarely labeled as terrorists.

From Pearl Harbor to Palm Harbor

In light of all of this, it is not surprising that the national imaginary about Pearl Harbor and the materiality of the place Pearl Harbor, morphed into America's imaginary about September 11 and the material sites of the 9/11 attacks, particularly New York City. Politically, socially, and culturally, re-releasing the film *Pearl Harbor* after September 11 allowed Americans collectively to exercise their individual patriotism by going to the cinema and, in so doing, to arm themselves with the rhetorical hardware they needed to fight the terrorist 'heirs of fascism' (Bush, 2001a).

Whereas Pearl Harbor provides America with a sense of historic destiny, moral duty, and heroic agency by making America's glorious past present, Palm Harbor disturbs each and every one of these American sensibilities and their connections to September 11. The most striking way in which it does this is through its grammar of repetition through imitation. Visually, this aspect of Palm Harbor is unmistakable, for Charles Bishop's act replicated in miniature the events in New York City on September 11. But why?

It is why Bishop did what he did that captured America's attention. Everyone seemed to wonder what could possibly drive a white, 15-year-old American male who 'earned straight A's, carried the flag at school assemblies, planned bake sales for his school, entered essay contests run by the Daughters of the American Revolution and wanted to join the Air Force' (Rosenberg, 2002) to commit suicide in solidarity with Osama bin Laden and the September 11 hijackers?

Answering this question became the focus of the US news media. Stories about Bishop's motives abound.[3] Maybe Bishop was a depressed loner who changed schools too often (Blair et al., 2002) or he could have been an acne-marked, Accutane-maddened adolescent made suicidal by prescription (CNN.com, 2002a). Or his parents' ineffectually-executed suicide pact as teens who were denied a marriage licence could have had lingering effects on their son (Associated Press, 2002). Or maybe Charles Bishop – formerly Charles Bishara – acted as he did because of his Arab Syrian (albeit Christian) heritage (CNN.com, 2002b).

By focusing on the question 'what made him do it?', the American media largely overlooked the question, 'what does Bishop's act do to how we think about the war on terrorism and about America itself?' Or, put differently, by circulating some silly yet captivating theories about Bishop's motives, the American media perpetuated the circulation of non-knowledge about the war and about itself, thereby keeping from America what it did not want to know.

What America did not want to know in the Palm Harbor case is that Bishop's crash stood not only as a memorialization of September 11 that ran counter to official American remembrances like Pearl Harbor and tidy narratives of treason and betrayal (as in the case of American 'Taliban' fighter John Walker Lind). Even more disturbingly, Bishop's crash caused the collision of two American narratives that hitherto had no connection – September 11 and school shootings.

In recognition of this, one American commentator dubbed Bishop 'Charles Bishara Bishop – Osama bin Columbine' (Vitello, 2002), a name that captures the multiple fears about what Americans thought they knew about the connections between terror, race, and religion and the fears Americans did not want to know about youthful exchanges and imitations of violence in public places. The naming of Bishop's Syrian heritage via his original surname, Bishara, and the linking of it to bin Laden recognizes, on the one hand, what Americans think they know about race and terror – that Arab races and terror go together. Yet on the other hand, this linking recognizes that Bishop's personal history challenges America's official national history around race and ethnicity, a narrative about assimilation of the melting pot to the incorporation and respect of benign difference through multiculturalism. Substituted in place of this particular national narrative by Bishop's name is one narrative that fails safely to incorporate personal histories or respect and celebrate their claims to difference, be they Bishop's Syrian ancestry (however distant and partial) or Bishop's repeated claims to his teachers and friends that for all he knows he might be Arab (CNN.com, 2002b). Instead, Bishop's personal history becomes a conduit for other evil influences to infiltrate America – Osama bin Laden, Arabness, terrorism.

And so through the name of Osama bin Laden seems to pass an infectious identification with – and indeed a glorification of – violence against America. By imitating the act of hijacking a plane and crashing it into an American skyscraper, Bishop's act seems to stand as evidence of the infectiousness of Arabness and terrorism for an America trying to protect itself against foreign terrorist forces. For this is a case of a home-grown American boy who identified with a foreign terrorist act by violently re-enacting a foreign terrorist plot, albeit in miniature. By reading Bishop's act as the infectious act of Arab terrorism, the act at first seems to fit neatly within the clash of civilizations rhetoric popularized after September 11, especially in the early days of the war. And yet it is not quite so simple. For Bishop's act makes a mockery of the US foreign policy position on the war against terror that 'you are either with us or against us' (or, in Samuel Huntington's terms, you belong to one civilization or another) by acknowledging that the 'us' in the US of A marks a fractured, multiple subjectivity, some aspects of which may well defy safe assimilation, be they (in this case) ethnicity or 15-year-old white American boys.

In so doing, Bishop's act also makes a farce of America's discourse on homeland security, for it locates dangers not only within America territory but within the American nation and its citizens. Bishop's act suggests that if America truly wants to secure its homeland, it must secure itself and its citizens from 'inappropriate' identifications. And this, of course, is something that Americans already know cannot be achieved.

Indeed, the failure – or really, inability – to secure America from dangerous identifications is articulated in the final part of Bishop's new name – Columbine. Charles Bishop is the ordinary name of an ordinary American teenager, whereas Columbine is the site of one of America's most violent school shootings. This part of Bishop's new nickname reminds us that ordinary American teens regularly commit dramatic acts of violence against their teachers, their peers, and themselves.

Bishop's act was, of course, not a school shooting. It did not involve his high school, take place on school property, or take as its target teachers or students from the school. Nor was it directed against Bishop's other school – his flight school. In spite of these obvious differences, Bishop's act and school shootings in the US share striking similarities, both in deed and in effect. As deeds, both are very public acts of violence carried out in and targeted against pubic spaces almost exclusively by white, middle-class rural boys (although this is changing). Both are carried out by children who are model students. So described, they are not usually marked as future troublemakers but seem to have assimilated into social institutions and rarely exhibit signs of alienation.

It is only retrospectively – after the violence – that these youths are characterized as 'troubled young men'.

Finally, school shootings and Bishop's act proceed according to logics of mimetic identification – identifications of acts with acts. Although of course there was an 'original' school shooting and, in Bishop's case, an 'original' episode of a teenager flying a stolen plane into a skyscraper, the original is less important than what the original copies (and subsequent 'originals' copy as well). School shootings often copy violence depicted in the media, be this on film, on television programs, or in newscasts and newspapers reporting school shootings. In the logic of school shootings, an identification is often made with an act of violence and copied, albeit in a slightly different form. The same can be said of Bishop's act. It is a copy of the September 11 hijacked jetliners crashing into New York City's Twin Towers. Bishop's act, like acts of school shootings, identifies through imitating prior acts of media/mediated violence.

Copycat violence

Because they adhere to logics of mimetic identification, school shootings and Bishop's act unleash a similar dangerous effect – copycat violence. As themselves instances of copycat violence, these acts glorify copycat violence and seem to encourage further repetitions of it, promising futures that repeat and repeat and repeat the violence of the present, albeit each time with a twist. The twist most school shooters use is to scale up their violence. Instead, Charles Bishop's twist was to copy the scale of the violence of the September 11 hijackers by scaling down. Just as the September 11 hijackers scaled down the means of their attack to make it possible, so too did Bishop's suicidal tribute scale down violence in his act (non-violently stealing a plane to re-enact 9/11 in miniature) (Firestone, 2002). In so doing, Bishop's act raises the alarm for America's homeland security generally and in schools. For how can America protect itself from itself, especially when the violence within it goes undetected, even when a violent act is in the making? This applies as much to the US Air Force declining to intercept Bishop, as he flew over their airspace on his way to his fateful collision in Tampa, as to the everyday rearing of American youth.

With all of these connections between Bishop's act and school shooting, it is surprising how little play it got in the American media. Of the sources I found, none analyzed how media violence – whether in the 'fiction' of film or the 'fact' of hard news – was ritually repeated by Bishop and by school shooters. Only one account remarked on how youthful re-enactors of media violence sometimes achieve cult status among teens and their violent acts are re-enacted by their admirers, sometimes as tributes, sometimes as attempts to do the originals one better.[4] And none recognized that youthful re-enactors of violence not only imitate violent events, but they also identify with the movements in the scale of these events – in school shootings by scaling up violence; in Bishop's case by scaling down. Even Michael Moore's recent film *Bowling for Columbine* (United Artists, 2002), which analyzes school shootings in America in the context of wider social and political phenomena, fails even to mention Charles Bishop, much less to analyze the relevance of Bishop's act for his topic.

Commentaries that in the immediate aftermath of the Bishop suicide urged a future increase in aviation security or suggested that under-18s be forbidden from flying misrecognize that contemporary violence occurring in America is not following a World War Two Pearl Harbor script. Morally, this violence is troubling because incidents like school shootings and Bishop's act are carried out by 'good boys' – even 'patriotic' boys (Rosenberg, 2002) – whose alienation (if it is alienation) is unmarked before they act, except by their youth. Yet because youth is a category often placed beyond morality since young people are seen as moving toward 'moral maturity', youthful acts of violence often blur clear good vs. evil moral dichotomies upon which stories like Pearl Harbor rely. Palm Harbor is a case in point, with the Bush administration agreeing that Bishop was a 'troubled young man' (Rosenberg, 2002), but explicitly pointing out that he was not a terrorist (Wald, 2002). Temporally, these American youth hold no promise of progress. They are stuck in time – forever young – because of their suicides. And their acts of violence are also stuck in time, abiding as they do by a temporality of repetition. As such, they break away from the American 'we will win' progressive narrative about American wars the Pearl Harbor story depends upon. And spatially, these acts of violence are not easily contained. Their movements are not *within* spaces but across cells, nets, and schools. They represent exchanges of violence *and identifications* and, as such, are not easily encircled or annulled.

Overall, the Palm Harbor 'collision' of 9/11 with Columbine results in 'the apparent cross-pollination of an angry extremist Islamic terrorist conspiracy with an emerging American archetype: the ravenously suicidal, male, loner, teenage killer' (Vitello, 2002). In so doing, it stands in stark contrast to Pearl Harbor. Yet read back onto Pearl Harbor, what is evident is that the disruptions that Bishop's act shares with school shootings are the same disruptions it shares with narratives about the 'war on terrorism'. Moving from Pearl Harbor to Palm Harbor morally, temporally, and spatially ruptures America's narrative about September 11 (for example, that it is 'winnable') and about America itself (for example, that it is the envy of the world, something that jars with the knowledge that in America children regularly shoot children).

Not surprisingly then, Palm Harbor quickly faded from America's headlines and nightly news reports. While it was the lead story, it was often just a load of CNN on CNN. And that I think is dangerous. It may be convenient and reassuring to have the American media not tell Americans what they do not want to know. But that does not help them understand their world, their war, or themselves. This is not to say that I believe there is any escape from CNN or CNN, nor should there be. Without the Cable News Network, we would know a lot less about what America thinks about itself. And without the circulation of non-knowledge, we would all be psychotic (the unconscious is there for a reason). I prefer a neurotic, narcissistic America to a psychotic one.

Yet I think CNN's and CNN's overprotection of America from a psychotic break is backfiring. By *not* telling Americans what they do not want to know, CNN and CNN help Americans increasingly lose touch with reality, living as they do in a Pearl Harbor past without much of a clue about their Palm Harbor present.

Notes

1   Thanks to Terrell Carver for pointing out to me that my term 'the circulation of non-knowledge' phonetically translates into the acronym CNN and suggesting the link to the Cable News Network.
2   I use the terms 'America' and 'America itself' to refer to imaginary representations of places and peoples that have some collective resonance for those who would refer to themselves as 'Americans'. I am not claiming that these terms actually refer to these places and peoples; rather, following the work of Lauren Berlant, I am suggesting instead that they represent national symbolics around which powerful national fantasies about America and Americans are invoked. See Berlant, 1991.
3   My sources are almost exclusively online sources. Yet, especially in the case of CNN.com and the *New York Times* on the Web, these reflect what was reported on television and in major newspapers.
4   This story appeared in the UK newspaper *The Guardian*, although I would not be at all surprised if it was also reported in the US press. See Burkeman, 2002. For another reading of school shootings see J. Webber, 2003.

References

Associated Press (2002) 'Parents of teen pilot tried suicide', *The New York Times*, Online Edition, 10 January.

Berlant, Lauren (1991) *The Anatomy of National Fantasy: Hawthorne, Utopia, and Everyday Life*. Chicago: University of Chicago Press.

Blair, Ronnie, Perretta, Beth and Haymon Long, Karen (2002) 'Teachers Did not see Freshman as a Loner', *Tampa Tribune*, Online Edition, 8 January.

Burkeman, Oliver (2002) 'Death Wish', *The Guardian* G2, 9 January, p. 3.

Bush, George W. (2001a) 'We're Fighting to Win – and Win We Will', remarks by the President on the USS Enterprise on Pearl Harbor Day, 7 December.

Available at http://www.whitehouse.gov/news/releases/2001/12/20011207.html

Bush, George W. (2001b) 'Islam is Peace Says President: Remarks by the President at Islamic Center of Washington, DC', 17 September.

CNN.com (2002a) 'Teen pilot might have taken acne drug', 8 January. Available at http://www.cnn.com/2002/US/01/08/plane.suicide.mother/index.html

CNN.com (2002b) 'Police: Tampa pilot voiced support for bin Laden', 7 January. Available at http://www.cnn.com/2002/US/01/06/tampa.crash/index.html

Doherty, Thomas (2001) speaking on *Four Corners*, BBC Radio 4, 5 November.

Engelhardt, Tom (1995) *The End of Victory Culture: Cold War America and the Disillusioning of a Generation*. New York: Basic Books.

Firestone, David (2002) 'Teenage pilot left note praising Sept 11 attacks', *The New York Times*, Online Edition, 7 January.

Harden, Blaine (2001) 'Pearl Harbor's Old Men Find New Limelight Since Sept 11', *The New York Times*, Online Edition, 7 December.

Rosenberg, Scott (2002) 'Bin Laden's other American boy soldier', *Salon.com*, 9 January. Available at http://www.salon.com/news/feature/2002/01/09/bishop/index_np.html

Vitello, Paul (2002) 'In Teenager, al-Qaeda meets Columbine', *Newsday.com*, 8 January. Available at http://www.newsday.com

Wald, Matthew L. (2002) 'Student pilot, 15, crashes plane into bank in Florida', *The New York Times*, Online Edition, 6 January.

Webber, Julie A. (2003) *Failure to Hold: The Politics of School Violence*. Lanham, MD: Rowman & Littlefield.

14

ICONS AND INVISIBILITY: GENDER, MYTH, 9/11

Jayne Rodgers

The chapter is not just about representations of women in the reports of 9/11. It is intended, rather, to shed some light on an area where our interpretations of news and its impacts are lacking. Regardless of personal perspectives on debates about media effects, the active audience, media imperialism and so on, most people will accept the premise that the mass media – global, local and glocalized – are hugely influential in most, if not all, contemporary societies. More difficult to swallow may be the notion that the news we receive suffers from a range of biases which render any claims to objectivity, neutrality or impartiality virtually meaningless. A number of scholars have examined the imbalances in mass media output. Racism has been highlighted (Shah, 1999; van Dijk, 1999), as have bias against some ethnic groups (Cuklanz, 1995) and class divisions (Kray, 1995). Indeed, whole books have been written about the many factors hindering journalists in their quest for balanced reporting (MacGregor, 1997). Overlaying these factors is the issue of gender, understood here as a form of conditioning which affects individuals – women and men – at structural and interpersonal levels.

Gender is not divisible from other dimensions of our ethnic, cultural and social conditioning but is singled out here as a hugely influential part of our understanding of life to which global news producers pay scant attention. It is perhaps only through events like the 9/11 attacks, when a sense of global crisis seems to prevail, that the role of news media in reading events for us comes into sharp focus. In such situations, the news is there to make sense of, as Jack Lule puts it, 'almost senseless events' and to 'explain and give meaning to terrible and complex events, telling stories of heroes and victims, of high tragedy and great loss . . . to understand a struggle between good and evil' (Lule, 2002: 276). This story-telling role of the media is the central concern of this chapter, which draws from Lule's article on the myth-making of media reports after the attacks on New York and Washington on 11

September 2001. It takes a different perspective from Lule's, however, and hopefully one that will serve to broaden our understanding of the attacks and how the global media responded to them. Lule asks what stories journalists tell and why, what the systemic and corporate constraints upon them are and who is left out of the archetypal stories of news (Lule, 2002: 288). These questions are addressed here from a gender perspective. It does not ask where the women were on 9/11, but rather why certain women were visible in our news reports when others were not and how they were constructed through characterization in media coverage during and after the attacks.

Research into gender and the news has tended to look mainly at the structural bias in reporting and there have been a number of case studies on male/female hierarchies in media organizations in general and in news production in particular (Byerly, 1995; Djerf-Pierre and Logfren-Nilsson, 2001; van Zoonen, 1994). These hierarchies, of course, have a significant impact on the end product, the news we watch, read and hear. They are not the only factor involved in the gendering of news output but their impact resonates through this chapter.

Compounding the gaps in our understanding of news production and output is the fact that surprisingly little has been written about gender and the reporting of crises and conflicts. There has been a good deal of research in the field of International Relations on gender and the military (Enloe, 1988, 1989, 1993, 2000), and there exists a sizeable body of work in communications studies on crises, conflict and the media (Shaw, 1996; Taylor, 1992 and 1997). There is little overlap between these literatures, however. This chapter links these issues – the gendered hierarchies of news production and the absence of detailed research into gender and the reporting of crises and conflicts – to examine gendered depictions of the World Trade Centre attacks and their aftermath. To speak of 'the media' may in some circumstances sweep a little too broadly. The emphasis here is on news output but, as the discussion on gender below demonstrates, there was a common framework to the responses to 9/11 which was applied by both the press and broadcasters. In this respect, 'the media', embedded in and a contributory factor to wider (gendered) social structures, is a valid object of scrutiny.

Gender, media

'Gender is a pervasive social and cultural regulating mechanism that is part of our everyday life, our thinking, our speaking' (Visser, 2002: 529). We are all, male and female alike, positioned by the societal structures we operate within. The workplace, the political system, the family and so on all bring with them gendered expectations of the roles we will play and the functions we will perform. While discussions about this have brought the notion of gender constructions to our attention, gender-media relationships have been under-researched (Hermes, 1997: 65). One of the difficulties of researching gender is that it is a complex composite. Whichever way we come at the subject, we encounter difficulties. An essentialist (i.e. biological) perspective is inadequate for understanding how societies' expectations shape our behaviour. A perspective which addresses our immediate environment – the home, the workplace etc. – gives us only part of the picture of how we interact as gendered beings. A macro-level position which addresses political systems, social mores and so on cannot adequately address interpersonal gender dynamics. To make sense, gender needs to be seen as operating in all of the above perspectives and more. To make matters even more complicated, the multiple-levels of gender are interrelated: 'In a vicious circle, culturally and socially determined gender perceptions will be reflected in gender roles, which in turn reinforce communally and unconsciously held perceptions and gender' (Visser, 2002: 529).

We cannot escape gender, but we are becoming more adept at comprehending it. The ways gender affects news output has been researched over the past couple of decades and, though this research has made little impact on mainstream analysis, it provides a good deal of evidence on how structure and agency can be mutually reinforcing in the news. As far back as 1978, Philip Schlesinger was struck by the gender imbalance in newsrooms. He highlighted then how the majority of women in the BBC newsroom he was researching were secretaries and typists, that the stories reserved for female journalists were 'soft' ones, that they suffered from what was then generally known as male chauvinism in the workplace and that their style of dress often attracted more attention than the work they did (Schlesinger, 1978: 154–157).

Ongoing research in this area would suggest that these and other, related, problems with the gender-media relationship persist today. The narrative structure of news has been criticized for its distorted representations, with Rakow and Kranich arguing that news should be seen as a 'masculine narrative in which women function not as speaking objects but as signs' (Rakow and Kranich, 1991: 9). Male technicians are in the majority, while women are disproportionately employed in administrative and secretarial positions; male journalists dominate in the 'hard' news areas, whereas 'women tend to prevail in those areas that can be seen as an extension of their domestic responsibilities: in children's and educational media, programmes or sections; in consumer and domestic programmes; in human interest and feature sections of newspapers; in entertainment programming etc' (van Zoonen, 1994: 51).

Women have traditionally been poorly represented in senior positions in most media industries (van Zoonen, 1994: 50; De Clerq, 2002) and, in newsrooms in particular, there often exists a culture of 'informal occupation socialization' based around pubs, bars and unsociable working hours that serves to exclude women (van Zoonen, 1994: 52). Gallagher's report into the findings of a project covering both press and broadcast news output in 71 countries demonstrated, among other things, that women were quoted less often than men and, where they were, they were more likely to be 'ordinary' people – office workers, students and so on – rather than 'officials' (Gallagher, 1999: 207). In addition, though they less often make the news, women appear more often in news photos, contributing to the 'objectification of women in media content, including news' (Gallagher, 1999: 207). The male-dominated areas of news such as international affairs and defence issues, it has been claimed, have higher status than 'female' ones in terms of headlines or news placement (Djerf-Pierre and Lofgren-Nilsson, 2001: 18) and male journalists dominate conspicuously in stories on international crises and national security (Nordenstreng and Griffin, 1999: 210).

Findings like these led van Zoonen to suggest that it is possible to make some crude generalizations, sustainable across different countries and different media sectors:

> . . . press and broadcasting are media industries dominated by men; the higher up the hierarchies, or the more prestigious a particular medium or section is, the less likely is it to find women; women tend to work in areas of communication that can be considered an extension of their domestic responsibilities and their socially assigned qualities of care, nurturance and humanity; regardless of difference in years of experience, education etc., women are paid less for the same work. . . . most women in media professions have experienced sexist behaviour of male colleagues.
>
> (van Zoonen, 1994: 53)

All of these issues could be seen as merely part of a broader critique of the media industries, were it not for the impact they have on the news that we, the audience, receive and, in turn, the impact the news has on how we interpret the world around us. The gendering – of women *and men* in their roles as journalists and broadcasters – feeds into the ways news is framed and its narratives determined. For all of its increasing sophistication (see particularly Bennett and Entman (eds), 2001), the literature on framing rarely acknowledges the role gender plays in shaping the news.

Media, myth

Much is written about the ways news narratives are framed for us by the mass media. Gitlin was among the first to deal with the issue, suggesting that 'media frames, largely unspoken and unacknowledged, organize the world both for journalists, who report it and, in some important degree, for us who rely on their reports' (Gitlin, 1980: 7). The picture is rather more complicated than a simple matter of imposing a given framework for interpretation of events. Structural constraints – political, cultural and economic, though perhaps less often these days technological – play an important role in determining what the news we receive consists of. It is reasonable to argue that a tendency to portray particular kinds of information in particular kinds of ways can exclude information, ideas and actors that may reasonably be expected to have a place in the reporting of events. For Entman, '*bias* defines a tendency to frame different actors, events and issues in the same way, to select and highlight the same sort of selective realities, thus crafting a similar tale across a range of potential news stories' (Entman, 1996: 78, emphasis in original). Audiences are 'not passively absorbent sponges but active "negotiators" of meaning in media "texts"' (Carruthers, 2001: 8). If we consider the largely hidden gender factors that come into play in shaping the news, however, we need to question what is and is not encoded in the texts in the first place – which 'selective realities' we are being given. We need to consider how gendered representations of events considered newsworthy influence audience interpretations, of the texts themselves and of how our own lives can be read in relation to them.

Adding the notion of myth to the concept of framing provides an analytical framework that recognizes both the constraints inherent to news stories (the framing) and the ways they evolve (their narrative trends). Myth is valuable in helping to deconstruct some of the dominant gendered themes in the reporting of 9/11, as it provides a basis for understanding how both structural constraints and personal experience can contribute to the ways a news narrative develops. Lule has drawn together the work of a range of scholars, including Barthes, Carey, Hall and McLuhan, to explore the concept of myth and mass media with renewed rigour. He points out that the notion of myth is not about false beliefs or untrue stories but is 'a societal story that expresses prevailing ideals, ideologies, values and beliefs. More broadly, myth is an essential social narrative, a rich and enduring aspect of human existence, which draws from archetypal figures and forms to offer exemplary models for social life' (Lule, 2002: 277). Myth is not about spin, nor about deliberate strategies to dictate how we should lead our lives. Myth is about creating order out of chaos, about identifying recognizably good and bad behaviours, heroes and villains and so on. All societies need it and, as we gain access to more information from more parts of the world than ever before, its import grows rather than diminishes.

Although myth does not emanate from single sources – governments, for example, cannot single-handedly create sustainable societal myths – it does depend upon the cultural contexts from which it evolves. Therefore 'news and myth are inherently social and political narratives that help support the status quo and maintain social order'

(Lule, 2002: 279). Research on framing gives a sense of the effect of structural constraints on news as a product, of how corporate goals, journalistic routines and so on have an impact on news output (Byerly, 1995: 109). Analysis of myth and the media identifies the ways stories with recognizable characters and character traits are told in the news, in ways that influence how events may be understood. We already know that 'the media is not a neutral, common-sensed or rational mediator of social events, but essentially helps to reproduce pre-formulated ideologies' (van Dijk, 1988: 11). What has been unexplored to date is the degree to which framing and myth in the media reflect the broader gendered societal structures within which we reside.

Myth, 9/11

News does not just happen but is:

> . . . the product of judgements concerning the social relevance of given events and situations based on assumptions concerning their interest and importance. The 'reality' it portrays is always in at least one sense funda-mentally biased, simply in virtue of the inescapable decision to designate an issue or event newsworthy and then to construct an account of it in a specific framework of interpretation.
>
> (Schlesinger, 1978: 165)

In a global media age, news providers are often drawing on the same sources and more importantly, upon the same implicit value systems and same understanding of what constitutes 'news'. The 'reality' put together in the global media following the 9/11 attacks was shared across far more disparate and geographically dispersed communities than coverage of any previous event, except perhaps the death of Diana, Princess of Wales. The 9/11 attacks, though, saw the construction of a 'reality' reflecting global security concerns, certainly a first for the media. The scale and unexpectedness of the events of 9/11 meant that any 'differences that usually separated local news from national and global news collapsed, as coverage was shared across media and news organizations' (Zelizer and Allan, 2002: 4). Al-Jazeera aside, this was a global news story, for which a common narrative rapidly evolved. In the minutes following the attacks 'news organizations – together with their sources – lacked a readymade "script" to tell their stories, a frame to help them and their audiences comprehend the seemingly incompre-hensible' (Zelizer and Allan, 2002: 1). In the ensuing hours, a common framework was clearly established and the gendered myth of 9/11 began to develop.

The language used to describe the attacks invoked horror, shock, tragedy and disbelief. The 'apocalyptic image of the falling towers' (Blondheim and Leibes, 2002: 272) stupefied the millions who witnessed it by proxy from afar. In the 'dazed days after' (Rosen, 2002: 29), the media worked to establish the story of 9/11. Most analysis of the reporting of the attacks identifies a need not to maintain order but to *restore* it. As Zelizer and Allan put it, some journalists 'recognized the crucial role they had to play not only in framing the story but in helping whole populations move from crisis to continuity' (Zelizer and Allan, 2002: 4). For Lule, the restorative role of the media in the days following the attacks centred on four myths used to portray events: The End of Innocence, The Victims, The Heroes and The Foreboding Future. (The Enemy, the other crucial element of 9/11 mythology, came later, when the role of bin Laden became more clearly defined). These were 'more than editorial "themes" or political "issues", these were myths that invoked archetypal figures and forms at the heart of human storytelling' (Lule, 2002: 280). In dealing with each of them, the media promoted gendered values, based in part on the dynamics of the production process and in part on a need to reassign roles to individuals and institutions in a newly-fractured world.

This is not to suggest that the news producers made conscious decisions to frame 9/11 in gendered terms or set out to create a stereo-typed myth of male-female relations more redolent of 1950s suburban America than of the twenty-first century. As Hall says: 'just as the myth-maker may be unaware of the basic elements out of which his particular version of myth is generated, so broadcasters may not be aware of the fact that the frameworks and classifications they (were) drawing on reproduced the ideological inventories of their society' (cited in Lule, 2002: 279).

The dominant 'End of Innocence' myth acted as the defining framework for the others, in gender terms at least. There is a sense when looking back at the reports, the bulletins and the editorials, that some more comfortable gender order than the one that actually existed prior to the attacks was being depicted.

The characters chosen to represent heroes and victims demonstrate the gendering of 9/11 reporting most clearly. Male deaths from the attacks outnumbered female deaths by a ratio of three to one. All of the fire-fighters who died in the attacks were male and of the 50 police officers who died, only two were female (WTC Statistics, 2002; Willing, 2001). Logic would suggest that, while women would not necessarily be the heroes, the victims of 9/11 were largely men. This was not the way the narrative developed. It evolved instead along two trajectories. On one of these, what we could term the iconic, the male hero and the female victim emerged. On the other, on what could be termed an invisible trajectory, men dominated the official responses and women were largely absent.

The iconic imagery of men from the towers depicts the fire-fighter hero, much to the chagrin of female fire-fighters in New York. There were 33 female fire-fighters and rescue workers on duty on September

11, working alongside their male colleagues in the towers (Carouba and Hagen, 2002). Floren, herself a New York fire-fighter, suggests that the language used in media reports served to diminish the role of female officers: 'when you say . . . "fireman" you imply a necessary connection between gender and occupation. "Firemen" is the perfect word to use when you want to say "all (real) fire-fighters are men". It is a deliberate rejection of the gender-neutral in order to define heroes as male' (Floren, 2002). The heroic myth – and this is not intended to deny the undoubted heroism of many who lost their lives in the attacks – was based on a strong sense of restoring gender, as well as social and political order. The portraits of heroism were almost all of men – of Guiliani, of fire-fighters, police officers and the rescue workers who raised the Stars and Stripes at the rescue site (Charlesworth and Chinkin, 2002: 600). Bush was criticized for going to ground immediately after the attacks, heading for a 'safe place' to assemble the National Security Council (Carey, 2002: 73). His absence was seen by many as an ('unmanly') act of cowardice rather than one of pragmatism.

While men – manliness, masculinity, maleness – were being constructed as heroes, women were being constructed as victims. There were, media coverage would lead us to believe, few if any female heroes on 9/11. Women were constructed first as victims of the attacks, then defined through narratives centring on the widows and children left behind. Finally, some months later, came the images of the '9/11 babies', born after the deaths of their fathers. In the hours following the attacks, pictures of stunned, weeping women on the streets close to the site were circulated worldwide, one of which was used by the *New York Times* no less than three times over a two-week period (Zelizer, 2002: 63). The days and weeks that followed saw the myth of the victim develop further, with coverage of the fiancées, widows and children of men who died in the attacks dominating the 'human interest' angle of media coverage. Little was heard about the men left behind with children and there was no male equivalent to the photographs that appeared some months later of the gathering of 9/11 babies and no group shots of tragic widowers. While the suffering of the 9/11 widows warranted attention, the imbalances in reporting are worth commenting upon. While these women were seen to struggle gamefully on, their role in the crisis was as wives and mothers, as women essentialized to their femaleness.

The invisible woman was, for obvious reasons, less evident. Condoleeza Rice was the only female in the US administration who played any prominent role in media coverage. Even then her role was limited and, of course, the male to female ratio of government officials meant that men were inevitably seen to define the US position. Indeed, this reflected the reality of the decision-making processes, with women as poorly represented in the defence sector as at the top of media industries. At the same time, the dominance of men as political and defence commentators determined that the media framing was male-led. Only two of almost 50 *New York Times* opinion pieces in the six weeks following the attacks were written by women (Charlesworth and Chinkin, 2002: 601). Women's status in news reports became more obvious only when the spectre of the 'war on terrorism' was raised. At this point, images of women in *burqas*, as victims of the Taliban regime, were widespread. Ironically perhaps, the media now made the (hidden) victim visible and gave her iconic status, using her to symbolize not only Taliban repression but also American freedom.

Charlesworth and Chinkin note that a 'feature of gender is that what is deemed masculine is typically assigned greater value than what is defined as feminine' (Charlesworth and Chinkin, 2002: 604). The dichotomization of character traits – masculine/feminine, active/passive and so on – has long been challenged by gender theorists as something that perpetuates fallacious impressions of male strength and female weakness, investing authority or the lack of it in 'male' and 'female' traits respectively. The application of dichotomies of this kind is at the heart of the structure of myths, which rely upon 'the juxtaposition of two principles, such as clever and stupid, big and small, . . . arrogant and modest and, of course, good and bad' (Schoenbach, 2001: 363). The dichotomized representations of maleness and femaleness linked with a broader ideological impulse not necessarily to position women in a particular way but to depict men – symbolizing authority – as strong and in control. Peterson and Runyan suggest that: 'depending on what the situation calls for, gender ideology may promote women as physically strong and capable of backbreaking work (e.g. slave women, frontier women), as competent to do men's work (e.g. Rosie the Riveter in World War II), as dexterous and immune to boredom (e.g. electronics assembly industries), or as full-time housewives and devoted mothers (e.g. post-war demands that women vacate jobs in favor of returning soldiers and repopulate the nation' (Peterson and Runyan, 1999: 42).

In the case of 9/11, the media helped to depict the courage of America by juxtaposing its female population – feminine, maternal, nurturing – with its male – vigorous, strong and heroic. The gender myth built up in media reporting of the attacks was of action man and passive woman, restoring, in theory at least, one element of societal imbalance.

Conclusion

So how can the gender balance be redressed in media coverage of events? This is a pervasive problem that operates at multiple levels. Rakow and Kranich suggested over a decade ago that 'any improvement in women's treatment in news will require not simply more coverage of women or more women journalists . . . but a fundamental change in news as a narrative form' (Rakow and Kranich, 1991: 9). There is no evidence to date that the narrative form of news is changing. Indeed, the consolidation of media industries and the globalization of news as a product are resulting in an expansion of the format.

The structure/agency problem runs as a theme through much of the research on gender and the media. Redressing the gender balance does not depend simply on women's agency (that is, introducing more women will not necessary make for gender-neutral news or something approximating it). The structures of production, which are influenced by gender roles and the gendered expectations of the people working within media industries, continue to militate against balanced reporting. There is something of a cyclical character to this structural bias: women do not do 'real' reporting, so when something as serious as the 9/11 attacks occurs, women are not seen to have the necessary skills to investigate and report on them. This is partly true, though inexperience is largely based on gender-based constraints on their career development. Why would any media organization send a journalist inexperienced in reporting political or security matters to report on events with enormous ramifications for global politics and security? The short answer is that it would not, and so the patterns of exclusion and imbalanced reporting continue.

Lule suggests that there is a need to take the role of myth in media output more seriously (Lule, 2002: 208). This is perhaps the area that warrants most attention. Why do we accept certain myths, largely without question? And, in classic media studies style, do myths lead or reflect our understanding of the world we live in? Adding more women into the media mix would no doubt influence the nature of the news product. Gendered media myths run much deeper than employment structures, though, and there is clearly a need to investigate in greater detail both their use and acceptance. Lule wonders what myths are told and to what purpose (Lule, 2002). Media coverage of 9/11 showed how societal ideologies feed into the myth-making process and, to understand news better, more information on how this works – in calm times and in crisis – is necessary.

None of this is intended to suggest that news producers should be blamed for gender bias in the reports on the attacks. Although some individuals were no doubt culpable of consciously positioning men and women in certain ways, the majority were working to deadlines, to their own and their audiences' expectations of news and what it should contain and to their employers' implicit or explicit directives on what to cover. We can probably conclude that any gender bias was neither designed nor deliberate. There was a need for comprehension, stability, order after a crisis. The news, as our modern-day myth-maker, was there to impose a rational discourse upon a world apparently thrown into chaos. With the communications systems available to us now, this became a need to create a 'global' (I use the term loosely) myth, a need to restore order for a near-worldwide community of viewers, readers and listeners.

While the characters of 9/11 in the news – the mythical creatures, we could say – were mainly Americans, they were held to symbolize the light against dark, good versus evil characteristics necessary to impose some semblance of order on the chaos. The character traits used to represent the society responding to 9/11 were, theoretically at least, universally recognized as elemental to the human condition. The heroes, victims and the lost innocence were all crucial to the telling of the 9/11 story. They were also applied in profoundly gendered ways. Whatever the rights and wrongs of the dominant characterization of events in the news, this is a layer of myth that should trouble everyone – male and female, news providers and audiences. In the twenty-first century, in an age of highly sophisticated global communications, women can be characterized, largely without question, as passive victims, with men as their dynamic, protective heroes. It is as if the twentieth-century never happened.

Acknowledgements

Thanks to Annette Davison, Sharon O'Brien and Emma Tregidden for their comments, and especially to Judith Stamper for her insights into life in the newsroom. I would also like to thank Colin Cuthbert, my research assistant for this chapter.

References

Bennett, W. Lance and Entman, Robert (eds) (2001) *Mediated Politics – Communication in the Future of Democracy*. Cambridge: Cambridge University Press.

Blondheim, Menahem and Liebes, Tamar (2002) 'Live Television's Disaster Marathon of September 11 and its Subversive Potential', *Prometheus*. 20 (3): 271–276.

Byerly, Carolyn M. (1995) 'News, Consciousness and Social Participation: The Role of Women's Feature Service in World News', pp. 105–122 in Angharad N. Valdivia (ed.) *Feminism, Multiculturalism and the Media – Global Diversities*. London: Sage.

Carey, James W. (2002) 'American Journalism On, Before and After September 11', pp. 71–90 in Barbie Zelizer and Stuart Allan (eds) (2002) *Journalism After September 11*. London: Routledge.

Carouba, Mary and Hagen, Susan (2002) *Women at Ground Zero – Stories of Courage and Compassion*. New York: Alpha.

Carruthers, Susan L. (2001) *The Media at War*. Basingstoke: Macmillan.

Charlesworth, Hilary and Chinkin, Christine (2002) 'Sex, Gender and September 11', *American Journal of International Law*. 96 (3): 600–605.

Cuklanz, Lisa M. (1995) 'News Coverage of Ethnic and Gender Issues in Big Dan's Rape Case', pp. 145–162 in Angharad N. Valdivia (ed.) *Feminism, Multiculturalism and the Media – Global Diversities*. London: Sage.

De Clerq, Mieke (2002) *Shedding Light on Absence – Women's Under-representation in the Newsroom*. Paper presented at the IAMCR Conference, Barcelona, July.

Djerf-Pierre, Monika and Lofgren-Nilsson, Monica (2001) *Sex-typing in the newsroom: Feminization of Swedish Television News Production, 1958–2000*. Paper presented to 15th Nordic Conference on Media and Communication Research, Reykjavik.

Enloe, Cynthia H. (1988) *Does Khaki Become You? The militarisation of women's lives*. London: Pandora.

Enloe, Cynthia H. (1989) *Bananas, Beaches & Bases: Making feminist sense of international politics*. London: Pandora.

Enloe, Cynthia H. (1993) *The Morning After: Sexual Politics at the End of the Cold War*. Berkeley: University of California Press.

Enloe, Cynthia H. (2000) *Maneuvers – The International Politics of Militarizing Women's Lives*. Berkeley: University of California Press.

Entman, Robert (1996) 'Manufacturing Discord: Media in the Affirmative Action Debate', *Harvard International Journal of Press/Politics*. 1 (3): 77–92.

Floren, Terese M. (2002) 'Too Far Back For Comfort', Women's Fire Service Incorporated. Available at http://www.wfsi.org/Toofarback.html

Gallagher, Margaret (1999) 'The Global Media Monitoring Project: Women's Networking and Research for Action' in Kaarle Nordenstreng and Michael Griffin (eds) *International Media Monitoring*. Cresskill, N.J.: Hampton Press, pp. 199–217.

Gitlin, Todd (1980) *The Whole World is Watching*. Berkeley: University of California Press.

Hermes, Joke (1997) 'Gender and Media Studies: No Woman, No Cry', pp. 65–95, in John Corner, Philip Schlesinger and Roger Silverstone (eds) *International Media Research*. London: Routledge.

Kray, Susan (1995) 'Orientalization of an "Almost White" Woman: A Multi-disciplinary Approach to the Interlocking Effects of Race, Class, Gender and Ethnicity in American Mass Media: The case of the Missing Jewish Woman', pp. 221–244 in Angharad N. Valdivia (ed.) *Feminism, Multiculturalism and the Media – Global Diversities*. Thousand Oaks, CA: Sage.

Lule, Jack (2002) 'Myth and Terror on the Editorial Page: The New York Times Responds to September 11, 2001', *Journalism & Mass Communication Quarterly*. 29 (2): 275–293.

MacGregor, Brent (1997) *Live, Direct and Biased? Making Television News in the Satellite Age*. London: Arnold.

Nordenstreng, Kaarle and Griffin, Michael (eds) (1999) *International Media Monitoring*. Cresskill, New Jersey: Hampton Press.

Peterson, V. Spike and Runyan, Anne Sissan (1999) *Global Gender Issues*. Boulder: Westview, 2nd edn.

Rakow, Lana and Kranich, Nancy (1991) 'Woman as Sign in Television News', *Journal of Communication*. 41 (1): 8–23.

Rosen, Jay (2002) 'September 11 in the Mind of American Journalism', pp.

27–35 in Barbie Zelizer and Stuart Allan (eds) (2002) *Journalism After September 11*. London: Routledge.

Schlesinger, Philip (1978) *Putting Reality Together*. London: Routledge.

Schoenbach, Klaus (2001) 'Myths of Media and Audiences', *European Journal of Communication*. 16 (3): 361–376.

Shah, Norbert (1999) 'Race, Nation and News in the United States', pp. 317–332 in Kaarle Nordenstreng and Michael Griffin (eds) *International Media Monitoring*. Cresskill, New Jersey: Hampton Press.

Shaw, Martin (1996) *Civil Society and Media in Global Crises – Representing Distant Violence*. London: Pinter.

Taylor, Philip M. (1992) *War and the Media: Propaganda and Persuasion in the Gulf War*. Manchester: Manchester University Press.

Taylor, Philip M. (1997) *International Affairs and the Media Since 1945*. London: Routledge.

van Dijk, Teun A. (1988) *News As Discourse*. Hilldale, NJ/Hove: Lawrence Erlbaum.

van Dijk, Teun A. (1999) 'Media, Racism and Monitoring', pp. 307–316 in Kaarle Nordenstreng and Michael Griffin (eds) *International Media Monitoring*. Cresskill, New Jersey: Hampton Press.

van Zoonen, Liesbet (1994) *Feminist Media Studies*. London: Sage.

Visser, Irene (2002) Prototypes of Gender: Conceptions of Feminine and Masculine, *Women's Studies International Forum*. 25 (5): 529–539.

Willing, Linda (2001) The Language of Inclusion, Women's Fire Service Incorporated. Available at http://www.wfsi.org/Inclusion.html

WTC Statistics (2002). Available at http://www.september11victims.com/september11victims/wtc_statistics.htm

Zelizer, Barbie (2002) 'Photography, Journalism and Trauma', pp. 48–69 in Barbie Zelizer and Stuart Allan (eds) (2002) *Journalism After September 11*. London: Routledge.

Zelizer, Barbie and Allan, Stuart (eds) (2002) *Journalism After September 11*. London: Routledge.

Part 5

CONFLICT AND THE CULTURES OF JOURNALISM

JOURNALISTS UNDER FIRE: SUBCULTURES, OBJECTIVITY AND EMOTIONAL LITERACY

Howard Tumber and Marina Prentoulis

The events of 11 September 2001 and the subsequent war in Afghanistan are producing considerable debate about the future of journalism. Dramatic and tragic events do not often change 'professional' behaviour overnight but they may accelerate trends. Globalization, concentration of ownership, increased competitiveness, new technology, and 24/7 news are all contributing to journalism's changing role within the public sphere (Tumber, 2001). At the same time definitions of war, conflict and terrorism are undergoing reassessment. This chapter examines perceptible transformations within journalism and, in particular, ambiguities within the subculture of war and foreign correspondents.

Journalism subcultures

It is a commonly accepted thesis that the development of journalism as a professional occupation in the course of the nineteenth century never fully managed to homogenize the range of the activities falling under the scope of the profession. The development of journalism as a distinct professional culture was a response to the concept of 'responsibility', first conceived during the 1920s, among editors and foreign correspondents (Carr-Saunders and Wilson, 1964: 265, 267).[1] This found expression in the conflict between journalists, who promoted the ideal of professional responsibility in relation to 'objectivity', and the publicity agents' distorted versions of truth (Bourdieu, 1996: 70; Bovee, 1999: 113; Trice, 1993: 7).

Objectivity, as the concept underpinning professional journalism as well as the expectations of the public, is in itself inherently ambiguous. As the major signifier associated with the occupation of journalism, 'objectivity' is associated and often confused with ideas of 'truth', 'impartiality, 'balance' and 'neutrality'. For example, a journalist's aim may be to reach the truth (and in order to approach the truth they may need to be impartial), but that does not necessarily imply that the means used or the means that could be used, are objective (Frost, 2000: 35–38). Similarly, balance refers to the equal amount of space and time provided for conflicting sides. It does not follow however, that this makes reporting either 'objective' or 'true'. Neutrality may also be problematic when one considers moral imperatives as part of the function of journalism (Seib, 2002: 85).

The confusion arising from the signifying processes associated with objectivity, leads to further ambiguities when examining the value of objectivity itself. From the 1920s onwards, different disciplines within the humanities and social sciences have convincingly demonstrated that reality itself and the knowledge about this reality, are both socially constructed (Schudson, 1978). It can be helpful, therefore, to treat 'objectivity' in two distinct ways: as a theoretical imperative underpinning reporting, and as a strategic ritual enabling the defence of the practice as a profession (Tuchman, 1972). In the first instance, objectivity is conceptualized as an impossible goal. However, 'objective reporting' is associated with ways of gathering news (knowledge about places, people, events) and conveying them in a detached, impersonal way free of value judgments. Nevertheless, the act of reporting itself places limitations (such as space, time, pertinence) on the ability to report the whole known truth. It follows, therefore, that the necessity of selection and the hierarchical organization of a story, suggests more of a subjective rather than objective outcome (Bourdieu, 1996: 21; Bovee, 1999: 114–116, 121). In addition, the structural environment of the institutions of reporting is also restricted by economic and political factors that lead to a subjective outcome (Schudson, 1978). Furthermore, the desirability of such reporting is becoming increasingly questioned (Bovee, 1999: 121, 124, 128; McLaughlin, 2002: 153–163; Seib, 2002: 85).

In contrast, objectivity used as a strategic ritual, allowing for the defence of the profession, becomes a convincing argument if one compares journalism with social sciences (Bovee, 1999: 123–4; Tuchman, 1972). The latter demands a 'reflexive epistemological examination', which the former does not and cannot engage with while processing information (Tuchman, 1972: 662). The procedures of the verification of facts, the separating of 'facts' from 'analysis', the presenting of conflicting possibilities and supporting evidence, the judicious use of quotation marks, the structuring of information in an appropriate sequence and the criterion of common sense in assessing news content, whilst enabling the claim to objectivity (which functions as a shield from criticism), do not guarantee objectivity. Instead, they only allow an operational view of objectivity (Tuchman, 1972: 662–679).

However, since the professional ideology of journalism is based on these claims, it is important to examine the effects of this ideology on particular subcultures within journalism. It is widely accepted that the boundaries of journalism are fairly broad, incorporating activities as distinct as 'investigative reporting' and book writing. (Trice, 1993: 14). Journalism is far from a homogeneous aggregation of professionals, all sharing the same cultural values. Shifting the emphasis from the examination of the occupation as a whole to the occupational subcultures, allows an exploration of the dynamic interrelations between the core culture of journalism and the subcultures incorporated within the profession. It is within this antagonistic dynamic that the embryonic modifications of wider cultural changes can be isolated and analyzed.

Journalism, as other professions, is founded on a claim that its practitioners have mastered the specific knowledge requirements necessary for the performance of a distinct set of tasks. Even if in the actual performance of the tasks, the required knowledge is more related to experience and practice rather then abstractions, the claim remains (Abbot, 1988: 7, 8; Bovee, 1999: 175; Trice, 1993: 7, 12). However, it is the presence of a background system of knowledge governed by abstractions that allows for the characterization of journalism as a profession rather than a craft. It is only through a system of abstractions that the redefinition of the problems and tasks associated with any profession is enabled (Abbot, 1988: 8–9). In journalism, the abstractions operating and modifying the specific tasks are grounded on notions of 'objectivity', and 'neutrality'. The practice that war correspondents adopt is similarly governed by the same abstractions, although this assumes a different form from other journalism sub groups (McLaughlin, 2002: chapter 8; Seib, 2002: chapters 3–4).

A second, related claim is the demands for control over the way tasks are performed, either formally through apprentice programs or informally via socialization processes (Trice, 1993: 12). Journalism differs from other professions, such as medicine and law, in that the profession is much less formalized, lacking a specific set of educational requirements and professional rules (Adam, 2001: 315–316; Frost, 2000: xii–xiv; Schudson, 1978). The absence of these inhibits journalistic professional prestige and legitimacy (Adam, 2001: 315; Frost, 2000: xiv). However, what journalism lacks in terms of formal rules and procedures, it gains through the claim to professional autonomy (Pedelty, 1995: 89). One manifestation of this is expressed in the attempt to restrict administrative control. 'Journalists', according to Janowitz, 'want to select their own stories, to treat them as they feel appropriate, and to avoid being rewritten and edited by members of the organization. [. . .] Journalists in the United States have been more concerned with their personal autonomy than with mechanisms for auditing their performance' (Janowitz, 1977: 92).

The demand for professional autonomy is particularly intensive for the foreign/war correspondent. Owing to the restrictions placed by government and military on reporting conflicts, professional autonomy can be seriously hampered (Hallin, 1986; Kellner, 1992; Morrison and

Tumber, 1988; Prochnau, 1995; Taylor, 1992). Whilst the management of the flow of information becomes more apparent during conflicts, clashes intensify between war correspondents, news organizations and the military over this flow. War correspondents however, rarely recognize the macro structures that constitute the system of power that manages the flow of information. Instead, they attribute the impediments of their independence to their editors[2] or specific organizations (i.e. the US State Department) (Pedelty, 1995: 90, 95, 145). It comes as no surprise then, that foreign/war correspondents are preoccupied with their relationship with their editors.[3] The commercial and social realities of news organizations that dictate restrictions and compromise professional autonomy are personified as flaws in the character of specific editors (McLaughlin, 2002: 17–18).

The macro dimensions that may restrict or enhance professional autonomy are also the forces that lie behind intercultural antagonisms and conflicts. Pedelty, in his study of foreign correspondents, follows Bourdieu's explanation of how social formations work by suggesting that the antagonistic and oppositional pairs within the culture of foreign/war correspondents are rooted in the wider social order (Pedelty, 1995: 78). For example, as the maintenance of specialist correspondents becomes more costly, the role of staff correspondents may be reduced as news coverage may rest increasingly on freelance journalists. This economic reality may be one possible factor behind the antagonism between staff and freelance correspondents. Both groups demand and desire greater autonomy and independence in order to perform their tasks. However, they operate under different norms which may differentiate not only their news products but also the place they occupy within news organizations. Whilst freelancers lack the resources, economic or otherwise, necessary for their task, they are perceived by the administration as more 'dangerous' and 'subjective'. Staff correspondents on the other hand, may have the resources, but are caught in stricter administrative controls (Pedelty, 1995: 76).

The diverse organizational perspectives that news administrations adopt towards staff correspondents and freelancers, coupled with the respective antagonism between the two groups, reveals that even within more or less collectively accepted norms and practices (i.e. the foreign correspondents' culture), there is always a degree of ambiguity and contradiction. 'Although each culture nurtures stability, harmony, and continuity, most modern cultures are awash with change and ambivalence' (Trice, 1993: 22).

Group identity among war correspondents

From its foundation in 1980, the Institute of Journalists placed an emphasis on establishing that professionals were qualified members, possessing the necessary theoretical and practical knowledge (Carrs-Saunders and Wilson, 1964: 268). While the status of professional qualifications progressed in the twentieth century, with Pulitzer anxious to establish the necessary standards to allow journalists to gain the same status and expertise as other professions (Adam, 2001: 315), debate continues today over notions of professionalism. For example, new genres associated with journalism, from eyewitness accounts to independent writers and thinkers, are inhibiting the fostering of a professional identity based on knowledge and expertise (Sreberny, 2002: 221–222).

What practitioners lack in terms of formal knowledge, they gain through the ability to absorb the occupational demands placed upon them. While the physical and psychological welfare of all journalists is to some extent at risk, war/foreign correspondents face the most severe conditions and demands. The identification with their specific practice is therefore re-enforced. Those war/foreign correspondents who work as 'parachuters' or 'firemen', having to cover geographically vast regions without a more permanent base, describe a life of 'constant work, confusion, and frustration' (Pedelty, 1995: 111). The permanently stationed foreign correspondents also describe their work as 'erratic' and 'frenetic', with no dividing line between work and free, personal time. For both groups, covering conflicts demands an ability to overcome social isolation, stress, absurdity, boredom and terror and at the same time cope with diseases and poor hygienic conditions that affect their physical welfare (Deeds, 1990; Pedelty, 1995: 113–114, 127). Furthermore, war/foreign correspondents and media personnel in conflict zones, together with the local reporters, are now often among the casualties of conflict (Tumber, 2002). The hazardous aspect of the occupation is emphasized through signifiers such as 'the fellowship of danger'. These extreme and dangerous demands create strong bonds among the practitioners who refer to those killed at the war zones as '"Brother Number One" among "brother correspondents"' (McLaughlin, 2002: 8).

The pervasiveness of work and the blurring of the line between work and private life are exemplified in the personal friendships of war/foreign correspondents. US staff correspondents, due to their privileged access to the American Embassy, often develop close friendships with United States Information Service (USIS) officials, relationships seen as a natural outcome of their mutual 'working relationship'. Similarly, freelance war correspondents (stringers) are not just a professional group. For long periods of time, the members of the group live, socialize and participate in the same recreational activities (Pedelty, 1995: 71, 75). The professional and the private often coincide, leading to a life which can easily be modified by the occupation. Christiane Amanpour of CNN, explained that she mainly dated her colleagues because this 'tight band of people' are the 'only people who understand that it's too sad, too shocking, too intense, or too fun and exciting' (*Newsweek*, 1996). In less fortunate ways, the private life of the war/foreign correspondents can be seriously threatened by the demands placed upon them, leading to severe psychological conditions such as post traumatic stress disorder (PTSD). In these cases, the personal lives of war correspondents seriously suffer (Tumber, 2002).

The factor that plays a decisive role in the construction of a war correspondent's identity is the forms of representation that permit them to communicate the central values associated with their identity to those outside the occupation. The importance of this communication is illustrated quantitatively in the number of autobiographies by war and foreign correspondents. It is possible to suggest that the validity of the social identity of war correspondents is constructed around three axes: service to the public; their professionalism (which may exhibit different peculiarities compared with journalism in general); and the internalization of the values associated with reporting conflict.

Tunstall's pioneering 1971 study on British specialist correspondents showed that foreign correspondents exhibit certain peculiarities when compared with other specializations such as political, crime or sports correspondents. First, they perceive their specialist role in news organizations as primarily non-revenue, while other specializations understand their role as advertising or audience revenue oriented. Second, foreign correspondents have the highest class background and spend more time in education compared with other specialist groups. Third, their entry into the profession was through an 'elite' route when compared with the 'provincial entry' of other specializations. Most foreign correspondents began their career either in London or overseas and had fewer separate employers than other correspondents. Finally, foreign correspondents were the most 'highly thought of' within the whole field of correspondents, which may be related to their 'non revenue' goal (Tunstall, 1971). Although many of the trends identified in the study may have undergone significant modifications, nevertheless, they still illustrate that the ideal of the 'service to the public', the importance of professionalism and of the values associated with specific news gathering, all contribute to foreign/war corresponding being a peculiar if not deviant group among correspondents.

Service to the public

Despite the fascination and addiction to war, and the excitement and glamour that is associated with the profession, many war correspondents refer to the crucial social values of their work. 'Truth' and 'a sense of making history' are primary motivations, leading to the elevation of the profession as a 'vocation' (McLaughlin, 2002: 15–16). Seib (2002) gives an insight into how journalists perceive their role in international conflicts: consciously or unconsciously, journalists try to grab the attention and sentiments of their audiences in order to make them aware of atrocities around the world. In some cases, neutrality and objectivity, the traditional journalistic standards, are perceived as factors contributing to the further continuation of war crimes. This personal commitment is enhanced when journalists see themselves as 'witnesses'. The public is perceived as more or less ignorant about world affairs, and the journalist-witness has to open their eyes to the world's brutal reality. Despite the contradictions with professionalism that may emerge, 'caution' is itself questioned and viewed as restraining correspondents from performing their public duty (Seib, 2002: 52–54, 70, 84, 85). The prioritization of the moral and ethical duties of the journalist towards the public and the world in general is part of the ideological framework within which contemporary journalism operates. This is clearly illustrated in the case of war correspondents acting as witnesses at the International Criminal Tribunals in The Hague. Although most journalists approach the decisions cautiously, fully aware of the dilemma between their professional position as observers and the moral imperative which may arise in certain (compelling) cases, war correspondents still have to deal with a new and unclear dimension of their professional occupation (News World Conference, 2002; Seib, 2002: 84).

Professionalism

The institutionalized and thus professional phase of journalism started with the elevation of objectivity to the dominant ideology within the profession (Trice, 1993: 60). Objectivity became the foundation for the social responsibility claims of the journalistic identity. Even in a period when traditional journalistic standards have been widely questioned and in many cases abandoned, the status of objectivity is an ongoing concern within the profession (Seib, 2002: 40). In war/foreign corresponding, the rules of objectivity may restrict the ability of the correspondent to present the socio-political framework of a conflict, since he may be accused of 'editorializing' (Pedelty, 1995: 87). At the same time, the practices that ensure the 'objective' coverage of a story are often restricted or negated during international conflicts (Morrison and Tumber, 1988).

Similarly, the condition of detachment, valued as a main imperative of professional journalism, has a double edge. On the one hand, it is attached to the criticism that the 'ordinary people' have been neglected due to their 'lack of newsworthiness'. On the other hand, however, as the reporters remain disconnected from the aspirations and anxieties of the ordinary people, detachment becomes a facilitator of objectivity (Pedelty, 1995: 100). Within the specific tradition of war corresponding, the principle of detachment is the locus of the antagonism between the two main axes around which the social identity of war correspondents is constructed i.e. service to the public and professionalism. For example, recent criticism has condemned the tradition of detached reporting for its dispassionate stance. Public service broadcasters, including the BBC, have come under fire for acting merely as 'transmission vehicles' (Bell, 1996; McLaughlin, 2002: 21). At the same time the 'journalism of attachment', the human, emotional face of war corresponding, has been criticized for opening the door to mistaken accounts of the conflicts, and for being 'self-righteous', and 'moralizing' (McLaughlin, 2002: 166–168; Ward, 1998).

Internalization of occupational values

The differences between the professional values of war correspondents and the social value of their occupation for the public, may point to a cultural shift in war corresponding. Nevertheless, the culture of war corresponding is not only constructed around rules and values associated with the end product of the process, but also with the internalization of the occupational values and the way it defines the very existence of the war correspondents. The attempt to attract world attention and evoke sympathy concerning war crimes does not end with the accomplishment of journalistic work. Frustration by the world's lack of response becomes a common phenomenon among correspondents (Seib, 2002: 52).

Furthermore, the internalization of the ethical and moral duties places enormous pressure on journalists: 'To witness genocide is to feel not only the chill of your own mortality, but the degradation of all humanity' (Fergal Keane quoted in Seib, 2002: 72). This internalization of occupational values is also evident in the identification of war correspondents with their news organizations. Newsworthiness and objectivity are associated with particular prestigious news institutions such as the *New York Times*. Pedelty's research among war correspondents reveals that *New York Times* correspondents believe their news organization covers all newsworthy events and ignores those lacking news value. As a result, objectivity and truth are intrinsic to the work of the specific news organization and define the line of occupational values followed not only by its own employers but also by the whole community of war correspondents (Pedelty, 1995: 71–2).

Cultural shifts

The axis, upon which the ideological framework of war correspondents depends is further reinforced by a set of cultural forms unique to the specific subculture. These may include myths, language, ritual and taboos, all of which are part of the subculture of war/foreign correspondents (Trice, 1993: 39). Occupational subcultures are dynamic as are the cultural forms in which the subculture finds expression. However, changes in the occupational subcultures may signal the beginning of deeper, more radical changes, related to the occupation as a whole. The first phase of the evolution of occupational changes may be marked by what is perceived as interruptions of the cultural expressions of the occupational ideology (Trice, 1993: 58). Before going into the cultural shifts associated with war corresponding, it is necessary to examine the cultural forms associated with the subculture.

Myths of professionalism and independence

The antagonistic relationship between stringers and staff inherent in the culture of war correspondents reinforces notions of professional independence and autonomy amongst both groups. Staff correspondents themselves differentiate between those war/foreign correspondents that exercise the profession on a full-time staff basis and the 'stringers' and freelancers who work more independently (Morrison and Tumber, 1985: 446).[4] For the excluded 'stringers' and freelancers, it is imperative to emphasize the professional identity and social validity of their practice. As a result, freelance journalists use 'the mythical figure of Ernest Hemingway, the archetypal foreign correspondent-freelancer, as the iconic evidence that one need not be staff in order to earn the title of "foreign correspondent"' (Pedelty, 1995: 79). Both groups seem to invoke the myth of professional independence in order to overcome the demands of an oppressive practice, brought about largely by the economic and political constraints placed upon them by news organizations and social structures. Peter Arnett, who emerged from the Gulf War as the archetypal figure of the war correspondent ignoring personal risk and hardship in order to get the story, claimed that the same public figures who criticized him for being too soft on Saddam Hussein had upbraided him before the war began for being too critical. The media, however, represented him as a legend, and emphasized the similarities between him and the World War Two journalistic legend, Edward R. Murrow (Zelizer, 1992).

The enmity between staff correspondents and freelancers is primarily the product of the economic condition of news organizations. Nevertheless, the animosity also exists around an antagonistic linguistic schema: employment status is used to determine degrees of professionalism and is reflected in the 'staff' vs 'stringers' labels. Freelance correspondents use the phrase 'A Team' for staff correspondents whilst referring to themselves as 'independents' or 'freelancers', terms that emphasize the professional value of independence. Staff correspondents on the other hand, call freelance correspondents, 'part-timers', while appropriating the term 'correspondents' for themselves. In this way, they associate professionalism with their own group (Pedelty, 1995: 78).

Rituals of war correspondents

Pedelty, following Kluckhohn and Levi-Strauss, defines rituals as 'an obsessive repetitive activity, often a symbolic dramatization of the "needs" of the society, whether "economic", "biological", "social", or "sexual"' (Pedelty, 1995: 120). Within journalistic culture there are a number of media rituals such as press conferences, interviews and photo opportunities which transform specific interests into the needs of society as a whole (Pedelty, 1995). The same rituals are evident in the culture of war correspondents. However, because of the specific demands associated with their practice, recreational rituals are especially prominent in the culture of war/foreign correspondents. The professional identity of war correspondents is often associated with sexual activities that function as a source of personal empowerment or liberation from the social inhibitions of one's own culture. Similarly, alcohol and drugs also function as rituals that allow war correspondents to escape from the demands of their work and the horrors of the war (Pedelty, 1995: 138–141).

Storytelling is another important ritual among war correspondents. When journalists cannot express their individual opinion, they tend to find alternative ways such as stories, editorials, cartoons or radio programmes (Gans, 1980: 187). Pedelty identifies two main types of storytelling among war correspondents: the first focuses on the extraordinary achievement of a journalist or photographer; the second, on the failure of others, which is used as a negative example of what should be avoided in professional practice. In both cases, storytelling becomes a mythological narrative with initiating properties that mark the entrance of the young correspondents into the veteran group (Pedelty, 1995: 129–133). These rituals, although not exclusively male, point to a 'macho' culture. In relation to storytelling for example, Rosenblum argues that women correspondents assume a 'participant-observer' role, which Pedelty attributes to the less 'public and boisterous' female ways of dealing with fear (Pedelty, 1995: 135). The constituency of the war/foreign correspondent group traditionally contributed to this 'all male' image. Despite the fact that today many women war correspondents stand at the peak of their profession, the stereotypical representation of the profession as 'male' continues.

The cultural forms associated with the subculture of war/foreign correspondents illustrate that despite sharing the core ideology of objectivity, journalism can and does incorporate multiple cultural forms, practices and ideologies. The different subcultures may be related to each other in enhancing or conflicting ways, or may have no bearing on other subcultures at all. Subcultures, however, are not only unstable but also ambiguous – often characterized by uncertainty, contradiction and confusion (Martin and Meyerson, 1988: 112).[5] Objectivity, the core ideology of war/foreign correspondents, progressively becomes more of an ambiguous area. This is illustrated in the changing cultural forms among foreign correspondents.

Ambiguity and objectivity

A decisive strike against the notion of 'objectivity' comes from 'New Journalism' and journalists-cum-novelists. Within this trend, factual journalism embraces fictional techniques and subjectivity (McLaughlin, 2002: 163–164). Another challenge that adds to the ambiguity of 'objective' ideology comes from the embracing of a 'journalism of attachment'. In this case neutrality, objectivity and detachment are suspended and emphasis is placed on the ability to engage the audience (Carruthers, 2000: 240; McLaughlin, 2002: 166; Seib, 2002: 68; Tumber, 1997, 2002). Critics of this kind of journalism explain this trend as an attempt to provide some sort of moral certainty, not only for society as a whole but also for their own personal lives (Mclaughlin, 2002: 169). Others associate the interest in the 'human' side of war reporting with the increase of female correspondents (McLaughlin, 2002: 171). In contrast, the desire to find the 'truth' and act as a witness of the horrors that journalists encounter (Seib, 2002: 67, 72) is perhaps a more relevant reason for its advocacy. During the Afghan War, for example, the risk taken by *Sunday Express* reporter Yvonne Ridley that led to her captivity in Taliban-ruled Afghanistan, was justified by the claim that she was prepared to take a 'calculated risk' in order to get to the truth (Morgan 2001; Tumber, 2002). Similarly, Janine di Giovanni of *The Times* argued that the risks associated with reporting international conflicts are taken because of the importance of being a witness in the middle of history (di Giovanni, 2001: 8; Tumber, 2002). Without claiming that the ideal of 'truth' necessarily leads to a journalism of attachment, there are cases where this may lead to crusading, personalized reporting (McLaughlin, 2002: 166). Whatever the stance taken in relation to these questions, it is clear that the notion of 'objectivity' points to increasing ambiguity.

This ambiguity stems from a number of changes related to modern warfare and as the structures of conflict alter, the subculture of war correspondents undergoes related changes. September 11, 2001 in this sense was a landmark: it forced an acknowledgement of changes in the macro as well as the micro structures of war. The face of war, which previously had largely taken place between nation states, has changed. Terrorism has become the dominant form of international conflict. Wars between uniformed armies, limited civilian casualties, proportionate use of force and agreed warfare conventions, are all aspects of the past. The aim, the proximity of the targets, the scale and the unexpectedness of the event, all contributed, at least temporarily, to the breakdown of conventional interpretative frameworks (Sreberny, 2002: 220–1).

Cultural shifts after September 11

In what ways did the events of September 11 change the cultural forms of war/foreign correspondents? First, the boundaries between war/foreign correspondents and other reporters have become less clearly defined. The attack on the twin towers, the anthrax incidents and the subsequent fears of more terrorist attacks throughout the Western world, created a new category of 'urban war correspondent'. Those covering September 11 were not necessarily war/foreign correspondents and, as such, may have had less experience in dealing with the anxiety, fear and trauma associated with the coverage of catastrophic events on that scale. Second, the antagonistic relationship between stringers and staff correspondents (as well as between war correspondents and 'others'), illustrated in the myths of each group, may in the future be ameliorated due to the increasingly dangerous conditions faced by all. Reporting September 11 became as dangerous as reporting in a conventional war zone: *New York Daily News* photographer David Handschuh, for example, was injured as the South Tower collapsed and was rescued by firefighters (CPJ, 2001a; Tumber, 2002). The International Federation of Journalists (IFJ) reported the highest total of journalists and media personnel killed for six years in 2001. The events of September 11 were responsible for the deaths of seven media workers, while by the end of December 2001 eight journalists had been killed in Afghanistan. The anthrax attacks on US media companies threatened the lives of several media employees and resulted in the death of a photo editor at American Media in Boca Raton, Florida (CPJ, 2001a and b).

Furthermore, the storytelling ritual of war correspondents became a wider practice not only among journalists but also among non-professionals who experienced the tragic events of September 11. Writing and verbally communicating the events became a form of catharsis from the trauma (Sreberny, 2002: 221). The repetition of eyewitness accounts, final messages of the victims and the proliferation of instant expert opinions all contributed to challenging the taken-for-granted norms of journalism (Sreberny, 2002: 221). Schudson similarly argues that the series of obituaries after September 11 were closer to feature stories than conventional obituary writing, representing a new type of journalistic writing that was at the same time tribute, homage and solace (Schudson, 2002: 39). These ritualized repetitive activities opened the door to emotional responses, not only for ordinary people, but also for journalists themselves.

This is illustrated in the call for a more 'human face' in war reporting and the rebuttal of an old culture of newsgathering and war reporting founded on a 'macho' attitude that prohibited any display of emotion or psychological anguish. Chris Cramer, CNN's president of international networks, unleashed an attack against the traditional approach to newsgathering and urged media employers to allow displays of emotion from reporters. Similarly, CBS News producer Susan Zatrisky argued that emotional responses to disasters such as that following September 11 make for better journalists (Hodgson, 2001). The change, however, is set to be neither immediate nor smooth. Tony Burman, executive director of the Canadian Broadcasting Corporation, characterized some of the responses as 'over the top' (Hodgson, 2001). Within the macho culture of war correspondents, the display of emotions or, even worse, the admittance of post-traumatic stress disorder, leads to stigmatization and is often perceived as a character flaw (di Giovanni, 2001: 8; Ochberg, 2001: 12; Tumber, 2002).

Emotional literacy

After September 11, the need to deal with trauma presented an urgent challenge not only for journalists but also for the general public. The re-enactment of storytelling rituals taking the form of eyewitness accounts and obituaries tells the story of a nation that is attempting to deal with a major trauma through the means of mass communication. As the nation tries to communicate with itself, journalism changes its features and its function. The traditional ideological framework of journalism is breaking down as a new culture of journalism, one that embraces emotion and trauma, develops. Journalists themselves acknowledge the change in two ways. From a more practical perspective, September 11 stimulated a demand for safety training among war/foreign correspondents. Two leading safety training companies, AKE and Centurion, aim not only to increase awareness and anticipation of danger in order to minimize risk (AKE, 2002; Centurion, 2002), but they both also offer training in dealing with Post-Traumatic Stress Disorder (PTSD) (Tumber, 2002).

A second change that goes further than simply acknowledging and treating PTSD, is the tendency towards adopting an emotionally literate engagement, articulated through less 'detached' and more emotional journalistic expressions. The notion of a 'journalism of attachment' requires re-assessment from its earlier expressions during the Bosnian conflict. The categories of objectivity, neutrality and detachment have to be re-examined as the cultural forms of war reporting in particular and the ideological framework of journalism in general, changes. Instead of leading to the 'feminization' of news values, a 'journalism of attachment' allows journalists to deal with traumatic events and to assist the re-creation of a balance between the emotional and rational lives of their viewers, listeners and readers. The problem posed for participant journalists, identified during research on the Falklands conflict in 1982, was how to respond when events force a choice between professional commitment and participatory loyalties (Morrison and Tumber, 1988). The events of September 11 and the subsequent news media response are perhaps accelerating a trend in which attachment and emotion eventually become fully embraced into the culture of journalism. As the journalist's role as an active interpreter becomes more pronounced and recognized, the psychological dimension of war reporting is opening up a new debate. In particular, discussion is taking place on journalistic norms with the possibility of the acceptance of a more 'human face' in war reporting. What we may be witnessing is a paradigmatic shift which unsettles even further the public/journalist distinction: from detachment to involvement, from verification to assertion, from objectivity to subjectivity.

Notes

1 Max Weber places a lot of emphasis on the concept of 'responsibility' by comparing it with scholarly responsibility: 'it is almost never acknowledged that the responsibility of every honourable journalist is, on the average, not a bit lower than that of the scholar, but rather, as the war has shown, higher' (Quoted in Weber, 2001: 25).

2 For the influence of editors in reporting process (as 'gatekeepers' and 'overseers') see Tuchman, 1978 and Pedelty, 1995: 91–2.

3 Foreign desk editor Victoria Brittain talks about her work as a 'facilitator', but admits the existence of 'a whole layer of editors who are only interested . . . in budgets and what is going to cost . . .'. The importance of a good relationship with one's editor is also illustrated in the relationship between H. Russell and his editor, J. Delane during the Crimean War (McLaughlin, 2002: 18).

4 Morrison and Tumber in their 1985 study of foreign correspondents based in the UK created their own definitions and distinctions between the two groups.

5 According to Martin and Meyerson: 'Uncertainty refers to lack of predicability in, for example, the organization's environment or technology. Contradiction refers to cultural manifestations and interpretations that are capable of double meaning, as in, for example, a paradox or an irreconcilable conflict.

Confusion is caused by ignorance or lack of information, rather than by awareness of contradiction' (1988: 112).

References

Abbot, A. (1988) *The System of Professions*. Chicago: University of Chicago Press.

Adam, S.G. (2001) 'The education of Journalists', *Journalism*. 2 (3): 315–339.

AKE (2002) www.akegroup.com

Bell, M. (1996) 'TV news: how far should we go?', *Critical Studies in Mass Communications*. 13 (3): 7–16.

Bourdieu, P. (1996) *On Television and Journalism*. London: Pluto.

Bovee, W.G. (1999) *Discovering Journalism*. Westport, CN: Greenwood Press.

Carr-Saunders, A.M. and Wilson, P.A. (1964) *The Professions*. London: Frank Cass.

Carruthers, S. (ed.) (2000) *The Media at War: Communication and Conflict in the 20th Century*. Basingstoke: Macmillan Press.

Centurion Risk Assessment Service Ltd. (2002) www.centurion-riskservices. co.uk.

CPJ (The Committee to Protect Journalists) (2001a) 'US photojournalist among World Trade Centre dead'. Available at www.cpj.org/news/2001/US20sept01na. html

CPJ (The Committee to Protect Journalists) (2001b) 'CPJ concerned about threatening incidents in the US'. Available at www.cpj.org/news/2001/ US13oct01na.html

Deeds, W. (1990) 'A much harder job now', *UK Press Gazette*, 3 December.

di Giovanni, J. (2001) 'Risking more than their lives: the effects of post-traumatic stress disorder on journalists', *Freedom Forum*. Available at www.freedomforum.org 12 April.

Frost, C. (2000) *Media Ethics*. Harlow: Longman.

Gans, H.J. (1980) *Deciding What's News*. New York: Vintage Books.

Hallin, D.C. (1986) *The Uncensored War: The Media and Vietnam*. Berkeley: University of California Press.

Hodgson, J. (2001) 'Let reporters show emotion', 19 November, *Media Guardian*. Available at http://media.guardian.co.uk/attack/story/0,1301,596093,00.html accessed 21 January 2002.

Janowitz, M. (1977) 'The Journalistic Profession and the Mass Media', in Joseph Ben-David and Terry N. Clark (eds) *Culture and its Creators: Essays in honor of Edward Shils*. Chicago: University of Chicago Press.

Kellner, D. (1992) *The Persian Gulf TV War*. Boulder: Westview Press.

Martin, J and Meyerson, D. (1988) 'Organizational Cultures and the Denial, Channeling and Acknowledging of Ambiguity' in Louis R. Pondy *et al.* (eds) *Managing Ambiguity and Change*. New York: Wiley.

McLaughlin, G. (2002) *The War Correspondent*. London: Pluto.

Morgan, J. (2001) 'Rivals backlash against "foolhardy" Ridley', *Press Gazette*, 11 October. Available at www.pressgazette.co.uk, accessed 21 January 2001.

Morrison, D. and Tumber, H. (1985) 'The foreign correspondent: date-line London', *Media, Culture and Society*. 7, 445–70.

Morrison, D. and Tumber, H. (1988) *Journalists at War: the dynamics of newsreporting during the Falklands*. London: Constable.

News World Conference, Dublin (2002) in *News World*. Available at www. newsworld.org/our_news/nw2002-conference_report-day2.htm accessed 25 November 2002.

Newsweek (1996) 'Christiane's World', 26 August: 41–45.

Ochberg, F. (2001) contribution to 'Risking more than their lives: the effects of post-traumatic stress disorder on journalists', in *Freedom Forum*. Available at www. freedomforum.org 12 April.

Pedelty, M. (1995) *War Stories: the culture of foreign correspondents*. London: Routledge.

Prochnau, W. (1995) *Once Upon a Distant War*. New York: Times Books.

Seib, P. (2002) *The Global Journalist: news and consciousness in a world of conflict*. Oxford: Rowman and Littlefield.

Schudson, M. (1978) *Discovering the News: A Social History of American Newspapers*. New York: Basic Books.

Schudson, M. (2002) 'What's Unusual About Covering Politics as Usual' in B. Zelizer and S. Allan (eds) *Journalism after September 11*. London: Routledge.

Sreberny, A. (2002) 'Reconfiguring the inside and outside' in B. Zelizer and S. Allan (eds) *Journalism after September 11*. London: Routledge.

Taylor, P.M. (1992) *War and the Media*. Manchester: Manchester University Press.

Trice, Harrison M. (1993) *Occupational Subcultures in the Workplace*. New York: ILR Press.

Tuchman, G. (1972) 'Objectivity as a strategic ritual: An examination of newsmen's notions of objectivity', *American Journal of Sociology*. 77: 660–79.

Tuchman, G. (1978) *Making the News: A Study in the Construction of Reality*. New York: Free Press.

Tumber, H. (1997) 'Bystander journalism, or journalism of attachment', *Intermedia*. 25 (1): 4–7.

Tumber, H. (2001) 'Democracy in the Information Age: The Role of the Fourth Estate in Cyberspace', *Information, Communication, & Society*. 4 (1): 95–112.

Tumber, H. (2002) 'Reporting Under Fire' in B. Zelizer and S. Allan (eds) *Journalism After September 11*. London: Routledge.

Tunstall, J. (1971) *Journalists at War*. London: Constable.

Ward, S.J. (1998) 'Answer to Martin Bell: Objectivity and Attachment in Journalism', *The Harvard International Journal of Press/Politics*. 3 (3): 121–125.

Weber, M. (2001) 'Political Journalists' in J. Tunstall (ed.) *Media Occupations and Professions: A Reader*. Oxford: Oxford University Press.

Zelizer, B. (1992) 'CNN, the Gulf War, and Journalistic Practice', *Journal of Communication*. 42 (1): 66–81.

JOURNALISTS AND WAR: THE TROUBLING NEW TENSIONS POST 9/11

Nik Gowing

I was a reporter at Independent Television News (ITN) for 18 years. That included 14 years at Channel 4 News where I was diplomatic editor for six years. Since 1996, I have been a main presenter at BBC World, the global TV news service. When I began working for the channel we barely had ten million viewers globally. In January 2003, BBC World had 244 million viewers in 200 countries.

I am very much involved in presenting conflict day in, day out, on air for anywhere between three and six hours a day. So what I want to discuss is something from the front line of TV news, which happens to be a presenter's desk in West London. I want to focus on what I see as very significant changes in covering conflict, particularly, but not exclusively, since 9/11. There are trends in my business that I do not think many people have detected because of the overwhelming nature of what happened on 9/11. I would argue that rather than being a pivotal moment in news coverage, 9/11 was the most graphic example of a trend which had already been changing exponentially our real-time business of news coverage, especially in TV.

We are still struggling in our business with the dilemma of news versus rumour. The business that I am in – real-time continuous news – is highlighting that more than ever. The key is to distil news from rumours in a timely way with credibility. Being first with a version of developments can have short-term commercial and competitive advantage. But there can be a long-term cost for credibility and reputation for accuracy.

In my early years at ITN, we used to record news on ten-minute cans of celluloid film. The film would have to be shipped back physically to a laboratory somewhere and then sent on to London. That could take a few hours or it could take a few days (developing the film itself took 90 minutes). Now with a video cassette and digital electronic signal the

Figure 16.1 BBC armoured vehicle hit in mortar raid in Macedonia, May 2001

cycle can be instantaneous or take no more than a few minutes for the signal to be beamed up on a tiny bit of highly portable transmission equipment from the middle of nowhere. This transformation is having a dramatic effect on our business, both for those of us dealing in video as well as for those dealing with audio and words.

I want to underline a phenomenon which I christened the 'tyranny of real time' in my 1994 Harvard University study (Gowing, 1994). I warned then it was coming; we are now in the thick of it. As confirmed by any dictionary, tyranny refers to something that is 'cruel and arbitrary'. That is the impact of new technology on the matrix of real-time journalism from conflict zones. Real-time is not just about broadcasting or daily journalism. It also applies to those who write news magazines articles, e.g. for *Newsweek* or *Time* for a few days hence. The writers are under the same kind of tyranny of compressed time lines as us broadcasters.

This may sound slightly odd when talking about war and all the horrors that conflict implies. However, in my view, although media reporting of war has been a dangerous business for a long time, it is now more dangerous than ever. Consider what happened to £80,000 worth of BBC armoured vehicle when hit in the wrong place by a stray mortar in Macedonia in May 2001 (Figure 16.1).

As journalists and news organizations it is our job to report the deadly business of war. The new, insidious development is that because of the impact of our real-time capability to bear witness immediately, we are being actively targeted by warriors, warlords and forces of even the most highly developed governments who do not want us to see what they are doing. This is the price for the new technological advances that we journalists can now use to work in conflicts. We have more transparency from more parts of the world than we have ever had before. But it is now even more dangerous to use this increasingly familiar, low-cost and lightweight communications technology.

Those journalists who went to Afghanistan and were murdered, probably by bandits or in revenge, as they drove down the road, provide evidence of this vulnerability in the new transparency of war. A Swedish cameraman was killed near Mazar-e-Sharif because he had a particularly large amount of money on him. TV teams need large amounts of money to facilitate coverage of war. The *Toronto Star* correspondent, Kathleen Kenna, was almost killed when her vehicle was hit by a mortar as she defied military controls to find out what was happening in Eastern Afghanistan back in November 2001.

And then, of course, there was the murder of Daniel Pearl, the *Wall Street Journal* correspondent in January 2002. I went through Eastern Europe at the time of *Solidarnosc* and Charter 77 and I remember being invited to go and meet dissidents in cafes or parks. I did not know who would be there or whether I would be picked up by the police. But we knew then that probably the worst thing that could happen, as happened to me on several occasions, was that we would be beaten up and thrown out of the country. For Daniel Pearl the equivalent of the dead-letter drop to a dissident in Prague, Warsaw or Moscow in the 1980s was the e-mail contact with those in Pakistan he hoped might reveal more about Al-Qaeda. Instead they used the new technology to trap him, and he paid with his life.

The Italian photographer, Raffaele Ciriello, was shot dead in Ramallah, West Bank on 13 March 2002 because he too was determined to do his job of bearing witness. A tank opened fire when Rafaelle pulled out a small video camera. It is the kind of camera that anyone – whether media or non-professional – can buy for £600 in a high-street shop and stick in their pockets or rucksack, but which is now essentially part of a real-time broadcast platform. For any journalist, the very act of pulling out a video camera now puts you at great risk if an army like the Israeli Defence Force (IDF) thinks you are threatening their operational security. According to the International Press Institute, this is now part of a concerted strategy by the Israeli Army to control reports on the recent surge in armed hostilities in the region.

I am trying to highlight the real tension that exists now because of the new lightweight, go-anywhere nature of our business. We are not just talking any more about £250,000 satellite dishes put on hotel roofs well back from the action. We are talking about new £20,000 devices linked to a satellite telephone which beam up video pictures of live war from the front line, or very close to it. This technology is now part of the new information dynamic of war that is making journalists far more intrusive, and therefore more vulnerable. This technology is much cheaper, we can take more risks with it and we can forward deploy it much more easily. But the price is that we are seen potentially as spies by some at the military and government command levels.

The risks go even further. In the *Media Guardian* of 8 April 2002, I summarized my findings after months of investigation into the bombing of the pan-Arabic television news network Al-Jazeera office in Kabul on 12 November 2001. The matter remains unresolved, with outstanding ominous questions. Why did the Americans bomb the bureau of a highly respected news organization? There are conflicting views about Al-Jazeera and their coverage. But they are brave journalists, many are BBC-trained and they are doing a very good job. Why did the Americans hit that building with two 500lb bombs? It may have been an error. However, after extensive phone conversations with US Central Command in Florida over many weeks, the US claimed that there was 'significant military activity' taking place inside the building. This raises the troubling question: how can the activities of a news organization reasonably be construed as 'significant military activity'?

By that analysis, our entire business of 'bearing witness' in conflict can be construed as 'significant military activity'. We record and transmit real-time information from a war zone that in many ways challenges and contradicts the official reported version of what is taking place. The Al-Jazeera office was there in Kabul for 20 months with a satellite up-link before the Americans hit it, although the US claims that the intelligence which led them to believe there was 'significant military activity' had not revealed that crucial fact. It is odd that all the capabilities of US intelligence can detect 'significant military activity' but not discover a basic fact that this was a news organization's office.

Nevertheless, US Central Command eventually claimed to me that the senior Al-Qaeda figure Mohammed Ataf was in there on the night they hit it. There are thus many deeply worrying inconsistencies. After many months of investigation for BBC News, the Americans now say that they will hit any office or uplink facility that they consider to have some kind of potentially hostile military use. This could include a videophone from a front line trench that is beaming up 'inconvenient' real-time details about fighting and targeting. They made clear to me they will not ask any more questions, even if we give them GPS co-ordinates of where we, as journalists, are working. We could be hit in order to remove what warplane pilots have described to me as 'the threat of the media'.

Moving on to 9/11, I was on air shortly after the catastrophe began to unfold live on our TV feeds from New York City. What happened on that dreadful day highlights the disconnection now between the real-time capability to transmit, particularly from a place like New York, and the complexity of discovering what really happened. In other words, it raises questions about the accuracy of the reporting itself.

Even in those first few minutes and hours when we had the video of the two planes hitting the World Trade Center, and then the catastrophic collapse of the buildings, we could not be sure what had happened. We could only speculate about navigational or avionics problems on the planes. Terrorism was probably third or fourth in our speculation. It took literally one to two hours before we had a pretty clear idea of what had happened. Reporting lagged well behind reality. The capacity to broadcast pictures and capability to broadcast real-time pictures from places like the West Bank and the Middle East is now ahead of our ability to do journalism and to find the answers to the questions 'why, what, where, when and how'.

A month after 9/11, an American Airlines plane went down at Kennedy Airport. I remember walking into the BBC World newsroom and saw smoke rising once again over the borough of Queens. I still recall thinking: 'this must be Al-Qaeda's second punch?' It was a reasonable, but incorrect, assumption. In the first hour, the word from Kennedy Airport was that an American Airlines 767 had crashed on landing. So we reported it. But within the hour, the explanation from the New York Port Authority had changed diametrically. The plane had been an Airbus A300 which crashed on taking off.

Now, even though we reported an official source in good faith, some would probably complain that this was bad journalism. Yet it was those who you expect to get basic information right – the official sources – who got it wrong in the first place. This is not only the tyranny of real time. It shows how all of the professions – whether media, government, military or diplomats – who are dealing with information in an unfolding crisis are confounded by the very basic necessity to filter and validate information at high speed. It is an imperfect skill, where expectations – especially of the audience – exceed our capabilities to validate and confirm reports, at least in the first few minutes or hours.

The need to report and get the facts clear leads to a new kind of tension that blurs the meaning of truth in a crisis. Truth and accuracy can never be absolute in real time. This is not simply the result of 9/11. Day by day, hour by hour we at BBC News have endured these conflicting pressures in a host of conflict zones like Kashmir, Sri Lanka, or the Intifada. In New York on September 11 the phenomenon was merely highlighted dramatically in the world's most connected city where there is so much telecommunications capability that virtually anything is available on a satellite somewhere and somehow in real time.

Overall, I think we are now seeing a dramatic asymmetry between our business and the government/official/military side in conflict. The US Military now have this massive new Unmanned Aerial reconnaissance Vehicle (UAV) called Global Hawk (Figure 16.2).

Figure 16.2   Global Hawk – US Unmanned Aerial Reconnaissance Vehicle

Its extraordinary (and secret) functions take up virtually as much bandwidth as the whole of the American Air Force put together – that is if every single piece of equipment on board is actually activated. It has the capability to create a multi-spectrum, 3D electronic matrix of almost everything happening anywhere in the battle space, including in a challenging and hostile location like Afghanistan.

Yet it cannot sense some of the things that we as journalists are able to report on the ground. Our new lightweight, cheap, mobile reporting technology can challenge the view from Global Hawk. This is the asymmetry in information power from the battlefield. A few hundred or a few thousand dollars worth of journalist equipment can now get under the wire of controls that the military expect to have in a war zone. It can thereby challenge the government version of what is happening, thereby deepening the tension with journalists.

We saw that very specifically in Afghanistan. The asymmetry is similar to that which enabled the 9/11 hijackers to use a few box-cutters to terrorise the aircraft crew and passengers, turn civilian aircraft into guided missiles, and thereby defy all the explicit security controls and military defences of the world's dominant hyperpower.

Let me illustrate this with three examples. First in Kabul where an International Committee of the Red Cross (ICRC) warehouse was bombed by the US on 26 October 2001 because the Americans said it was being used by the Taliban. When a single digital picture emerged in defiance of Taliban controls using this new technology, US defence secretary Donald Rumsfeld initially argued that the ICRC had exaggerated the situation. But within 48 hours the US had to admit that it had indeed hit the ICRC warehouse. There was similar US embarrassment over the bombing of the UN de-mining depot, an act it had initially denied.

The same happened when, via Al-Jazeera, the Taliban produced a picture of a clearly identifiable US helicopter wheel. They claimed that this proved a US helicopter had been downed. Rumsfeld again said that this was an exaggeration and a lie, even though the picture told us – it bore witness – that something had taken place. Two days later the

FIRST SIGHT OF SPECIAL FORCES

Figure 16.3 Front page of *Evening Standard* 5 November 2001

Americans had to admit that a Black Hawk helicopter had lost its undercarriage when it had taken off and hit the top of a building somewhere. This is evidence that the media's very cheap, low-tech capability can challenge the stories of governments and the military who believe that they have the right – and the resources – to control everything.

The third example is the front page of the *London Evening Standard* on 5 November 2001 (Figure 16.3). I can make a personal comparison here. I broke the news twelve years ago that the Russians were leaving Afghanistan. I was about the only journalist in Afghanistan and all I had was a telex machine. This picture was taken by a photojournalist working for the *Evening Standard* on his little digital camera. He took it and two hours later it was on the front page of the *Standard* from a remote place called Golbahar. I was giving a lecture recently at the NATO College in Rome, among the audience was a Special Forces officer who was on the MI-17 helicopter. He came up and told me that none of them had realized they had been seen, let alone recorded and splashed across a front page like this. But that is the new transparency, and we saw the principle in operation time and time again in Afghanistan. We even had Donald Rumsfeld showing a picture of Special Forces operating on horseback – probably pretty uncomfortably. Apparently the Pentagon was very worried when they suddenly got a request for 15 saddles and drops of hay into Afghanistan until they realized that Special Forces were operating there.

There is, however, another side to this. We have up-link satellite technology that can be packed into two 5-kilogram attaché cases and carried as hand baggage onto an aircraft (see Figure 16.4). As a presenter, I could even carry this myself in order to broadcast live from a location close to the thick of battle. No longer do we need just bulky, expensive satellite ground stations. And as bandwidth capacity expands swiftly, the quality of the signals from these videophones will soon approach the best digital quality.

7E Communications, the company that developed this device planned to build 50 in its first year, 2001 (Figure 16.4). Such was the demand that they built 600 in the four months immediately following 9/11. 300 of those were deployed into Afghanistan in the first few weeks of conflict, thereby creating this exciting new media transparency.

But this transparency has generated a new and disturbing paradox: it has helped to create the new dangers for journalists to which I have already referred. And these dangers have in turn created a new, self-restricting ordinance. Too many of the places from which our new technology can facilitate graphic reporting have become too dangerous, in particular due to the threat that our up-links will be bombed Al-Jazeera-style because our reporting and electronic signatures can be construed as 'significant military activity'.

So in Afghanistan the dangers are forcing journalists to live and co-exist at Bagram Airbase with the military. Hacks try to sleep under canvas alongside a 24/7 runway where there are air movements at all hours. They rely on the military not just for sparse and suspect military information but also for food, water and sanitation. This puts immense emotional and professional pressure on journalists who feel corralled by the military and denied information even about the Special Forces they can witness on the base a few tents away.

Such arrangements are a Faustian bargain. It is a deeply uncomfortable situation which leads to questions about how much information media colleagues really receive, and how independent news organizations can really be. They are the kind of controls that many in the military have wanted to re-impose for a long time and it has happened because of the dangers of working in this transparent environment. The new strains between media and military have confirmed the bad impact on long-term relations which may take a considerable time to improve, if ever.

Finally, a note on the conflict in the West Bank. The Electronic Intifada website (http://electronicIntifada.net) declares its function as 'to equip you to challenge myth, distortion and spin in the media in an informed way enabling you to affect positive changes in media coverage of war'. In other words the primary intention of the reporting on this site is to challenge the versions of news broadcast and published by the well-established, well-known media brands. The E-Intifada is

Figure 16.4 Videophone used by reporters, developed by 7E Communications

challenging headlong their (and our?) legitimacy, especially among the younger, more radical Palestinians and Muslims who are attracted by the site's form of journalism.

That is why I ask the question: who are the media now? And how true or at least accurate is everything we see and hear reported? The way the IDF operation in Jenin in April 2002 laid siege to the refugee camp and cut off all access, highlights how electronic information can evade a military cordon and emerge. But what is the efficacy of the emotional reporting that somehow seeps out via the internet or mobile phones?

At the time of the IDF operation, the issue in Jenin was whether a massacre of Palestinians was taking place unseen by journalists and humanitarian workers. Human Rights Watch and Amnesty International later published investigations which confirmed there had been no massacre in the strict meaning of the word. However, 52 Palestinians were confirmed as dead and they raised questions about the conduct of some IDF soldiers under the laws of war and their humanitarian obligations. Internet and mobile phone coverage challenged the very limited IDF version. The emotion of its haphazard reporting from often traumatized writers or amateur correspondents created a very clear picture of what might be happening. It created a perception that at the time could never be checked. It also created a dilemma: should we as the big news brands report uncheckable claims from unknown sources? It is tempting to report without question the most emotive descriptions and claims. Some did, others restrained themselves.

As with all conflict, reporting what we have seen is a real crunch between traditional and new forms of journalism facilitated through the internet and digital recording systems. It is often unfiltered, polemicized and radicalized. As such it can produce the most horrendous images of people being killed or maimed in a host of different ways.

These new tensions are thus distorting the matrix of information in which we as journalists are working in conflict. At this moment the most important aspiration is to be sensitized to the pressures, and to question material, whichever source it comes from.

Reference

Gowing, Nik (1994) 'Real-Time Television Coverage of Armed Conflicts and Diplomatic Crises: Does it Pressure or Distort Foreign Policy Decisions?' Joan Shorenstein Barone Center, John F. Kennedy School of Government. Cambridge, MA: Harvard University.

17

CONFLICT AND CONTROL: THE WAR IN AFGHANISTAN AND THE 24-HOUR NEWS CYCLE

Kieran Baker

'Act of War' was the *USA Today* headline on 12 September 2001 'as jetliners strike US landmarks, America's sense of security is shattered'. The lead article went on to say that 'it may have been the bloodiest day in US history, when our two biggest office towers were obliterated and the Pentagon, symbol of our military authority, was ripped open like an egg carton. Our commercial jetliners were turned into weapons of mass murder, and we had to stop doing things we always do, from trading stocks to going to Disney World'.

It was a Tuesday evening Hong Kong time, when I got an almost unbelievable call from my boss in Atlanta: a plane had gone into the World Trade Center in New York. We were to be prepared to do any type of reaction coverage out of Hong Kong regarding the economic or market impact of the events. It was not until the second plane hit the other tower that we were put on a more mobile footing; the thinking, of course, was that this was no accident, but a perceived terrorist attack.

By the following morning, news organizations had identified Osama bin Laden as the prime suspect. CNN immediately deployed crews not just to assist in the coverage for New York but also to make a mad scramble to head, as soon as possible, to Pakistan. A logistical race of sorts was already on for the various news organizations. I was based in Hong Kong, coordinating the entire Asia coverage and Pakistan and Afghanistan were on my beat. We were also 12 hours ahead of Atlanta, who were, not surprisingly, sent into a 'news panic'. 'Who can we get in first? Who has a visa for Pakistan? Where are our videophones?' These were important logistical questions, and part of my job was simply making the necessary connections. CNN was one of the first teams into Pakistan because it had covered the recent elections, and the

Bangkok team had obtained multiple entry visas. A quick start paid off well later.

We also understood that we had to report on the unfolding reaction to this quite incomprehensible news. Back upstairs in our Hong Kong bureau we sent out crews to the busy international airport, where flights to the United States had been stopped, and asked people simply what they thought. In our office we watched in disbelief: every network we monitored was showing and repeating the same stunning pictures. If a universal impact was possible, it was clear that the world was mesmerized by what it saw, over and over again. This was an event that broke out live and in front of people, not only the poor desperate people dashing for cover as debris fell from the sky in Manhattan, but a world audience familiar with the famous skyline. To me, the destruction of the World Trade Center seemed to rock the United States in almost biblical proportions – here was a country that appeared invincible, yet had taken an epic blow.

My first trip to Afghanistan was in the October of 2000, when I accompanied Madame Ogata, then Head of the United Nations High Commissioner for Refugees (UNHCR), on a trip to Herat. Most news organizations took every opportunity they could to get into Afghanistan to report on this desperately isolated country, so the idea of following a 'soft-news' related trip always had the potential for more and at least provided a window into what I could only describe as a medieval world. As a news organization it was important to keep a presence in such a remote location – after all it took days to get there and sometimes weeks to gain a visa. On this particular occasion the Taliban wanted publicity and in fact the whole trip was, by their standards, well organized. Upon arrival at the dilapidated Herat airport we were treated to a military welcome which, while not textbook army academy style, showed off in full the Taliban's control over the country. This was a 'control' that found favour with some, but created fear for the majority. My most vivid memory is of a boy, maybe eleven or twelve, coming up to me and asking if I could teach him English. He said that he had had to learn in secret with a woman teacher and when I asked him how life was here in Herat, he just looked at me with desperate eyes.

It was such examples of fear that were cited by the United States in its military campaign in the winter of 2001. In fact the propaganda war began in earnest almost immediately after the twin towers fell, as President George Bush described the act of terror as 'an attack on freedom'. This helped to pull together a coalition and allow a sense of mourning amongst international politicians as they sent letters of condolence or visited New York in person to acknowledge the fall of the twin towers. Also, over time, the US administration was to take the unusual step of going on Arab television to present its case for what would be essentially an attack on a Muslim country. Its primary purpose was to reach the growing and influential Arab audience that was now able to view news from regional channels, the most notable of course being Al-Jazeera.

One of the most dramatic moments in the television coverage of the Afghanistan conflict was the emergence of certain audio and video tapes that were hand-delivered to the Kabul offices of Al-Jazeera. They showed bin Laden often in a cave or in a military training camp discussing his view of the world and how he thought he was going to change the world. Such tapes and the broadcasting of them sent shockwaves through Western media outlets, as well as the US State Department. Newsrooms were forced to debate the airing of them and discuss whether they were in fact subliminal messages being broadcast on national and international television. Al-Jazeera, for their part, had no problem with using these tapes. In fact, they had an exclusive and used it to their advantage, like any broadcaster who had been given such primary evidence. Some questions have been subsequently raised by US news organizations that now seek to place significant checks and balances on the usage of such bin Laden tapes. This is a reminder that, even with a free press, there is a determination to prevent terrorist messages from reaching their desired audience. Al-Jazeera, to their credit, say that Western news groups published and interviewed IRA representatives during 'sensitive' times. Interesting parallels on how the Arab and Western media have covered the 'war on terrorism' will continue to be a source of study for scholars and journalists alike, particularly as we move closer towards another conflict: Iraq.

Both stories – Afghanistan and Iraq – however, demand the same crucial components: covering conflicts on the scale of major international wars requires an ability to present information, sometimes under fire, in a fast and accurate fashion, the key ingredient to the 24-hour cable or satellite marketplace. Add in the competitive and commercial pressures of various news conglomerates and the emergence of rival regional news channels in the Middle East and Asia, and one can see how the 24-hour news landscape has changed dramatically in just the last five years. Producing television newsgathering in a 24-hour cycle places an incredible burden on resources, both technical and human, with teams working literally around the clock under harsh conditions, trying to meet hourly deadlines and to maintain an editorial edge. It is no wonder then that news channels, operating with the 24-hour ethos, lend themselves to criticism that accuracy is sometimes sacrificed for speed.

Also, does television find itself manipulated by local minders or officials and are there elements of subjectivity and added pressures of pandering to certain politicians during times of crisis? The answer is probably yes: a little of everything comes under the banner of television news because politicians and military regimes understand the power of television news, even though good journalism, whatever its medium, should always win through.

Other arguments made by the detractors of 24-hour news culture are that the repetition of live shots of reporters prevents an accurate understanding or acknowledgement of the 'real' news, because so much time is spent standing by the live-shot location rather than gathering 'real' and informative journalism. Substance, in other words, is sacrificed for style. This was never more apparent than in the coverage from Pakistan in the days after 11 September. The immediate criticism was that we were all suffering from the same problem of 'rooftop journalism', locked into 24-hour a day live shots from the top of the now famous Marriott Hotel. I even saw a *Vanity Fair* piece with photographs of 'that rooftop' explaining the limitations and frustrations for journalists covering those early days of the conflict. In fairness, this was the closest logistical spot we could all get to in a timely fashion. As the weeks and months went by, most TV companies expanded their operation to Peshawar and Quetta, and a few even tried to get into Afghanistan, either dressed in a *burqa* or being pushed across in a wheelbarrow.

For this journalist, seeing the frontlines and accessing the story as far as I could would always be my number one priority, and by sitting in Hong Kong I would see nothing. After staying up for all of 11 September and most of the 12th, and after continually pressurizing my boss, on the morning of the 13th I left Hong Kong for Singapore, then direct to Lahore, where I changed planes for Islamabad, arriving in the very early hours of the 14th where I joined my recently arrived London colleagues.

This was my second trip to Pakistan, which, while it did not make me an expert, meant that I knew some good people and understood the environment. I had been there almost exactly a year earlier to help train a *Time* magazine correspondent to work in television and to set up an Islamabad bureau, and had grown to like the town, if not the country. My home, like the last time, was the Marriott, a fairly well equipped four-star hotel, but this time I was not to be alone. Some 1,500 journalists were to come through the hotel doors over the next few months, taking over the building in ways it had not been designed for. The growing demands and expectations of television news reminds me increasingly of how the film industry operates: by the end of this operation we had ten drivers, a fleet of four-wheel drive vehicles, five fixers and translators, and over 50 staff.

Big television newsgathering budgets allow you to hire hotel suites to make sure there is enough accommodation, not just for personnel, but also primarily for the equipment. We had to decide where to set up the edit area, where to put a tracking booth and how to organize a news desk. In particular, everything revolves around where to place the satellite dish and its proximity to the camera and live-shot location. We needed a flat rooftop space, some shelter from the sun for the satellite engineers and a tent to protect the satellite dish from the elements. On one occasion, a storm came in so quickly that it blew a dish and other equipment off the roof, only to end up in the swimming pool seven floors below. We eventually had to ask the hotel to build a platform, so that the limited space available was maximized to facilitate all the networks' requests. While we were one of the first to arrive and pay for our space on the roof (yes, we were charged a daily rate), we knew over time the hotel would have to provide more space for other networks too. Sometimes television teams work well together on location, sometimes they do not.

CNN was in a unique situation in reporting the events of 11 September. Rather than just relying on the rooftop space at the Marriott, CNN had a reporter actually in Afghanistan. Being at the source of a story is the overriding force that drives any journalist, and being inside Afghanistan was everyone's priority. Yet as the weeks went by, it became apparent that the Taliban were not going to allow any more journalists to enter, and in fact they expelled those that were in Kabul. Only by pushing hard were CNN allowed to travel down to Kandahar to plead its case direct to Mullah Omar's press person. While networks struggled to grapple with this problem of access, the Taliban's embassy in Islamabad became the focal point of their view of the events of 11 September, and the increasing isolation that they were now facing. CNN managed to cover live and exclusively the daily press conferences that were being held at the Taliban's embassy.

As weeks went by we began to realize we would never get our visas to go into Afghanistan, so Pakistan became a focus for a variety of reasons. With the world's media in town, Pakistan President Parvez Musharraf came under considerable scrutiny. However, he handled being in the spotlight extraordinarily well and in fact rose to the challenge. He was quick to address the Pakistani nation, explaining that they faced a new opportunity, in backing the US on a proposed 'war on terrorism'. He was smart enough to use these television addresses as a public platform to also push the issue of Kashmir onto the agenda, a tactic that later was to bring India and Pakistan back to the brink. But as a nuclear power, the US looked on Pakistan as a pivotal ally, hoping to secure its help, although Pakistan always said that it would not allow US planes to land and take off from military bases.

For me, I was to become part of CNN's operation in Quetta, south-western Pakistan, in the remote region of Baluchistan, a frontline state with strong Taliban connections and a rabid, radical religious element, made up of high profile supporters of the fundamentalist *Jamiat-e-Ulema Islam* party.

On the face of it was a somewhat scary place. However as I found out when I arrived, journalists were to be kept in the lap of luxury at the Serena hotel, serene by name and by nature. An oasis within a town that hadn't seen rain in over five years, water flowed into the garden close to the verandah where we all had breakfast. However, we were essentially guests of the Pakistani intelligence service for weeks on end, as they went to elaborate measures ('for our own security') to keep us all together and prevent us from travelling to the border region where the refugees were massing – firstly because of fear of air-strikes and then because of the reality of them.

The Serena hotel was a confine for all journalists; our names had been taken when we arrived at the airport, they were taken again in the hotel, our rooms were cross-referenced and our ability to leave was highly restricted. Armed guards accompanied us on even the most banal trips to the bazaar; they also barricaded the gates of the hotel to prevent any of the locals from running in and machine-gunning the lot of us. In hindsight, it turned out to be a very good precaution. As each Friday's 'day of rage' came and went, the pre-bombing campaign tension rose, culminating on the day after the air attacks on Afghanistan began with a massive demonstration outside the hotel that turned very nasty. In town, a cinema was burnt as well as other buildings, including one housing an aid agency.

But as weeks went by, things died down and the numbers of demonstrators dropped dramatically. Musharraf's policy of locking up the key religious leaders proved effective. Without them around to whip-up the frenzy, support drifted away. However the sentiment was still there, particularly when you moved closer to the border where feelings among the locals ran very high. One of our colleagues, Robert Fisk from the *Independent*, broke down in his car in a remote town and when he got out to ask for help he was very badly beaten up. This was a reminder of some of the hazards, but nothing compared to the deadly problems that faced journalists as they made their way towards Jalalabad after the fall of Kabul that resulted in a convoy being attacked and its occupants killed.

As the military campaign broadened so did the aspirations of television news executives, who were trying hard to maintain interest for the audience as the initial ratings declined. MSNBC's Ashleigh Banfield had created the format for a solo anchored show 'live' from a remote location. Like any good idea in television it eventually gets copied. The CNN executives in Atlanta hit on what they thought would be a winning formula, a half-hour broadcast hosted from a regional location and always produced 'live'. It helped that CNN chief international correspondent, Christiane Amanpour, was the primary presenter for this slice of TV, providing her with a platform that capitalized on her unique ability to retain information, juggle different international stories and solo anchor a show. So, weeks later, arriving at the barren and dusty Quetta Airport in the heart of Baluchistan, Pakistan's remote desert, mountainous and tribal hinterland that borders Afghanistan, I was relieved to see Christiane Amanpour and her producer Pierre Bairin unloading their equipment into one the many four-wheel drive vehicles we had recently hired. There was no time for them to stop at the Serena Hotel, because we were heading straight to the Afghan border to set up for a programme called *Live From. . . .* It involved, however, some difficult logistics as we were eventually heading on the journey to Kandahar. A satellite dish had been placed on the back of a truck, a house at the border at been hired, supplies, sleeping bags and tents purchased. This would be a rough trip of sorts, but another example of what it takes to get things done.

Looking back on how the media covered Afghanistan, and the access journalists were given, however, raises some interesting parallels with the impending conflict in Iraq. The control Iraq exerts over the media is not dissimilar to the Taliban in Afghanistan, but perhaps the Taliban were not as well organized. The Iraqi Government now employs a coordinator in addition to the regular minder that accompanies every journalist. Fears of hostage taking, chemical weapons and worse, however, remain ahead in this conflict.

In fact the more I look back at the build-up to the American air assault on Afghanistan I am reminded of the same diplomatic approach and rationale. A bullish Bush being held in check, only temporarily, by a pragmatic Powell, the latter adding the only intellectual checks and balances to war. But why now? Many in the Arab world despise Saddam Hussein but prefer a more peaceful means of removing the problem. The conflict in Afghanistan and the control exerted over the media may be nothing compared to what happens in 2003. The Iraq conflict will be another defining moment in the fate and future of the American empire.

18

IN THE FOG OF WAR . . .

Yvonne Ridley

Instead of writing the news in 2001, it was I who became the story, which was a rather alien position for any journalist to find themselves in.

I was a Sunday newspaper journalist, which is quite a different style and branch of reporting to that of the daily newspaper journalist. Both roles are very demanding but the pressures are different. Daily reporting usually involves tight, daily deadlines and reacting to the day's events. Sunday newspaper journalism requires more lateral thinking and trying to second-guess the news agenda five or six days ahead.

As a Sunday journalist, when I arrived in Islamabad for the build up to the war, I therefore avoided being spoon-fed with propaganda being spouted from Washington, London and anywhere else. I was trying to think ahead to what would be interesting for our readers and so went for stories that would entertain and inform the readers and give them an idea of what life was like in Pakistan and neighbouring Afghanistan.

After three weeks it became obvious the bombing would not start for at least another ten days and so I looked ahead, with difficulty, to see what I could write for the coming Sunday. After several days of pondering and speaking to locals in Pakistan, I decided that I would sneak across to Afghanistan and do a humanitarian feature on the life of ordinary Afghan people living under the Taliban. I wanted to know their hopes and fears for the future and, more importantly, how they viewed the prospect of being bombed by America and Britain and being dragged in to a war as a direct result of the September 11 terrorist strike in the US.

I had already written at length about the plight of Afghan refugees who were living in camps in Pakistan, some of them for a period of 20 years. I had also spoken to clerics in one of the most 'notorious' *madrasas* which had awarded an honorary degree to a Mr Osama bin Laden. So my main reason for going into Afghanistan was to try and come up with a different angle, one that would be interesting for readers and one that rival newspapers would not be publishing. I was actually working on two projects that week. One involved going into Afghanistan undercover while the other involved going to a suspected Al-Qaeda training camp thought to be in a remote location in Kashmir. My guide decided that the latter would have been a very, very dangerous thing to do, which made the Afghanistan project look like a breeze in comparison.

While I was busy ferreting around for 'Sunday' stories, I was quite amused, in the build-up to the war, to see TV reporters spending much of their time on the rooftops of the Pearl Continental in Peshawar or the Marriott in Islamabad. It is very difficult for television because you need exciting pictures and backdrops, and some journalists became quite inventive in making viewers think that they were in the thick of the action.

The reality is that many of them never left the rooftops of the hotels and the majority of those with the Northern Alliance were up to seven miles away from the frontlines. It was very difficult for journalists stuck with the Northern Alliance to give an accurate idea of what was going on with this war, to such an extent that when it did start, some TV reporters paid Northern Alliance soldiers $5 a round to start firing off as the cameras rolled. They could broadcast their piece looking very combative, dressed for a frontline situation when, in actual fact, it could not have been further than the truth. One of the stray bullets from a Kalashnikov fired by a soldier, who had been paid by one particular television company to provide good sound effects, actually hit and killed a little girl some distance away.

This was always going to be a war without witnesses. The Taliban certainly did not want the media in their country. They had kicked out most, if not all, of the Western journalists. As I mentioned, the journalists who were with the Northern Alliance had great difficulty because some of them were quite a few miles away and could only rely on soldiers telling them what was happening and so there was no accurate reporting. It was a very difficult war for everyone to cover.

The British and the American press were on the whole quite gung-ho, with the exception of the *Independent*, *The Guardian* and strangely enough the *Mirror*. The *Mirror* had what some people said was quite a 'good war' because they actually did step back and take an alternative view of what was happening out in Afghanistan. One of the classic examples of poor reporting was the liberation of Kabul, which, if you listen to the Pentagon or to Downing Street, was quite a fantastic liberation: women were throwing off their *burqas*, men were shaving off their beards. The reality was quite different. This was definitely nothing like the liberation of Kuwait or Port Stanley. Basically Afghanistan actually swapped one nasty, little regime for another nasty, little regime and this was captured perfectly in the *Mirror* with a dramatic picture of some Northern Alliance soldiers about to blow the head off a Taliban soldier who was begging for his life. The headline was along the lines of 'Welcome To Our New Best Friends'. The other newspapers all carried nice war-like picture of tanks rolling through Kabul with flowers being thrown. I have been back to Afghanistan twice since then and believe me, there is nothing great to celebrate there.

The American press pretty much followed the Pentagon line for the first eight months. In fact the Pentagon have since admitted that they had a propaganda machine that was basically churning out lies and were quite unashamed about that fact. It is quite unfortunate because the American people, who rely on their newspapers to find out exactly what was happening, were being very misinformed. It was beginning to smack of the old Soviet style of misinformation which spoon-fed propaganda to a tame media.

However, to tell the truth was regarded as being unpatriotic and disloyal and not the thing to do. In fact newspapers in the UK were criticized by the British Government for not supporting the country in its hour of need. But some of the propaganda that came out was very misleading. Reading the newspapers after my release I noticed that Tony Blair was savage about the Taliban and really demonized them before the bombing, saying that these people were so evil they won't even let children fly kites. Now I had heard this about the Taliban before and I actually asked them: 'why don't you let children fly kites? What's the harm in flying a kite?' And they said: 'Well, you know, we don't let them fly kites in built-up areas because they get their kites wrapped around the power lines, they electrocute themselves, they plunge villages and districts out of power for two or three days at a time and that's why we don't let them fly kites'. This actually made sense, and I reflected about flying a kite up Oxford Street in London and wondered how far I would get before being arrested. It was pure propaganda but because the Prime Minister is saying it you just think that this must be the truth. Either that or he is lying or has been lied to.

Certainly when I was captured by the Taliban I did not think I was going to see the sun set that day because I too had fallen victim to propaganda – that I had been captured by the most brutal, evil regime in the world. My imagination was running riot as I thought 'what are these people going to do to me?' In fact they treated me with the greatest courtesy and respect. They were so concerned that I had gone on a hunger strike (because I wanted to use the telephone) that they got a doctor in case I was ill. In fact they tried to more or less kill me with kindness rather than anything else. So this was quite strange for me, because, as I say, I had also fallen for the popular line that they were indeed evil and tortured women. At least I was not bound, gagged, shackled and flown halfway across the world to wake up in a cage in Cuba.

When I was released, one of the first questions I was asked was 'how did the Taliban treat you?' Headlines were being written in advance, even by my own newspapers, and I understand that some of the head-lines included mentions of abuse, rape and torture. You can therefore imagine the disappointment of the headline writers when I said that they had treated me with courtesy and respect. This is not what media people wanted to hear and so the press, especially the UK media in Peshawar who were waiting for my arrival, were feeling quite hostile that I had said kind words about this 'brutal and evil' regime. So much so that when my car finally emerged outside the political agent's office in Peshawar, the Western journalists crowded around it and one jour-nalist got in and took out the keys to disable the car. They then started shaking the car and demanded that 'the bitch get out'. This was quite strange for me, having just been treated for ten days with the utmost courtesy and respect.

There is one thing that I do have to thank the British media for, as there were two pieces of information that would have actually caused me a lot of damage while I was in the hands of the Taliban. Had they found out that I had actually spent six years with the Territorial Army or that my ex-husband was an Israeli, I think I would have been executed on the spot. There were pictures of me circulating in the London press wearing a British Army uniform; trying to explain the concept of the TA to the Taliban would have been quite difficult. They would have just seen me in a khaki uniform, seen that I was a captain and that would have confirmed all their suspicions that I was a member of Special Forces (which was quite funny in itself).

The editors had all agreed that they would not report this fact and the *Times* pulled the information from one of their first editions when the Foreign Office asked them to do so. The other fact was that my ex-husband was an Israeli which was also not reported in the British press apart from the *Mail on Sunday*, and, I understand, the American press. However, the Israeli press reported about a conspiracy of silence among the Western media to protect Yvonne Ridley and quite happily pub-lished photographs that could have endangered my life. Fortunately the reputation of the Israeli press is so bad that nobody believed the stories, which I think probably had a reverse effect. The most amusing take on my arrest was a telephone call from a German journalist who said 'I've done an investigation on your capture and detention by the Taliban and I now know what you were up to.' And I said 'Oh, well do tell me' and he replied that 'We know that you were on a suicide mission'. I said 'Well, it worked really well, didn't it?' And I asked 'Why on earth would I do that?' to which he replied 'to kick-start the war'. I said that 'If you want to write that story, feel very free but you know you will become an absolute laughing stock'.

There are lots of conspiracy theories going around about my deten-tion. The saddest thing for me when I came out was that I had become a story and had taken the headlines. What upset me more than anything else was the second wave of reporting when people began focusing on

Yvonne Ridley, the mother. I just thought that male journalists never get stopped in the war zone or an area of conflict and asked 'What are you doing here? What about your children at home?' I just thought it was absolutely outrageous that, in this new millennium, one of the biggest points of debate over my decision to go into Afghanistan was the fact that I was a mother. It was something that actually split people and caused quite a debate. In some ways this was healthy but I just felt it was incredibly sad that the issue should even have been raised and it was raised particularly in the British press.

At the beginning of 2003, we seem to be gearing up for another war in this endless 'war on terror'. The target this time is Iraq and Saddam Hussein, the master of spin and propaganda. No doubt he will welcome in selective Western media to cover the war, but it remains to be seen how many will report the conflict from a hotel rooftop in a neighbouring country. I do not want to see Iraq being attacked, but if there is going to be a war, I shall head for Baghdad . . . with an Iraqi visa, hopefully!

THE NEED FOR CONTEXT: THE COMPLEXITY
OF FOREIGN REPORTING

Gordon Corera

I cover foreign affairs for the *Today* programme, the morning show on BBC Radio 4. My particular focus is the United States and the Middle East, the areas where I travel to and work out of most. I am interested in exploring some of the differences between the United States and Europe and, in particular, how they covered the 'war on terrorism'. I also want to touch on the challenges for journalists and the constraints in trying to explain the war on terrorism and some of the mindsets behind terrorism and foreign affairs.

Straight after 11 September 2001, I was in Washington and I remember well a speech President George Bush gave to the US Congress on 20 September. In this speech, he posed the rhetorical question 'Why do they hate us?' and the answer was 'They hate what they see right here in this chamber – a democratically elected government. They hate our freedoms: our freedom for religion, our freedom of speech, our freedom to vote and assemble and disagree with each other'. Now, I think most people in Europe would find it hard to agree with that. As, I think, would most people around the world. What are the causes of anti-Americanism? Why do people dislike America? They would not say it is because people are envious of Congress. They would give a whole host of other reasons to do with everything from economic, cultural and military power to US intervention and the failure of many an intervention. What interested me most about Bush's statement was the fact that he could make it without really being picked up on it. The questions 'Why don't people like us?' and 'Why are we quite unpopular'? were undoubtedly buzzing around Washington. The thing that struck me was that it was partly a failure of the US media to explain to the American public how the rest of the world sees America. Foreign coverage in the US media has declined dramatically since the end of the Cold War with the associated closure of a number of foreign bureaux.

Only about five or six per cent of the American evening news before September 11 was about foreign news. Instead it was the story about California congressman Gary Condit's relationship to his former intern Chandra Levy that made the headlines. However, if you read the *New York Times* or the *Washington Post* or you go on the internet, there is some of the best foreign reporting one would find anywhere. But it was not necessarily on television and in the places where most Americans get their news from. And it is one of the biggest struggles for journalists to explain to your own audience how other people think, how other cultures think, how other groups of people (communities) think. This is especially difficult during war and, I would say, in the context of terrorism. But it is critical to our understanding of the world, and it has real consequences in terms of policy, that ability to hear and listen to critical voices about what is happening and to hear alternative voices.

Another example is the big difference between the United States and Europe in the way they see the Middle East. An American reporter I spoke to saw European support for the Palestinians simply as anti-Semitic. Now many people would disagree with that: there is a difference between being sympathetic to the Palestinians and to being anti-Semitic – it is possible to be anti-Israel without being anti-Semitic. But there is a perception in the US that there is some deep-rooted European problem with Jewish people. Equally, I think Europe misunderstands the way America sees the Middle East in that I read a lot over here about the power of the Jewish lobby in Washington. However, the reasons for US support of Israel are a lot more complicated. The Jewish lobby is important in Congress particularly, but its impact on the White House is less so. American support for Israel post-September 11 is much more to do with the perception of terrorism, seeing terrorists destroying the Twin Towers and also seeing terrorists blowing themselves up in cafes in Tel Aviv. They see both events in the same context as being part of the same problem of terrorism. There is a fundamental difference there in the way in which we see the world which comes out of our cultures. It is tempting to say that Europeans sometimes see more of the context and as a result sometimes lose some of the clarity as they get bogged down in some of the history, while Americans have a slightly more simplistic view.

Explaining the motivations of suicide bombers and what is happening there is a challenge. Because if you try to do a report on the *Today* programme explaining why someone becomes a suicide bomber (as we have done), you have to go to the family of the suicide bomber. The immediate response is that you are explaining, and by implication, that you are justifying someone being a suicide bomber and you come under a lot of pressure as a journalist for doing that. Equally if you explain the way in which Israel reacts to terrorism and the mindset of the Israelis towards terrorism and the impact of daily bombs going off in cafes and restaurants amongst civilians, you are accused of justifying the

Israeli response and the Israeli aggression. So there is a serious problem in trying to convey why people are doing things around the world in the context of terrorism and war: why people are being suicide bombers without justifying suicide bombers. One of the things which we have been accused of on the BBC and on the *Today* programme is that every time we have Hamas on we are accused of justifying them, and equally every time we have Israeli ministers on we are accused of justifying them by allowing them to explain Israeli actions.

Why is it so difficult for the media to convey these mindsets and motives of other cultures? It is partly because, as journalists, we are not always specialists. Some of us are in certain areas but I think, particularly with the war on terrorism in Afghanistan, there certainly were not many people in journalism who knew a lot about Afghanistan at the start of it or who understood that much about the culture in the region or even about Islam. A lack of understanding on the part of journalists is one of the problems. There are also the political pressures that we come under. On the BBC and on the *Today* programme we come under a lot of flak for criticizing government policy, particularly when we question the war on terror, whenever we question whether the bombing is working in Afghanistan or whether our troops should be there. There is a lot of pressure on journalists who are seen as unpatriotic for raising any criticisms, which is a very dangerous situation to be in. It is partly the consciousness of government that there is a battle for public opinion going on – whenever they are most worried about public opinion not being on their side, that is when they are most critical of the media for not toeing the line.

There is also peer pressure within the media as well on how we cover the war on terror and the difficulties in conveying critical alternative voices. I remember the *Sun* attacking Steven Sackur, one of the BBC's Washington correspondents, for interviewing Donald Rumsfeld and questioning him about the treatment of prisoners at Guantanamo Bay. I think that the *Sun* said he, Steven Sackur, was pro-Taliban for asking these questions. That was unfair, but it reflects the combative media environment in the UK and the pressures the BBC especially faces due to its commitment to impartiality. Guantanamo Bay was another interesting situation because of the different mindsets. The Americans could not see anything wrong with the way they were treating the prisoners at all. I went to Guantanamo Bay to have a look at it and one of the things I saw on the plane on the way over was a film about Arizona prisoners and one of the toughest sheriffs in America. They showed these prisons which were amazing because they still had chain gangs and kept them in corrugated iron huts and you then realize that in the context of the American criminal justice system Guantanamo Bay is not actually that much more extreme than the way in which they treated some of their own prisoners. Now we can disagree, we think that is too tough, but to Americans that does not seem too tough, because that is their view of crime. I think that is one thing that journalists need to get across more clearly, the need to look into a country's mindset to understand its motivation.

Why do we have trouble doing this as well? Everyone knows that the military and governments restrict heavily what we can report on and that they put political pressure on us when we do not report something they like. That does not stop us doing it at all. On the *Today* programme we get lots of complaints from all sides but it does not tend to stop critical coverage. What is more dangerous is when you have an atmosphere in which the media finds itself swept up in patriotism of an event and for that reason finds it hard to raise any critical dissenting voices. I think President Bush's comments that 'you're either for us or against us' and that 'this is a battle of good and evil' makes it harder for journalists because if you say anything that is critical of government policy or conduct you could be called unpatriotic. If you explain anything that the other side is doing – if you explain the motivations behind Osama bin Laden for example – you become accused of trying to explain and justify evil.

What are the other problems involved in reporting on conflict? One of the hardest stories to cover is the Middle East because whatever you do you get flak from either side. Opinions from both communities are so polarized that almost anything you say as a result of being in the middle, as a reporter, leads to criticism. I went to Jenin recently and it was definitely one of my hardest experiences. You had one side who would say it was clearly a massacre and the other side people who would say it was a legitimate action against terrorism and not many people were killed. Trying to say anything more than just presenting those two views is very hard without a lot of work. To substantiate whether or not there has been a massacre takes a lot of work and more time than most journalists have (unless you are working for a weekly publication). What happens is that you get sent in there by an editor and you turn up and are told that you have to file something the next morning. You interview some refugees and they say 'there has been a massacre'. It is then very easy to go on air and play a little tape of the refugees with the translator saying 'there's been a massacre' and you have got a great story. But to substantiate whether or not there has been a massacre takes a lot of interviewing and a lot of work and time and is not necessarily the type of thing you can do in daily journalism as much as you would always like.

You end up taking a great deal of flak just by presenting conflicting perspectives on a specific event. This was particularly evident in Jenin where many European journalists jumped to the conclusion that there had been a massacre and reported it as such when in fact it was more complicated than that. American journalists, on the other hand, for whom the idea of tough anti-terror action fits with their idea of what is necessary in the war on terrorism, gave it very little coverage. I think that because people understand the power of the media, one of the main obstacles in trying to get inside people's mindsets and finding out what is actually happening is that people, including ordinary people, do not tell you the truth. Refugees in Jenin, because they knew we were journalists and were going to report what they were telling us to the outside world, would exaggerate and lie. Both sides were lying to us quite a lot and that is quite a hard thing to get through and try and deal with, particularly when you do not have enough time to substantiate and research events.

It is vital for journalists to tell the public and opinion formers about the complexity of the world out there and to try to explain to them the way different people and cultures think: to create some understanding of why people hate America, why people become suicide bombers and why people think they need to crush terror in the West Bank. As journalists we have to be willing to confront people with these quite harsh realities and they might not necessarily like to hear about why these things are happening. Too often I think journalists, because of the constraints on them, do not have the ability to do that and end up giving a much more simplistic story or sometimes pandering to stereotypes. I do not think it is impossible to convey this complexity and I think the best journalists do it, but it is definitely far from easy.

SUBJECT INDEX

AUTHOR INDEX